Sexual Bullying

Gender conflict and pupil culture in
secondary schools

Neil Duncan

London and New York

First published 1999
by Routledge
11 New Fetter Lane, London EC4P 4EE

Simultaneously published in the USA and Canada
by Routledge
29 West 35th Street, New York, NY 10001

Typeset in Goudy by
M Rules, London
Printed and bound in Great Britain by
Clays Ltd, St Ives plc

British Library Cataloguing in Publication Data
A catalogue record for this book is available from the British Library

Library of Congress Cataloging in Publication Data
Duncan, Neil, 1956–
     Sexual bullying: Gender conflict and pupil culture in secondary
schools / Neil Duncan.
         p.   cm.
     Includes bibliographical references (p.) and index.
      1. Sexual harassment in education—Great Britain—Case studies.
2. Bullying—Great Britain—Case studies. 3. Education,
Secondary—Great Britain—Case studies. I. Title.
LC212.83.G7D85 1999   98-33129
371.5′8—dc21   CIP
ISBN 0–415–19113–0

To Carol and Alex

Contents

Author's note

All names of schools, pupils and staff have been changed to provide anonymity. For the same purpose, certain contextual details of people and events have been altered where they are considered not to significantly change the meaning of the events.

In the interview transcripts, the notation: . . . denotes a pause. The notation: (. . .) denotes material removed for clarity. Other bracketed text denotes the author's notes.

Acknowledgements

I am indebted to all the staff, parents and pupils who were involved in this project, especially those at 'Blunkett Rise', for their time and interest. My thanks also go to Rhiannon Taylor for her assistance with the interviews, and to Jenny Williams and Paul Willis for their supervision and much-needed encouragement. My special thanks go to Kevin Magill for his support and advice throughout my endeavours, and to my family for their forbearance.

The words to the Kinks, 'David Watts', used by permission. Words and music by Raymond Douglas Davies © 1967 Davray Music Ltd and Carlin Music Corp.
The words to k. d. lang, 'The Queen of Popularity', used by permission.

Introduction

Lend me your ruler.
No.
You tight bitch, fucking slag.

Interchanges such as the above are commonplace in schools. They may not often be carried out blatantly in front of authority figures, but I would expect most adults who work in schools to be aware of their currency. Many other adults outside of schools have been surprised, offended or shocked at the language of teenagers whom they overhear on buses, in cafes or out on the street.

These interchanges can sound fearsome with their blasphemous, scatological, violent and sexual imagery, and are all the more shocking for the casual delivery and acceptance by boys and girls in the group. A friend of mine recently caught a bus that later filled with adolescents on their way home from school. She described it as 'like being dropped into a Quentin Tarantino scriptwriting workshop'. The *Independent* newspaper recently carried a feature on women's safety on public transport: 'A woman of about 30 snapped at a boy – I had seen his schoolbag thwack her in the face as he pushed past her. Egged on by his school-uniformed mates, he kept up a torrent of obscenities for a full three minutes: "you're a fuckin' interfering ol' cow, you're a fuckin' twat, you're . . ."'(Welford 1998).

So what was going on here? Why would such a vehement tirade follow a minor reproof? Why the language of sex-hate? Would the abuse have been in a different mode or intensity if the actors had been the same sex or age? Would the aggressor have been so aggressive if his audience had not contained his peers? These questions relate strongly to the social identities of the actors and their immediate and intimate social context, particularly the projected identity of the schoolboy.

During my time working in schools I became very interested in the processes of identity formation and the apparent dissonance between how parents and schools perceived the same child, and how the child perceived her/himself. Frequently, even fairly minor problems that the school was experiencing with the pupil, illicit smoking for example, would be absolutely denied by parents until admitted by the pupil him/herself. The parents would then display utter confusion and despair over how they had been deceived by their offspring – remarking that they had been aware of their friends' children's errant behaviour but not of that of their own.

One of the critical factors regarding the behaviour of adolescents is the absolute importance of their social selves. The peculiar self-image and contrary attitudes which people often embrace at this stage of development is testimony to a deeper turbulence. Adults researching any aspect of adolescents' lives must be sensitised to their egocentricity and its vulnerability. They must try to recall the intensity of feeling involved in having a crush on someone, the paralysing fear of a bully, or what it feels like to be caught up in the craze of a fad, fashion or hobby.

The nomenclature of these feelings is in itself telling: mad for . . .; fan of . . .; crush; craze; mania and so on. Teenagers career between ecstatic vibrancy and crushing ennui. They remain oblivious of enormously obvious 'facts' while being acutely aware of the minutiae of seemingly inconsequential trivia. Their values and interests are often completely at odds with those of the adults who are closest to them. For much of the time, adolescents just don't seem to be in control of their feelings. This book may stimulate memory of this condition in the reader. By remembering emotions from their own adolescence, adults can travel some way towards the empathy needed to understand the (often excessive and obsessive) attitudes structuring adolescents' relationships with one another and their ensuing behaviour.

Disjunctions between the lives of young people at home, at school and amongst friends raise fascinating questions about the existence of multiple or fluid identities: what are the enduring characteristics that they retain; are these chosen or ascribed by others and what are the social and emotional processes at work during that period? Of greatest interest to me was the way this largely hidden social system operated as a virtual closed institution ripe for fostering oppressive social relationships such as bullying.

This book explores the phenomenon of a particular form of bullying in schools, namely sexual bullying. It examines inter- and intra-sex conflict at four secondary schools in the central region of England where much of the original research was carried out as part of a Ph.D. study. Prior to an outline of the main areas of interest and their related sub-themes, I feel it is appropriate to offer some background information to the antecedents of the study and my personal motivation for undertaking it.

For several years after qualifying as a teacher in the 1970s, I worked in a number of residential special schools and units for young people with social and emotional difficulties. All the institutions in which I worked were, except one, co-educational. They accepted boys and girls with many forms of special needs and provided social care and education for them via a twenty-four-hour curriculum. These young people presented a high degree of challenging behaviour, both singly and collectively, and as a teacher working both in the classroom and in the residential sphere I was involved in an intensity of institutional life that has remained clear in my memory twenty years on.

Sexual tension or gendered hostility?

I was charged specifically with dealing with emotional and behavioural problems rather than learning difficulties and, within that working context, certain group-behaviour patterns emerged that presented such serious difficulties amongst the peer group that they became dangerous to ignore.

One of the questions that presented itself to me almost every working day, but which I never had time to explore, was why mixed-sex groups of young people were so much more volatile and difficult to work with than single-sex groups. There is no need to elaborate here upon those problem behaviours other than to say that they centred on powerful emotional events where one or more boys or girls would be verbally or physically attacked over seemingly trivial matters. Relatively settled groups of socially relaxed young people would suddenly change their character and become fractious, hostile and dangerous with the arrival of another member, and this change seemed to be related to the dynamic of gender as much as anything else. This is not to say that the behaviour of single-sex groups of these young people was unproblematic but, as a worker, taking a girls-only group rock-climbing or a boys-only group swimming was generally easier on the nerves than just watching a video with a mixed group.

This problem was most acute with age groups 12–15 years. Although the client group were by definition 'special children', it seemed from other colleagues in mainstream schools, at least anecdotally, that sexual tension contributed to a great deal of distraction from lessons and a lot of emotional stress to individual pupils. This view was often expressed in an attenuated mode, avoiding references to 'real' or 'normal' sexuality[1] or eroticism, but highlighting the exaggeratedness of a 'natural phase'. Comments frequently took the form of blaming the girls for badly handling this naturally occurring phase: 'it's their age'; 'it's their hormones'; 'they are lad-daft at the moment'; 'the boys are all right on their own'.

In the residential schools, both male and female staff appeared to find the adolescent girls the most difficult group to manage in respect of their preoccupation with romantic relationships instead of academic effort or social compliance. The sexual rivalry that was always bubbling amongst the girls frequently erupted as sudden violence. The boys, on the other hand, were figured simply as needing external controls placed upon their 'natural' sexual activity, not because it was deemed deviant, but due to the fact that they were in residential care and the staff would be blamed 'if anything went wrong'.

It may seem to the reader that professional staff should have recognised and understood such phenomena at the time, and enacted positive strategies to alleviate any difficulties. I am sure that many staff had, and still have, very insightful readings of different behaviours and systems, but there was just never an opportunity to develop a critical understanding of them. As one of my teaching colleagues put it:

> you are so occupied on the treadmill you can never get off it long enough to see how it works. If you do get off, the last thing you want to do is spend time

thinking about it. If an explanation offers any sense, you just accept it and get on with surviving other pressures without dreaming up more problems.

Over the years it became clearer that the common-sense interpretative framework I had been repeatedly trying to force around these behaviours was inadequate in accounting for them. The stereotypical notion of silly over-sexed girls chasing after arrogant over-sexed boys was continually being challenged by my experience as a practitioner. When it came to mutual or unreciprocated sexual or romantic attraction, these boys and girls did not appear to be operating within the popularly received ideals of the beautiful or the strong, of the clearly delineated femininity and masculinity models. One case in particular focused my attention on how the anticipated gendered power differentials could be radically overturned.

Paulette was a 13-year-old Chinese/African-Caribbean girl who had severe asthma as well as another medical condition that caused her mobility problems, and she had become obese. In addition, she had moderate learning difficulties: her reading age was so low she was functionally illiterate. On paper, Paulette seemed to be disadvantaged in so many ways that she was expected by the staff to need a high degree of protection from other older, mainly white, boys and girls: Paulette was constructed as an ideal victim of bullying.

In the event, she turned out to be highly sexually precocious with both boys and girls and suffered high levels of hostile reaction when she made her initial overtures. After a couple of weeks, however, she had so severely beaten up three of the other girls that she was made an honorary senior girl by them. Paulette was also frequently pitted physically against new boys and girls as a sort of initiation ceremony. Her status thus elevated, her opinion was always consulted before any boy–girl pairings were enacted, and she was given a deal of respect from the senior boys as a result.

It seemed so unlikely that a fat, disabled, black girl (as she was known to her peers) could wield such power in this situation, even given her unusual physical strength, that I wanted to explore the case further. Constructions of social power, as in the above example, seemed to offer all sorts of possibilities outside the 'normal' kinds of gender relationships, and raised questions for me about the existence of such subcultural systems in mainstream schools.

Initial attempts to learn more

In order to learn more about adolescent inter- and intra-sex conflict and social power, I searched for literature on the subject, but found surprisingly little. Disruptive behaviour by boys in schools was well documented, as was violence and aggression,[2] but the secondary school as a site for boys and girls to interact in such vehemently negative ways seemed curiously unexplored. Some feminist literature covered the effects on girls at the sharp end of name-calling and some went further with investigations into actual sexual assaults inside schools (Mahony 1985; Weiner (ed.) 1985). These studies, however, were more concerned with framing the phenomena of male-to-female sexual harassment within a female-hating society, rather than examining interactions between genders within the highly specific social institution of the school.

Areas vital to my own experience and observations were missing: what structures supported a physically impaired mixed-race girl in her dominion over her able-bodied, older, white male and female peers? How could all the official mechanisms at the disposal of an experienced staff group fail to prevent threats and attempts to wound a member of the pupil group, when a spontaneous whim of one of the gang could defuse the situation as if it had never happened? I had hoped that literature on bullying in schools would illuminate these questions, but until the publication of Besag's *Bullies and Victims in School* in 1989[3] there were no books dedicated to bullying generally available. One had to access academic libraries for journal articles to provide any serious information.

Using the method most common in contemporary research into bullying, the anonymous questionnaire, I investigated the nature, frequency and distribution of inter-sex bullying in four secondary schools in the Midlands. From the data, both boys and girls reported being sexually 'touched-up' against their will. There was also a statistically significant correlation between girls who were singled out for frequent casual sexual abuse and their vulnerability to other forms of vilification such as being called 'slag' and being spat upon (Duncan 1991).

The project failed, however, to provide any sympathetic narrative regarding the experience of the respondents or the micro-cultural conditions that prevailed for them. Pagelow, on research into 'woman battering', states that: 'Numerical tabulation of slaps or kicks produces raw material for the computer to feed upon, but we miss out on more than we get . . . what have we really learned about the interactional dynamics before and after those acts . . . ?' (Pagelow 1981: 346). Interesting though the findings of my survey were, they were not satisfactory in understanding the milieu in which the activities were produced: the pupil culture. Quantitative methods reveal only a frozen tableau of actors fixed in *a priori* roles and categories developed from the researchers' repertoire of expectations. The respondents' experience is channelled into a narrow range of replies that could mislead rather than enlighten through the pursuit of an ever-expanding list of ideal types of behaviour and actor.

As I had never met any of the respondents to my questionnaire, nor spent more than a few hours in each of their schools, I had no sense of empathy with their answers. When a boy claimed on paper he had been 'touched up' against his will by a girl, what did that actually mean? What was the relationship at the time? Was the act for retribution, lust or fun? My sense of the limitations of quantitative methodologies in this field was further reinforced by a change in employment.

Secondary observations: refining the research themes

In 1991 I was employed as a special needs teacher at Blunkett Rise School, a mainstream comprehensive secondary school. The brief for this post gave me a rare, perhaps unique, opportunity to observe pupil and teacher behaviour as a 'legitimate' rather than 'guest' extra adult in the classroom. Having an ordinary subject-teaching slot (Humanities) and my own mainstream form group enabled my full integration into the life of the school, whilst retaining a privileged position as floating observer in the capacity of support teacher. Over the following seven years I was able to see any pupil group in any situation with any teacher, and to share in the documentary knowledge available to members of staff, all within a substantial historical context: the full secondary careers of three pupil cohorts.[4]

In this capacity I was overwhelmed by the seeming omnipresence of gender as a constituent of pupil conflict in school life. Even in interactions that bore no overt reason for the deployment of sexualised verbal abuse, language was funnelled through that discourse. The interactions ranged from the socially trivial to the physically dangerous, a range which one might expect in any large community, but whilst individual interactions were constantly challenged by staff, their ideological underpinning of gender identity[5] and conflictual gender relations went largely unremarked. It appeared that the old 'treadmill syndrome' was still alive and well.

Within these conditions I formulated a project to examine in detail the gendered socio-cultural practices of adolescents within the secondary-school system. I specifically wanted to explore abusive gendered power relationships amongst peers: a cluster of behaviours, attitudes and material practices that I refer to as sexual bullying.[6] As Connell points out: 'Theories of gender, with hardly an exception, focus either on one-to-one relationships between people or on society as a whole. Apart from discussions of the family, the intermediate level of social organisation is skipped. Yet in some ways this is the most important level to understand . . . The practice of sexual politics bears mostly on institutions' (Connell 1987: 119). It was important for this study to convey the sense of institution (the school) and time (adolescence) in which these human activities were played out: to bring some sense of the messiness, contradictions and confusion that real actors experience and must somehow negotiate to survive.

The micro-personal world of adolescent relationships is a very private zone that can quickly become barred to intruders such as parents, teachers or researchers. But this volatile and 'natural' world exists in its most intense social forms within the highly rationalised and bureaucratised institution of the school. A methodological approach was required that could enable the researcher to hear what the young people in the study wanted to say and then relate it meaningfully to a wider audience.

I wanted to present the pupils' highly coloured and subjective accounts, invested with layers of shifting meanings related to specific time and place. I wanted to sound out the submarine topography of their subjectivities, to explore their cultural expressions of the experiences of schooling, adolescence and gender. This demanded an ethnographic approach designed to engage with those expressions.

Approaching the problem

In arriving at the methodology for this study, I was first influenced by essentially practical considerations: how to achieve the most illuminating results within the logistical constraints of a very minor piece of research. The disadvantages of solo, unfunded practitioner research are fairly obvious: academic isolation, financial hardship and pressure of paid work commitments. The advantages are not so evident, but they do exist in the form of flexibility and absence of collegial and sponsorial expectations. In addition, as an official 'second teacher' in many mainstream classes where I was supporting special-needs pupils, I had default access to participant observer status in my workplace school.

At another level, my training and professional background (and perhaps my gender) directed me towards the use of quantitative methods, whilst my political and philosophical standpoints were more consonant with those of Wolpe (1988), Mac An Ghaill (1989b) and Troyna and Hatcher (1992). It was the inclusion of the perspectives on race and masculinities, both informed by feminist methodological theory, that suggested possibilities for a multi-method approach to my own work where each element would support the other.

Access and credibility

The managers of the participating schools were very aware of the sensitivity of their schools' public reputations. A research project touching on the sexual mores of pupils in their institutions might reveal problems that they could be blamed for, or at least obliged to respond to with already stretched resources. With current discourses on education centred upon odious comparisons through league tables of competing schools, head teachers might well have been expected to avoid the extra trouble a researcher would bring. It was creditable to the individuals concerned, and indicative of their confidence in their staff and pupils, that permission was given.

Gaining access to schools to carry out research is difficult. To arrive 'cold' with a brief to examine gender relations amongst pupils, with a sub-text of sexual harassment and assault, would have been the kiss of death for the project. Some staff in the schools, usually pastoral staff, were aware of earlier investigations by radical sociologists and their impact on school life, for example, on the moral order: 'Radical feminists within education . . . have no reservations about alienating the educational establishment' (Weiner 1994: 69). The schools' relationships with educational psychologists were altogether more cordial: 'The relationship (between education and psychology) is institutionalised in myriad organizational, administrative and ideological forms: the conceptual tools at the teachers' disposal and the vocabulary in which curricular objectives are set . . . are those of psychology' (Sinha 1986: 401).

I quickly learned that the gatekeepers were more convinced of the credibility, respectability and usefulness of psychologists researching bullying than of sociologists studying gender. My project was presented as an extension of my earlier survey on bullying (carried out in three of the same schools), but it would be an ethnographic account of the problem informed by grounded theory in the generation of concepts and the analysis of data. The payoff for the schools would be the provision of some quantitative data to augment the 'soft' qualitative data. These quantitative features were:

- provision of statistical data as a service to the schools in return for permission of access
- the deliberate choice of a sample larger than would commonly be found in ethnographic research. This was constituted from four schools in order to draw out any potential for comparison and generalisation, as opposed to a singular case study of one school or pupil group
- organisation of the sample (for age, sex, school and social characteristics as nominated by teachers) along quasi-experimental lines to provide comparative statistical information
- adoption of specific techniques and practices more usually associated with psychological investigation, for example Q-sort technique,[7] scripted prompts and interview schedules, to enable replication of some parts of the study should schools or other researchers wish to use them.

Selection of schools

The four schools were chosen for convenience and similarity. All were drawn from the same geographical region but represented two culturally distinct localities, and apart from the addition of the workplace school, they had been used by me for a previous study. The selection criteria for that study were believed to be equally appropriate to this one:

- all were co-educational local-authority comprehensive schools
- each had a roughly similar number of pupils on roll, between 850 and 1,100 pupils at the time of visit (excluding sixth forms where applicable)
- all had multi-ethnic populations in varying proportions
- all were of a similar architectural construction and layout: concrete multi-storey on a single campus
- all were urban
- social class is very hard to ascertain in large comprehensive schools, but the population might reasonably be described as predominantly working class, with a few professional and many unemployed families making up the mix.

Selection of pupils

The pupils themselves were obviously the most crucial people to the study. Even before selection they had been observed by their teaching and pastoral staff and marked out as young people who had certain attributes.

The selection of pupils from the host[8] schools was made by the pastoral staff who had in-depth knowledge of the young people and their families. Their choice had to be based upon the grouping of either three or four young people of the same year group,[9] who were known to have a mutually supportive relationship with one another. They had to be self-confident, articulate, socially skilled students in the eyes of both staff and peers. They should not have been known or suspected bullies or victims nor unusually active in any socially undesirable practice, but should be 'street-wise' or knowledgeable regarding those who do engage in socially undesirable behaviour.

By meeting these criteria, it was hoped to give the unusual opportunity of listening to 'ordinary', or 'middle-of-the-road' pupils, who are often overlooked by researchers interested in the more flamboyant examples of youth culture (Skeggs 1993). Their articulacy and self-confidence would be helpful in preventing hours of tape-recorded silence. Their social skills would give them access as witnesses and informants within the peer groups' counter-curriculum, as well as offering thoughts on the official discourses of such behaviour in the school.

The prospective pupils were approached by their own teachers and asked if they would like to take part as a group in a recorded interview to discuss how boys and girls get on with one another in school. The interviews were to take place whilst their peers were timetabled for Personal and Social Education (PSE) – a subject that deals with topics in a similar vein.[10] Virtually all the pupils approached took up the offer, and were given clear information that they could opt out at any point.

In each of the three host schools, two groups of Year 7 (Y7) pupils and two groups of Y10 pupils were formed and interviewed. Half of the groups were boys only, and half were girls only, as during the pilot interviews mixed-sex groups had tended towards domination by boy members with some negative and offensive one-upmanship. The Y7 pupils were chosen to give a live experience of their first term in secondary school and the Y10 groups were chosen to represent older pupils in the school. Sixth formers were discounted as they were somewhat removed from general pupil society and, in any case, not present in all of the schools.

Y11 pupils were not included in the host school sample for logistical reasons. Y11 students have an especially hectic school year – compressed into less than three terms are mock exams, course-work assessments, work experience and final exams. Additionally, any unforeseen follow-up work required by the research would be nigh impossible, as they would all have left school at the end of that year. Nevertheless, the continuing relationship with my own tutor group in the workplace school meant that I was able to use some interesting data from their Y11 experiences.

Data gathering

After permission was granted and access arranged, I ran pilot studies to help refine the data-gathering techniques. The study was then organised into phases.

Over two terms, we[11] interviewed groups of boys and groups of girls from both years 7 and 10 in each of the three host schools. Between these sessions, I raised the themes and issues with pupils in my workplace school, both in formal interviews and in informal discussion as opportunity presented. After data collection from the host schools was completed the observations and interviews continued in the workplace school for more than five years.

By these means a template of the respondents' concerns from the host schools could overlay the observations from the workplace: emergent themes and discourses from one school could be explored in depth at another. Interview responses from boys' groups could be re-presented to the girls' groups, and vice versa, and by this means a 'safe' dialogue could take place with anonymity and power imbalances controlled.[12] By triangulating non-participant and participant observation, in-depth interviews, structured interviews and Q-sort techniques in selected sites amongst the participating schools, it was hoped that the result would be a richly textured picture of secondary-school life.

Although the sample was not of the magnitude usual in a questionnaire survey, it was considerably larger than is usual in an ethnography. This was to enable the development of a number of themes, as well as to provide the quantitative data requested by some of the schools. The study interviewed around sixty pupils at the host schools, and a further sixteen in depth at the workplace school. More than another twenty pupils were also observed and researched in detail at the workplace school.

Some ethical considerations

Poking about in other people's lives earns a living for many types of professional. Social-science researchers take more seriously than most (as they should) the impact of such intrusion upon the subjects involved, but there are always lingering worries about how hygienic each project is in that respect.

The young people who volunteered for interview could have exposed aspects of their life that they themselves had never confronted, far less discussed with adult strangers. They were brought together as a group to consider attitudes and behaviours of themselves and their peers. This raised their consciousness on important issues and carried an emotional risk. The ethical problem of minimising the risk was hindered by the difficulty of articulating an appropriate caution to the respondents (Okley 1978, cited in Herbert 1989). Given the intellectual and emotional immaturity of the pupils, the age and power differential between subjects and researcher, and the culture of deference to men wearing ties that is immanent in most secondary schools, it was possibly futile to attempt to deliver a cogent caveat to pupils' enthusiasm. It was unfathomable how effective such empowerment was in each case, but several groups showed a robust nonchalance regarding their participation.

My own concerns on this issue were somewhat allayed by the sophisticated post-modern joking of some 15-year-old girls regarding my assurances of participants' anonymity:

ND: All the names will be changed when it is written up . . .

SARAH: What are you going to call me?

JACKIE: I'll only do it (*the interview*) if I get to be called Kim! I always wanted to be called . . .

ND: Eh? Are . . .

JACKIE: I mean it Sir! You'd better promise . . .

*

In a matter of seconds the serious researcher had been re-positioned as confused functionary courting permission, and the girl does appear as Kim in the transcripts which follow. Considering the existing formal relationship between teacher and pupils, there was a great deal of openness and a declared satisfaction from many pupils of the benefits and pleasures of 'just talking and thinking about stuff'.

Heartening though this lack of fear of objectification and scrutiny was, doubts and worries did (and do) remain with me about my interference in the lives of the young people. As a practising teacher it seems paradoxical that I should get on with the paid job of forcibly pumping information into pupils' heads every working day despite their obvious resistance, yet become squeamish about listening to *their* information in a permitted and caring way. Although I did not resolve this conflict, it had a profound effect upon my classroom practice.

Apart from the risk of emotional intrusion, the other major ethical concern was that of sex/gender bias in the research project. In the months prior to the commencement of the project I had discussed the impact of my gender on the prospective interviewees with a number of women academics and colleagues who were informed about feminist research. I had already decided to use a female collaborator in the host-school girls' interviews, but there were also considerations of sexist bias pervading the whole project.

At times I felt that this type of enterprise ought really not to be undertaken by a male at all. Issues of 'championing of schoolboys in the face of feminist attack' concerned me (Wetherell and Griffin 1992), as did the idea of investigating the sexualised behaviour of school children. There is no glib response to such concerns, and I would be among the first to test the integrity of another researcher taking up the same position, but the only fair test is to judge the finished work. As long as my research questions remained I felt I should take an active part in exploring them.

Eichler (1991) asserts that whilst control for the sex of the researcher is often not possible, mention should at least be made of that fact and its possible effects. There were times when a girl's response (in the workplace school) could be detected as guarded due to my maleness, but other girls at other times were very forthright about the same questions. As Rhiannon's discussions with boys also varied in mood and climate, differentiated responses may have had more to do with group dynamics and personal style than pure gender differences. The time and space given to boys' and girls' experiences in this book are perhaps not equal but, hopefully, equitable.

An attempt has been made to be 'non-celebratory' in recounting some of the views expressed by interviewees. It is ethically important to try to remain aware of the difference between releasing voices that hold otherwise silenced feelings, and accepting expressions of oppressive opinion. Given the nature of the topic – sexual bullying – careful selection was made of the published data to minimise erotic or sensational content.

Data analysis

All the interview transcripts were read and coded for the larger themes. The texts were read for key words and phrases that related directly to Q-sort items[13] or what would have been items had I thought of them prior to their compilation. These key words – for example, 'gay', 'slag', 'two-timers', 'users' and 'sconners' – opened discourses on interpenetrating themes that were coded as major areas for investigation.

Some of these themes emerged during observation in the workplace school. When such incidents occurred that, in my opinion, concretised abstract concepts previously raised in interviews, I was able to follow them up in a number of ways. Permission was given for in-depth interviews with some of the protagonists and some of the bystanders. These young people were selected opportunistically and entered into dialogue with me, some of them on an ongoing basis. Observed activities and events were reflected back to these respondents for their own analysis, sometimes as groups, sometimes in pairs and sometimes in individual sessions. These observations were written up directly, and the recorded interviews were transcribed and coded as before. The themes were basically the same, but with some considerable elaborations. Race, age-seniority and female violence were among the extensions.

Case-study material, presented below on particular young people and events, was accumulated through a process of direct and indirect observation and taken from several witness sources in each case. This data was often supported by interview: if I wanted to know more about an incident or activity, I would just find the appropriate person and ask them.

Few formal field notes were taken, and usually these were recorded after incidents, a fight for instance, that required some official intervention. Notes on these incidents were first attached to running notes I made following the interviews, then later incorporated into my analyses of the scripts. In choosing the pupils with whom I wanted to talk, I tried to select those that I felt could throw light upon the observations I had made, either of themselves or of peers of whom we had shared knowledge. Through this triangulating process there emerged a reinforcing or weakening of various themes throughout the project.

Once the data had been collected from the host schools, quantitative analysis was applied to the Q-sort results. The participating schools were sent a short interim report on a list of sexualised anti-social peer-group behaviours to inform their anti-bullying policies.

All the material from this multi-method study was analysed from a cultural-studies perspective as an ethnography, with case studies on individual actors as well as themes. This hybridised design was intended to be exploratory and descriptive rather than explanatory or prescriptive. As a result, the following chapters may not answer the questions I have raised in this introduction with precision or finality. Throughout the book there are instances of contradiction and speculation, of dualities of meanings and misapprehensions, but, because this is one subject that every post-adolescent will have first-hand experience of, the reader can use that experience to draw their own interpretations from the presented data.

Interviews at the host schools

The pupils taking part were called from their normal PSE lesson to a private room in a quiet area of the school where the link person, usually the head of year, made the introductions. The boy and girl groups took separate rooms with either Rhiannon or myself.

The confidentiality ground rules were established and respondents were reminded that they could leave at any time, or declare their non-compliance with any aspect of the research. The tape was set running and the agenda set out. The prompt-scripts were read aloud by the interviewer (about three or four minutes of orienting material), and then the pupils were asked if such exchanges were typical in their school, but *not necessarily in their experience*.

At some point when the conversation grew strained, the Q-sort cards would be passed around. The individual pupils would be asked to rank order the behaviours described on the cards, thus generating debate amongst the onlookers over choice and definitions, frequently stimulating memories of incidents. The cards were usually introduced after about ten or fifteen minutes and the practical activity invariably stimulated further discussion and activity for the rest of the forty- to sixty-minute session.

The script below was taken from one of the pilot interviews at Blunkett Rise School. It was used as one of the prompt-scripts that stimulated discussion in the groups and oriented them towards the themes I wanted to explore under the general heading of sexual bullying. Although the Q-sort items and textual and verbal prompts were all drawn from pupils' definitions of bullying with a sexualised character, the terms 'sexual' and 'bullying' were not used by the researchers to begin with, instead the problem was framed simply as 'boy–girl hassle'.

In addition to stimulation and orientation, the prompt scripts helped to explicate the expectations for anonymity of the data, and to signal the more relaxed use of language acceptable in the interview situation compared to the classroom. Rather than relegate the prompt to the appendices, the text is offered here to give the reader the context of the following transcript extracts.

Y7 boys

RESEARCHER: I'm interested in finding out the sorts of things which some pupils do that get other pupils upset, particularly what boys do that upsets girls and vice versa. What things would you say you get upset about? Is there much bother ever between boys and girls?

PUPIL 1:   Not really.

PUPIL 2:   No, it's usually them that gets wound up by us, isn't it?

PUPIL 1:   Yeah, we take the pee out of them.

RESEARCHER: How do you do that?

PUPIL 1:   Just for the laugh like.

RESEARCHER: What do you actually do that you know they don't like?

PUPIL 3:   Well, if you ask to borrow something like a ruler or something, you know, that you might need, and say they won't let you borrow it, they go mad when you call them. Don't they?

PUPIL 1/2:   Yeah, especially Karen and Jackie.

RESEARCHER: What do you call them?

PUPIL 2:   All sorts you know, slags and that.

RESEARCHER: Why slags particularly?

PUPIL 1:   'Cos that's what they are . . . especially Karen, she's OK one minute then she gets really snotty, doesn't she?

PUPIL 2:   Yeah they're a right pair of bitches them.

RESEARCHER: I've heard the name 'slag' before, but I'm not sure why you use it. What does it mean exactly?

PUPIL 2:   Well it means, like, slag means a girl who you don't like, you know, someone who isn't nice to you, you know who is tight, and acts like a bitch.

RESEARCHER: When I've heard it used before I was told it meant a female who would have sex or act in a sexy way with lots of blokes . . .

PUPIL 2:   Yeah, well that's right, but they don't have to, they might just act bitchy like not give you something, and you call them slags to get your own back.

RESEARCHER: What do you think the girls think you mean by calling them slags?

PUPIL 2:   Well, like you say it's like calling them a prossie or something, it gets them mad, don't it?

RESEARCHER: But calling them names to do with sex is a bit strange to me. You said slag and prossie, which really mean 'you go with lots of blokes for sex' or 'you get paid for sex by blokes', is that right?

PUPIL 3:   Well not really, I mean I suppose so, but see you're just trying to get them mad, aren't you? If you weren't you'd just ignore them, wouldn't you?

RESEARCHER: Yeah I see what you mean, but what I mean is that you're using sexual insults when really they have nothing to do with what's going on, like the ruler or whatever. Do you see what I'm getting at?

PUPIL 3:   Yeah I know, but if you called them anything else they wouldn't mind . . . like say you said 'Oh Karen! You are so nasty!' That wouldn't get them mad would it? They would just think they'd won!

PUPIL 1:   The way they carry on they ask for it, though. Some of them think they're so brilliant 'cos they go out with fifth years.

RESEARCHER: Does that make you jealous, then?

PUPIL 1:   No way, I wouldn't go out with one of them, they're a bunch of dogs.

PUPIL 3:   Yes you would, you fancy Sophie . . .

ND (*to 'live' group*):   Does that sound familiar? Do you sometimes have that sort of hassle between boys and girls happen in this school?

At this point the group would begin discussion of some of the emergent themes. The discussion was led by the interviewer who kept up the tempo of the discussion by asking questions germane to the topic. Starting from cold with a deadline of about fifty minutes necessitated overt leadership.

Many ethnographers might view this type of interrogative interview style as contaminating data by its domineering approach. Such criticisms are valid to an extent, as the researcher can manipulate responses at that level by his/her control. But the researcher can just as easily, and more subtly, manipulate and distort data at every other level too. Even when data is gathered, the researcher can edit to fit the selection of his/her own agenda. Referring to participant observation, but just as applicable to interviewing, Willis draws attention to the false virtues of objectivity and researcher sterility for their own sakes: 'There is a clear sociological fear of naked subjectivity' (Willis 1980: 90). This dread of accepting the reality of the researcher as an historically real and active figure contradicts one of qualitative research's main strengths, engagement with the subject. Instead of pretending that there was no power differential, no agenda and no time limit, we made our roles as interviewers as obvious and open as we could.

Whilst the respondents were amenable to being directed on topic, the majority were clearly not swayed by our personal opinions. Occasionally we would mis-hear a comment and make a positive remark about it only to be corrected by the individual for misrepresentation, even if it meant rejecting our approval. Here and there we made explicit our value position, challenged comments and pontificated on subjects that were, at least, at the limits of our competence, and generally behaved like teachers, all of which was treated with patience, tolerance and good humour by the young people.

The next chapter gives an overview of the main concerns voiced by boys in the interviews. As noted earlier, an intermittent mediated dialogue took place between the age and sex groups, with points raised in one session re-presented to another group then back again. Chapter 1, and Chapter 2 which deals with the main concerns of girls, are not tidily sectioned reports. They are an attempt to give a wide-angle view of the principal themes and issues before detailed analysis in the case-study ethnographies later in the book.

1 Boy troubles

Overview of problems experienced by boys

In the host-school interviews, for the most part, the boys, especially the younger ones, began by giving predictable examples of trivial disputes with girls where gender seemed irrelevant to the hostility. Their specifically gendered complaints included girls' 'cliquiness' and their lack of interest in matters that the boys thought important. These usually included (detailed knowledge about) cars and motorbikes, sports and computer games.

In the greater part of the literature boys figure as the perpetrators of sexual harassment against girls, and some feminist writing presents all schoolboys as benefiting from a junior-league patriarchy mirroring gender relations in the wider society (Mahony 1985; Jones and Mahony 1989). Early evidence appeared to support this view as it was perceived by the female respondents. The picture seemed less clear-cut and direct than previous research, however, and attempts to explore the underpinning conditions promoting this situation in schools were made as described below.

As the interviews developed it became evident that there were particular difficulties faced by adolescent boys *vis à vis* relationships with, or around, girls. The problems were much the same from school to school, but significant differences were apparent between the 11-year-old boys and the 15-year-old boys. One of the general findings from the research into bullying in schools is the evidence of age as an important variable of frequency.[1] This pattern has been attributed to a number of influences such as an increase in pupil cognitive awareness of different types of conflict, and of school organisation altering from primary to secondary phase, thereby offering different opportunities for bullying. There does not appear to be any strong academic interest in the coincidence of sexual maturation and formation of gender identity.

Lower-school boys

Most of the boys interviewed clearly perceived a fundamental difference in the attitude, interests and actions of boys and girls. They were keen to avoid any blemish through acknowledgement of victim status: nothing much affected boys adversely. They could have a laugh and fall out and make up again in the space of a school day and they could slag the girls off but still expect their moral and material support when they wanted it. A characteristic difference between the boys' and girls' interview groups was the restless energy amongst the boys. They gave the impression that they needed always to be jockeying for position within the group: they were relaxed in terms of being confident in the interview situation but less so with one another.

The younger boys had very few concerns with their sexual identity, at least they did not seem to be worried about attacks from girls. They tended to unify their sexual and gender identities up to the first stages of visible, physical pubertal change. This sexual identity, or enduring sense of oneself as a sexual being fitting into a culturally prescribed category (Savin-Williams and Rodriguez 1993: 80) did not become an issue until challenged by peer heterosexual relationships two or three years later.[2] Expressions of sexuality by the younger boys tended to be mediated through their collective common-sense view of gender, rather than individualised.

Their main concerns were focused on bullying episodes from older boys where their own lack of sexual development might be used as an additional humiliation, their loss of dignity thereby disadvantaging them amongst their own friends. These fears of male–male sexual humiliation are discussed below, but for most younger boys there was no overt sexual element in this type of bullying. It was seen as coincidental that the older boys were more fully sexually developed, they were just bigger, and represented a dominating seniority in pupil relations.

There was no evidence of the younger boys 'fancying' girls in any serious respect, although they did admire some of the most senior girls whom they thought glamorous. Girls of their own age were talked of as gendered but anerotic. The boys obviously recognised them as biologically and socially different from themselves (with the social differences predominating) but seemed not to recognise their development, actual or potential, into women. Neither did they seem to question why girls might have a different set of values or practices. The situation to them was unproblematic: as they were boys it was a comfortable given. The boys did not especially value the friendship of girls, or seek their company.[3]

Naming of names

Those problems that the younger boys did have with girls centred upon the girls' resistance to the boys' pretensions to mastery. Some girls had the temerity to refuse help to boys who were having difficulty with classwork, or who had no pen or book, for instance. The lower-school boys in these interviews saw nothing unusual or remarkable in their expectations or their indignation when resisted. In such cases the boys acted swiftly to make an example of the obstinate girl by calling her a sexualised name, for example 'bitch' or 'cow', to publicise the perversity of her girlhood in not servicing the needs of boys.

What seemed straightforward petty disputes were distorted into sexual conflicts where the language seemed far removed from the purpose of either of the parties. This sexualised name-calling was entirely unproblematic to the boys, it seemed the only natural response to girls challenging their authority. Only certain boys however, in certain conditions would succeed in this sort of domination, as most girls would attempt to fight back.

Y7 Baker Street boys

ND: What is the worst thing they could call you?
BRIAN: Gay.
ALAN: Gay.
BRIAN: Pervert, or poof.
ND: And would that upset you?
BRIAN: No.
COLIN: A bit.
ALAN: No.
BRIAN: We'd know that we'd get them back.
ND: But do you think there are some lads it would upset?
BRIAN: Yeah.
ND (*to Colin*):   You said you wouldn't like it.
COLIN: Some lads can't take it but if they said it to us . . .
BRIAN: If they said it to us four, well, we'd just ignore them, but there is some lads that would start hitting them.

Clearly the boys in this interview did not regard this type of retaliation from the girls as effective against their attacks, but recognised that some of their peers 'can't take' verbal abuse from the girls. In observation and discussion two types of boy *did* seem to be affected by the girls' name-calling.

The first was the low-status, socially isolated, but perhaps academically capable, boy. Such boys were prone to low self-esteem and would be unsure of the outcome of hostile engagement with the girls. Despite often appearing pleasant and successful to teachers, this type of boy was likely to be unattractive to many of the girls, and his name was in danger of becoming a byword for undesirability. This process worked like an inversion of the well-known 'sex-symbol' tag. It could be seen on many occasions in the workplace school, that the more a boy was praised by (some) teachers, the more he would squirm uncomfortably at the thought of his class-mates' disapproval. These boys were often called 'gay' by their enemies, and in this mode the term signified weakness and compliance to adult expectations.[4] Such boys may do very well in some schools or streams within those schools, but represented a disapproved form of masculinity in the peer groups in the research schools, and their low numbers reinforced their isolation. It was unlikely that these boys would need any type of service from the girls, but would in fact be used themselves to supply help to the other boys if the girls refused.

The second type of boy who could not take the girls' retaliation was the more reactive and generally aggressive boy. Some girls may have seen those traits as exciting and fun at times, but the boys' poor social skills, low academic achievement and early resort to physical violence reduced their stock and could lead to their being labelled 'nutters'. Despite all the schools having strict and well-publicised discipline regulations, the opportunities for violent behaviour were still available and the culture of 'not grassing'[5] to teachers was strong everywhere. The second type of boy to which Brian and Alan referred found themselves in trouble with the school's authority quite frequently. On those occasions the gendered or sexualised aspects of the conflict were usually misrecognised by teachers or played down as an unnecessary complication unless obviously central to the incident.

Every boy and girl has, of course, a unique life experience, and one of the limitations of the quantitative approach to this field of research is the loss of that sense of individuality. In this project, the individuals are seen against patterns and clusters of ideal types constructed by the pupils themselves. The dynamic nature of peer-group relations in schools prevents easy generalisation between participating schools.

Although there was an attempt to research schools that were similar in pupil intake, slight differences in the numbers of pupils considered disruptive or diligent affected the relative power and status of the individuals seen to belong to those groups. What appeared an acceptable level of compliance to authority in one school could appear as 'soft' or 'square' in another, and depended upon a form of critical mass of subcultural practice. Normative gender relations amongst the pupils followed the same pattern of development, with occasional moments of disruption caused by a convergence of conditions catalysed by the agency of a particularly powerful individual.[6]

The pupils in these interviews were recruited by staff who judged them to be the most 'middle of the road' pupils and, therefore, able to give a popular view of pupil life. The conflict between boys and girls and boys and boys was often reported as using two extremes of masculinity to punish one another. The boys in the above extract didn't want to be seen as either 'gay' or as a 'nutter' whose only response to challenge is excessive force, but of the two, 'gay' was the worse.

'Gay' seemed to have a duality of meaning against boys in much the same way as 'slag', 'cow' or 'dog' were used against girls. The word was recognised as meaning homosexual, but for most purposes it denoted a wider negative male role within the school group. Features of this role for Y7 boys included being undesired by the girls who matter, and being accepted only by the less popular girls 'as a friend'. The ascription of 'gay' replaced qualities which other boys had, such as sporting prowess, being a good fighter, cheeking teachers and hanging around with cool[7] mates doing cool activities such as smoking and swearing.

One of the shields against being hurt by the term 'gay' was the sure and certain public knowledge that one was not gay in any sense, and this meant a reinforcement of homophobia as a positive masculine trait, as well as the membership of a popular boys' group. These two goals were often contradictory (one didn't wish to appear too fond of one's friends, or over-keen to acquire them), and produced stress and conflict within individual boys and inside friendship groups.

Being shown up by lasses

The Y7 girls from the same class were very firm about their response to victimisation of any member of their social group, and particularly aware of the advantage of isolating boys before attack.

Y7 Baker Street girls

RT: How would you handle a boy that was being nasty to your friend?

ANGIE: Well, if there was a few of them onto one girl, that isn't very fair.

CATHERINE: We'd tell a teacher at first but later we would do something on our own as well.

RT: Have you ever done that?

CATHERINE: Yeah, after school . . . hit them a few times. (*Laughter*)

ANGIE: Hit them, yeah.

RT: Really?

BABS: When them by themselves them chicken.

The potential for girls to operate indirectly as bullies against boys is not explored in depth in the literature other than to remark that boys rarely report being physically attacked by girls. Only in extended discussion at Blunkett Rise School did any of the boys admit to feeling physically threatened directly by a girl or girls, but this may well have been due to this study's design limitations. These same girls went on to describe the dreadful shame attached to a boy who loses face in contest with the girls. The practice of 'debagging'[8] a boy – a mob pulling his trousers and underpants off him – was a popular form of attack.

CATHERINE: In our old school we was doing this sort of a play. We was all in the library and there was this one boy who nobody liked much and they debagged him and he run off crying. And he never came back to that school.

RT: Oh? Right!

CATHERINE: And it wasn't all the girls who did it, it was his mates too.

The boys seemed to place a high degree of importance on being part of the mainstream, especially in lower school. The need to belong to a popular group, not to be seen as an individual, was a strong underlying theme, and one played upon by the schools' disciplinary systems: equality meant uniformity, individuality meant selfishness, abnormality and thinking you were special. Pupils of both sexes detested being singled out for attention by staff, for praise or condemnation. When behaviour occurred which teachers disliked, the word 'normal' was often used in an attempt to redirect the behaviour towards more accepted limits.

In fact there was much unacceptable and anti-social behaviour which occurred between pupils which made those activities 'normal' by virtue of their frequency alone. This did not appear to be recognised by teaching staff who, despite suffering these behaviours on a regular basis, would often remark on abnormality of behaviour as a means of social disgrace. This might take the form of a PE teacher cajoling a pupil to co-operate thus: 'Everyone else gets showered without a fuss, what makes you so different?' (cf. Seltzer 1982). Other situations were described and observed where a boy might be fidgeting and the teacher asked whether there was 'something wrong with you?' with the undertone of unfavourable comparison with the rest of his 'normal' class-mates.

In some instances, the boys' main concern was the amount of trouble girls could cause by spreading rumours, in others it was the girls' ability to marshal other more powerful males to threaten their status or safety. The case above refers to boys and girls dispensing justice collaboratively to a boy that 'nobody liked'. Although the details were not explored in this case, there were other incidents reported where the effect on the male victim was considered much more powerful because both sexes had been involved, and a consequent sense that an important boundary had been crossed.

Accounts of this type fit closely with Pikas's (1989a and 1989b) concept of mobbing, but with an additional sexualised element. The older girls were also aware of debagging as a way of getting at boys, and they reinforced the view that the strategy was not universally applicable: targets had to be carefully chosen or a backlash might occur.

Y10 Baker Street girls

CELIA: Yeah it's mainly name-calling though, you don't get many girls going round debagging them, do you?

BEL: You might for a laugh, every now and then, but . . .

ANDREA: Yeah, but not often.

RT: Would that be to a particular type of boy you would do that?

ANDREA: Yeah, wimpy.

BEL: Yeah the kind that . . .

CELIA: Yeah the one that would run. (*Laughter*)

ANDREA: Yeah the one that everyone thought was a right wimp . . .

CELIA: Because they would get more embarrassed . . .

ANDREA: Because it would be easier to get at him . . .

CELIA: But if it was one of the lads who went around slagging off the girls, well that would just make him worse for ourselves. Because he'd be back on them even worse.

As with the Y7 girls, Andrea pointed out the virtue of seeking a soft target, one not popular or strong enough to retaliate effectively, and whose victimisation could be enjoyed by both boys and girls. This brought the sexes together and clarified which were the dominant masculinities and femininities. Boys who hit back at girls in retaliation for any provocation were likely to be seen as unacceptably unmanly. These Y7 boys maintained what they thought was the correct macho response to being called a poof by the girls.

Y7 Baker Street boys

BRIAN: If they said it to us four, well, we'd just ignore them, but there is some
     lads that would start hitting them.
ND: What, really hitting them?
BRIAN: Yeah.
ALAN: Hard, in the face and everything.

This response by boys towards girls who have called them poofs was seen (paradoxically) as entirely the wrong way to react. Real boys preserved a studied cool,
they knew they would 'get their own back' later; but in attempting to prove their
masculinity the weaker boys used physical force against the girls, which only
showed that 'some lads can't take it'.

The code of 'not really hitting girls' was elaborated upon by these Y10 boys who
saw their gender as subdivided into 'two lots'. They affirmed that some of the weaker
boys, even at the age of 15, were still repeatedly beaten by very aggressive girls for
their amusement. These relationships were impossible to break: once the girls had
discovered a vulnerable boy, he would be abused in this way for his school career. If
he tried to fight back he would be the victim of both the boys and the girls.

Y10 Blunkett Rise boys

PINXI: Yeah, the lads in our year, the ones who aren't dweebs, like there are two
     lots. One lot, and our lot who all hang around together, and if one of the
     dweebs picked on a girl in our year, we would get him, all the lads in the top
     level, we would come down and it wouldn't matter, 'cos we know we could
     batter him easy.
BOOT: You don't question it you just do it, do you?
ND: What! You would join in and beat up a little lad because he defended him-
     self against, say . . . Tammy Clegg?
BOOT: (*Laughter*) It's the way you put it. (*Laughter*) Yeah, though, I would. I
     know she is in the wrong but it is just something us lot . . . we all agree on.

Real boys simply didn't fight girls. They might verbally abuse them, try to touch
them up, give the odd nonchalant punch or kick to someone when they felt like
it, but real boys didn't fight girls. Resorting to fighting a girl would confirm one's
status as not a boy, therefore either a girl or a 'gay'. It was a test, a hardship one had
to endure if one wanted to wear the mantle of dominant masculinity. The policing of this unwritten law was carried out by the most securely masculine of all the
lads, thereby consolidating their own position, the chivalry extending in this
example even to Tammy Clegg, a girl who was earlier named as physically frightening to the toughest lads in the school. But this maladjusted chivalry may be read
in another way: an easy way for most boys to avoid defeat in a straight fight
between themselves and a hard[9] girl.

The interviewees agreed that such occurrences were infrequent, but happened
often enough to remind boys that certain types of boy could not get away with

certain types of behaviours. Strauss (1988) points out that the *effect* of rare but regular attacks on schoolgirls by boy peers is akin to the terror caused by occasional racial lynchings in the southern states of the US: it didn't need to happen often, just enough to assume a pattern. The foreboding atmosphere surrounding the attacks multiplied their effects on potential victim groups. A similar system operated against those 'wimpy boys' in this study.

Unfortunately for the girls, the benefits of scaring a few 'wimpy lads' by occasional debaggings or beatings was not likely to stop the rare attacks from the truly nasty boys, the 'nutters'. What it did achieve was the closer grouping of the 'ordinary' boys afraid of falling outside their own self-constructed reputational margins, and only a little girl-influence on the dominant mode of hyper-masculinity. These cultural expressions of gender relations amongst the peer group were understood but normally unspoken by the pupils but were presented as so prevalent that they constituted the material of adolescent experience. Everyone had to know their position within the peer group, and spend much time improving and consolidating it, or else run the risk of others assigning them a place which was dangerous to occupy.

The two extremes of male identity – being 'gay' and being a 'nutter' – were to be avoided if one wished to acquire a good reputation. One's personal identity was closely tied to that of the friendship group's. Younger boys had to be wary of the group turning against them, and it appeared sometimes that ritual sacrifice was one way of keeping the group together and strong. By colluding with the dominant boys in targeting weaker boys for debagging and the like, the girls reinforced and sharpened the norms of the two dominant gender codes.

The behaviour of some of the girls unwittingly reinforced this mode of masculine representation. Boys who were not seen to have the attributes valued by the dominant male group were jeered at and sometimes singled out for sexual persecution with or without the help of other boys. This threat may have pushed some quiet boys into a more reactive personal style in their dealings with girls. Boys and girls were deeply implicated in the construction and policing of their own sexual identities that were limited by their knowledge of the range of gender identities available.

Orchestration of romance

On occasions, girls would set up schoolboys against other boys, especially older ones, by involving them in disputes over relationships and slanders. This would be most likely to occur in the upper school where the older schoolboys were beginning to be attracted to their female class-mates in a sexual way, but where the attraction was not reciprocated by the girls. But in the lower school the girls also deployed an adaptation of this technique to upset the boys.

Y7 Baker Street boys

ALAN: And the girls say, if they want to get you, and there is a girl you want to go out with, but you don't know her to ask, they go and ask all the scutty girls if they will go out with you.

ND: What's scutty?
COLIN: All the horrible ones.
BRIAN: We call them gippos[10] as well.
ALAN: Like all the ugly girls, the tramps, all the gippos.
COLIN: Frankenstein.
BRIAN: Not smart.

Organising other people's affairs was presented as a girl-dominated practice in many of the interviews, and was seen as a powerful determinant for boy–girl relationships in all the schools. The practice might be construed as the control by sabotage of 'natural' choices of romantic partners by a small clique whose motivation was to maintain its importance and power in the peer group.[11]

In Blunkett Rise School, these cliques of girls could be clearly observed busying themselves by acting as advisers and go-betweens for relationships which were often no more than oral texts and could be spawned and smothered in the space of a lesson. John could be Sandra's boyfriend, Sandra could chuck him, become betrothed to Phil, Tina could be assigned to John; then the whole thing aborted without John even knowing about it. The cliques tended to conform to a fairly restricted model: three or four girls, usually of some academic ability, all very assertive but with at least one physically tough member, behaviourally disruptive in the eyes of teaching staff, and usually with at least one older sister within the school. The presence of an older sibling in the school was often a key point in determining social rank amongst the lower-school pupils. An older member of the family was a useful knowledge resource for many things, but also provided social contact with older boys and girls which was considered very prestigious. Not every younger sibling could, or wished to, utilise this potential: it needed to be associated with a personality that could manipulate situations and enjoy the thrill of causing trouble. After adopting their role as peer group sex-police, the cliques then spent hours of school time carving out pairings and groupings with themselves central to the baroque design.

Alan's problem of being matched to a 'scutty' girl is one example of how the cliques can operate. He likes a girl who is not a member of the clique and is not approved by them. They interfere by approaching another girl who is generally unpopular or considered untouchable in some sense, and propose to her on his behalf. The girl he does fancy will realise what is going on and will likely back away from the boy for fear of angering the clique.

The fact that the cliques actually used their less-favoured class-mates, the scutty girls, as weapons against the boys declared their own status by contrast as important and desirable. The message was 'If you don't treat us with caution you will be left with only the scutty girls as friends'. This tactic was a powerful one: not only did it draw a line between 'nice' and scutty girls, but the perpetrators knew that under those conditions no scutty girl would say she fancied the boy, as that would merely set her up for more ridicule. Instead, she was likely to put on a display of revulsion at the idea, thereby ingratiating herself with the powerful girls and entrenching her own miserable position. This then allowed the clique the opportunity to mock the boy for not being fancied by even the scutty girls, thus demonstrating the all-enveloping nature of peer group culture.

By this process even pupils who had no desire, or even had an actual disinclination, to be involved in the politics of pupil romance, were drawn into it as players without any hope of success.

Style, sexual identity and ethnicity

At St Joseph's School there was a substantial number of African-Caribbean (about 20 per cent) and Asian (about 30 per cent) pupils with a well-established culture distinct from the parent ethnic culture and the indigenous white pupil culture.[12] Mac An Ghaill (1995) illuminates the specificity of each school as a unique site for production of gendered ethnic identities mediated by staff and students. Social class of intake, school ethos and academic achievement interact with varying ratios of racial or ethnic groupings to ascribe certain characteristics to those groups. In working-class schools where there was a majority of Asian pupils succeeding on the school's terms, and a lumpen white failing minority, the Asian boys were ascribed the trait of slyness and complicity, and were considered less masculine as a result. The African-Caribbeans, however, stood in contrast as anti-authority, carefree and exciting, and were sometimes emulated by the macho, disaffected white boys.

Unlike their counterparts at Blunkett Rise School and Patten Avenue High, where African-Caribbeans were in a very small minority, those St Joseph's boys who were attracted to black cultural styles could find ready role models amongst their peers. In Baker Street there was a small but significant number of African-Caribbean pupils and they did not conform to the swaggering stereotype in ascendancy at St Joseph's.[13] Not all working-class boys felt affinity with such styles, nor approved of 'wannabe blacks': this group of boys included one African-Caribbean, Alan, and one mixed-race boy, Brian, along with two white boys.

Y7 Baker Street boys

ALAN: There is one kid in our class and he is really like clean (*sic*) and everything, and he acts hard, thinks he can deck anyone, he smokes and acts hard, he thinks he is a coloured person. And he talks all black languages. He likes reggae . . .
BRIAN: Tries to sing.
ALAN: . . . dances all round class and that, and the once . . .
ND: He is a white kid but you think he wants to be black?
ALAN: Yeah.
BRIAN: But if you fall out with him he'll call you a Negro or half-caste if you are black . . .
ALAN: . . . once when we were in geography he went to the back of the class and dropped his trousers.

ND: Did he?
COLIN: Just to attract attention.
ND: I suppose it worked, eh?
ALAN: Yeah.

This buffoonery seems linked in the group's minds with the adulterated cultural style described above, and re-presents black culture as shallow pop entertainment. The non-white boys in the interview appeared to want to distance themselves from that set of images, whilst acknowledging its appeal to others through its signification of a threatening masculinity.

Even boys and girls at Blunkett Rise, the most homogeneously 'white' school of the four, were aware of the high status given to popular black culture via three signifiers of subcultural style: music, dance and clothing (Gilroy 1987). These commodities commonly appeared amongst the pupils in a watered-down whitened way. 'Fashionable' white boys would wear clothing and hairstyles that approximated those favoured by black male stars, but which lacked an authentic edge. This phenomenon has been an enduring feature of western youth culture and fashion for several generations.

Although the cultural form of 'gangsta rap' had been around for several years, it had only really been picked up by the Blunkett Rise pupils in its emasculated form of mainstream pop. The genre's provenance is the urban crime culture of black gangs in the US, and has attracted notoriety for its assaults on white middle-class mores and its overt glorification of violent crime, violent sex and racial militancy. A small number of white *cognoscenti* were aware of its heavier elements and were attracted by the illicit nature of its sex/race/drugs/violence canon, and this eventually became popular with older boys in Blunkett Rise. Much of the lyric content is still considered too obscene to be given airtime on radio or television. Snoop Doggy Dogg raps titles such as 'For All My Niggaz And Bitches'. Cypress Hill have track listings which include 'Killa Hill Niggaz' and 'How I Could Just Kill A Man'. The lyrics are often blatantly pornographic with imagery such as male anal rape with a hand-gun. The Blunkett Rise boys were aware of the powerful modes of masculinity inherent in the form, and the attraction of those sexualities to their female peers even after weakening by white pop 'boy bands' such as East 17 and their like.[14]

A certain type of macho black style had become *la mode de rigueur* for lads who wanted to express their tough masculinity. With the assimilation of black American rap culture into the white pubescent culture in Blunkett Rise, corridors began to fill with boys wearing outrageously baggy trousers, and teachers' lockers became constipated with confiscated baseball caps. Pressure was on boys to subscribe to the heavy gangsta rap style, and to mimic the rappers' dress code and posture. The piss was taken out of those who preferred milder forms of entertainment, and this form of cultural expression became the identifier of the dominant hetero-masculinity.

Being one of the boys

The younger boys were aware of their own disappearing childhood, and seemed uneasy at having to put away childish things. The boys revealed a dread of unavoidable and imminent change: they were being forced to earn respect in an adult world where their old credit was no longer valid. One noticeable exception to the increasing pull of gang/publicly visible activities was fantasy role-playing games. These games exerted a strong attraction for the lower-status isolates whom the majority of boys felt were 'geekie'.[15] In the main, though, the fetishes of boy-hood (toys and hobbies) were increasingly left behind for more manly interests to which sport, especially soccer, figured as a bridge.

Sport is the most obviously institutionalised continuity agent in male lives. Its currency is good from infancy to the grave, whether as novice, spectator, expert, enthusiast or old sage. Along with being 'a good fighter' it is the most likely means of young boys achieving interest and approval from older males. Fathers are often keen to extend or improve their own sense of sporting success through their sons' activities (Cherry 1984).

The boys' masculinity was expressed in ways that paralleled competitive team behaviour and ethics. They knew they relied on group membership for survival and success, but they also needed to survive the group itself, and a major require-ment for group membership seemed to be individual toughness with a maverick self-reliance. Putting others down to keep yourself up was a common trait. Fear of being the weak link or becoming the fall-guy was a necessary concomitant of team membership. 'The fear and shame of losing was always there for boys . . . the flip-side of winning and success' (Salisbury and Jackson 1996: 206). The subculture of the boys was very rule-bound by the group ethic but, instead of providing a stable moral code, the climate was unstable. Contradictory pressures sprang from con-flicting rules: don't grass on your mates, but take the piss out of them as often as you can; don't hit girls, but make their lives a misery in any other way; don't appear too cocky, but don't reveal your weaknesses; pick on an individual within a group, but never on the group itself. If you can't defend yourself from bullying, tough luck.

Competition for teachers' praise or official recognition of personal status was never mentioned in any positive context. Official discourses of competition and of normality were deployed by staff as means of pupil management, discipline and control. What was important was success in sport, being an independent actor within a high-status and physically robust friendship group. This group identity was, in lower school, constructed in opposition to the values and modes of girls, and represented at times a hyper-masculinity which the boys were incapable of attaining other than by outbursts of sexualised verbal assaults on the girls. A heavy residue of this learned behaviour was present in the practices of upper-school boys, particularly those who were deemed less successful in the eyes of the girls.

Crushed crushes

Some Y7 boys reported the hazards of being just friendly with girls, or of having a girlfriend bring shame upon one. Arthur, below, was not unusual in expressing his fear of social disgrace by having the object of his desire turn him down. Here he clearly prefers the potential physical assault from an older boy to the public humiliation of a knock-back, although he does stress that it is the public aspect that would upset him most.

Y7 St Joseph's boys

BILLY: Yeah they take it the wrong way, if youm talking to a girl they say 'you fancy her, don't you?' And you say 'no, I'm just talking', but . . .

ARTHUR: But they say 'yes you do' and it starts an argument and it turns into a fight.

ND: And does that put you off making friends with a girl, does it affect you?

ARTHUR: Yeah, it does. I have had situations in this school when I have wanted to ask a girl out, but you don't know if they are going to say no, and if they did and it got out, it might get all round school.

ND: And would that be really bad? Would you feel bad about it?

ARTHUR, BILLY, CIARAN, DAK: Yeah.

ND: What about if they did not spread it about *(the rejection)*, what then, would you still feel bad?

ARTHUR: That would be fine. But I wouldn't take that risk.

ND: How about this? Which would be worse, being chased round school by a sixth former who wanted to take your money *(earlier reference)*, or being turned down by a girl?

ARTHUR: The girl. That would be if they told all their mates they had turned you down . . .

DAK: Yeah, being . . . *(Unclear)*

CIARAN: You can run away from the boy . . .

BILLY: I would charge into the next class and escape . . .

ARTHUR: When they have done that it is over, but *(when a girl turns you down)* it can carry on for weeks and you never hear the last of it.

The fear of public knowledge of having been spurned was not eased by Arthur's awareness that everyone felt the same way but no one let on. The fear was of the group of girls knowing something and being able to use it against him, but especially important is the phrase 'never hear the last of it'. This became a recurring theme in the interviews: the fear of being negatively labelled due to some failing perceived by one's peers.

ARTHUR: I have told him *(Ciaran)* secrets about who I have fancied, and he won't tell 'cos he has told me some secrets as well.

CIARAN: I wouldn't tell who he fancies, 'cos at my old school I had this friend who told me he asked this girl 'would you go out with me?' And she said yeah, and then one day he was in the team and he was playing football and she said she would come along and cheer him. Well she did come along . . . with another bigger boy!

ND: Oh no!

CIARAN: . . . he went up to him and he said 'excuse me, that's my girlfriend' and he just pushed him out of the way and decked him.

ND: So, the one who was playing football thought his girlfriend was turning up to watch him, she turned up with another bloke, the footballer complained, so the older lad decked him?

CIARAN: Yeah . . .

ND: So he had a bad day out! He lost his girlfriend and got pushed around in front of all his mates.

CIARAN: He got chased out of school because everyone went on at him and calling him names. They all got at him saying 'why don't you go and ask her out again?'

ND: And he left this school because of that?

CIARAN: No, our old (*primary*) school.

ND: Well can you put into your own words why he did that?

CIARAN: Because everyone kept on at him to go and ask her out, to stop letting himself get pushed around like that. And he said no I don't want to, because she is just two-timing me. And they kept on calling him names and saying that he was an idiot.

The social disgrace felt by this primary-school child for being cuckolded was sufficient to lose him the respect of his mates and make him leave the school. Everyone knew that, had he stayed and faced it out, he would have been reminded of his humiliation any time someone wanted to hurt him. Like the other anecdotes presented here, the 'facts' of the historical event are not as important as the preservation of the myths and meanings. Ciaran's story was recounted as a cautionary tale, and the audience accepted it and used it to frame the cultural experience of managing girlfriends as highly dangerous, an experience for which they were not yet ready.

Body talk

The pressure felt by boys was linked to their relationships with girls, but was usually mediated through their social relations with other boys. The biggest threat to most of the Y7 boys was that of older, bigger, tougher boys, or gangs of boys, making sport of them in ways that would cause long-term damage to their masculine reputations. A peculiar regional method of attacking a young person's credibility was the invocation of the name-tag 'sconner' against a youth with no pubic hair. These older boys in the same school explain the term and its use.

Y10 St Joseph's boys

AARON: We would say sconner to first years usually.

ND: Why sconner?

AARON: Because it looks like a scone.

ND: What's like a scone?

AARON, BEN, CARLTON: *(Laughter)(Unclear)*

ND: I'd see a doctor if that's the case! Is that really why? Because a scone has got no hair on it?

AARON: Yeah, that's why.

ND: *(Laughter)* . . . but neither has . . . a potato!

ALL: *(Laughter)*

CARLTON: The name has just developed, and it's caught on. It's popular all round the school now.

ND: And all the kids in Fordwell would know what sconner meant?

AARON: If you were to say to anyone 'what is a sconner?' they would know. If you said to any kid in Fordwell 'belly-sconner' they would know.

Use of the name was often tied to publication of one's low-status masculinity through the practice of debagging.

Y10 St Joseph's boys

FAZAL: And this kid called Sykes, they debagged him, and the next day he was called a sconner.

GRAHAM: And they debagged him, didn't they? And all the girls *(unclear)* a pube plucker!

The Y7 boys were less enthusiastic about the humorous element in this nickname. Still being at the sharp end, they showed reluctant acceptance of its use against them.

Y7 Baker Street boys

ND: Does it upset you? *(Being called a sconner)*

COLIN: No.

BRIAN: No.

ALAN: No.

COLIN: Not if you were the right age, but if you was 14 or something.

ND: But boys and girls mature at very different rates though . . .

BRIAN: Girls mature faster than boys.

Most of the young people were aware of their situation in the hierarchy of their own sex's pubertal maturation. This awareness was founded on three sources of knowledge: the family, the school and contact culture. The knowledge gained from the family was often prefixed with 'my mum says', and most often was couched in terms of acknowledgement of physical size, becoming a woman or man, or a hazy caution about the pitfalls of teenage life. Research by Martin (1996) supports the differential advice given by parents to boys and girls found here. Boys were told to go out, stand up for themselves and be independent; girls were warned to be careful, stay with friends, keep within safe boundaries. School sex education provided the official discourse of sexual development for the pupils, with many references made to science or PSE lessons. Almost always these references were devoid of human emotions or personalised involvement (DES 1987). The 'hot' material of the interviewees' sexual knowledge was derived from cultural texts such as peer group conversations, observation of older opposite-sex or same-sex behaviour and, occasionally, from the mass media or pornography.[16] These constituted illicit knowledges: knowledges which could not be used within the official conventions of the school, but which rewarded their keepers with enhanced social status, especially when used to access 'adult' humour.

Despite being able to rationalise the unfairness of the sconner epithet due to his knowledge of normal pubertal development, Brian was clear about the defining power of the word, and its abuse by older boys to undermine younger boys' masculinity. The seniority of age was not just exemplified by adults running the school, but was indicated by the bestowal of privileges incrementally through the years. Different rules that may well have seemed trivial to the staff were picked up and amplified in the peer culture. Some schools had different uniform ties to mark off the age bands. Some schools had preferential queuing arrangements for lunches or assemblies. Some schools gave over facilities to the upper-school pupils, such as use of the music suite or gymnasium at break times. In most of the schools there was a special common room reserved for the most senior pupils. Prefect or similar roles were assigned to those pupils who were older but also more conforming to school ideals. The amplification and distortion of these privileges were replayed in the peer culture through an expectation of casual abuse of power.

BRIAN: Like, just 'cos I was new to this school, right, and I was walking around, these second years (Y8) were acting big and they came up to me and asked me if I was a sconner and everything.

ND: They were asking you if you were?

BRIAN: And I said 'no,' and they said 'I bet you am', and I said 'no'. They kept saying 'you am, ant you?'

COLIN: They've got to be pervs to want to know stuff about your private lives, ain't they?

ND: (. . .) If you said 'mind your own business whether I'm a sconner or not, you must be a pervert if you want to know', what would they do if you said that?

ALAN: It depends on what type of person they am.

BRIAN: They'd deck you.

COLIN: If them bullies they'll have you, punch you and that.

ALAN: Like I was walking home, and they said 'if youm a sconner, jump the fence'. And I was walking and I daren't jump the fence right, and they pushed me over it and a nail went through my foot.

Brian, Colin and Alan were aware of a moral wrong being perpetrated against them by the Y8 bullies; they saw themselves as young children deserving of pro-tection within the school regime. Here they entered into the school's official discourse of equal opportunities, fair play and value of the individual, but they were also aware of the real power imbalance in the peer culture, of their physical and perhaps numerical weakness. Whilst actually impotent to do anything about the problem, they found some succour in the face of these contradictions by naming the bullies 'pervs', thereby reinforcing their sense of righteousness.

The usage of the terms 'gay' and 'perv' to denote very different types of dis-approved male behaviour gives some further clues to the actual meanings of each. The term 'gay' was reserved not as abuse for sexual deviance, but for a weak sub-dominant masculinity. Brian, Colin and Alan recognised the activities of debagging and sconner-baiting due to their direct or vicarious experience. The boys' anecdotes support the view that such a male-to-male form of sexual harassment was seen not as 'gay' but as 'pervy'. The sexual dimension is acknowledged as differentiating these activities from common bullying, but it cannot be called 'gay', for that would imply a physical weakness on the part of the bullies which manifestly contradicts their actual power position. Instead, their power is interpreted as excessively masculine but perverted: a gang of boys sexually bullying a smaller immature boy, when perhaps they should be pester-ing girls instead.

Schoolboys, lads and blokes

The problems that faced the older boys were very different. Whereas the Y7 11-year-olds co-existed with the girls in a fairly formal and dispassionate way, the 14-and 15-year-old boys were much more sexually charged and found the close proximity of attractive sexually mature females very difficult to manage. These girls, below, give their assessment of boys' shortcomings. The gendered differ-ences of their interests at the same age level is marked: even their mutual preoccupation with sex can be seen to take on very divergent cultural forms, with the boys claiming masculinity through technical expertise and knowledge, and the girls valuing the social venue of the night-club.

Y11 Blunkett Rise girls

RONA: They are so immature, aren't they? You could be talking about seeing your boyfriend in the club or somewhere, and they butt in and go on about 'what sort of car has he got?' If you tell them they say it's rubbish and start going on about the type, and who they know that has a better one and all this . . .

RT: Would you say that is just jealousy . . .

RONA: It is and it isn't. They say it, I think they say it to get at you, 'cos there is nothing you are interested in that is the same, so they say something about your boyfriend.

CLAIRE: They talk a load of rubbish though, don't they? I mean look at Steven White in our year, can you even imagine him with a girlfriend? What would he talk about? His idea of a good time is making a fire up on the mount (*recreational area*).

RT: Why do you think they pester you in school so much if they have nothing in common?

RONA: They are sex mad! They are all sex mad! (*Laughter*) I swear it, they are!

CLAIRE: So are we though!

RONA: Well, yeah, but we *do* it! (*Laughter*)

AMY: Hey! Not all the time!

ALL: (*Laughter*)

RONA: No, seriously, though, it is all they seem to think about, they go on as though they are real studs, but they are just desperate to get a girlfriend. They will have to grow up a bit first.

CLAIRE: But all the little third years (Y9), they think the boys in our year are gorgeous, don't they? Look at your sister, she fancies Clarkie in our year, doesn't she?

AMY: Yeah . . . tart! (*Laughter*)

CLAIRE: But we used to fancy the fifth years (Y11) when we were younger, didn't we?

RONA: Not all of them, one or two . . .

Whilst boys and girls recognised the mutuality of their sexual inclinations at this stage, the principal and repelling gender difference was the boys' public dissociation of the sexual from the social. Boys' sexual interest was in physical relief, and if that could be achieved without committing to any emotional relationship it would be perfect. Where boys did gain pleasure from social aspects of sexual relations, they tended to be couched in terms of enlarged reputation or popularity. Any evidence of boys' romantic feelings towards particular girls was purged by the male group, and seen as 'gay'.

Senior girls' sex-police

In each school visited there was always an exceptional handful of boys who were considered worthy of courtship by girls of their own age. In Blunkett Rise, two such were Pinxi and Boot, but despite their elevated status (of which they were very aware), and their initial insouciance towards anything challenging the mastery of their own destinies, they revealed underlying forces in the peer group which were more powerful than comfortable. In particular, 'hard' girls seemed to be able to bless or damn personal relationships by remote control.

Y10 Blunkett Rise boys

PINXI: Last night at the disco, my ex-girlfriend (*Y10*) and a girl that wants to go out with me (*Y9*), the ex didn't like it and decided to go with all her mates and talk to her. Then I had to go to Marchfield and when I came into school today I found that they had hit her.

ND: So are you still going out with her?

PINXI: No, not her. See there was my ex and this younger girl, the one that wanted to go out with me is a third year. My ex didn't like it so she and her mates said to the third year 'if you touch him we will kick your head in'.

ND: And they did!

(. . .)

PINXI: At the end of the day it doesn't affect me. She doesn't rule my life. I decide who I go out with.

(. . .)

PINXI: A lot of lads think if a girl finishes with them 'oh well', and carry on. But if a girl is finished then they cry and all that. The lads aren't bothered they just walk away. But then they get hassle from their *(ex-girlfriends')* mates to go back out with her, and they end up back together again anyway. That happens to me. I finish with a girl, my mates want me to go back out with her and put pressure on.

ND: Do they?

PINXI: Yeah all the time! It is 90 per cent of the reason.

BOOT: That is a pressure situation. Ha ha!

ND: Why do mates do that?

PINXI: I don't know!

ND: But what has it got to do with them?

BOOT: We all do it!

ND: But why?

BOOT: It's the norm, isn't it?

ND: But why?

BOOT: We think 'this is normal'. *(Laughter)*

Pinxi's choice of a girl whom he particularly liked but who was disapproved of by the group obviously did cause him some emotional conflict. He had begun the interview by announcing how much he was his own man, but later verified the irresistible pressure of the group. Towards the end of the interview Pinxi returned to the incident outside the disco, this time with a rather more sensitised view of events.

ND: What sort of things can girls call or do to boys to hurt them?

PINXI: Like, you know that girl that was with me last night? It's my life, what I want to do with the other girl, but they really got me with her. They said they were going to beat her up and it got to me. I was really cut up, really upset, I had to leave the disco at half past eight, it didn't finish till 10, and I was that cut up that they were going to hit her I asked her to come with me, but she wanted to stay with her friends. I was really cut up with that at home. They got to me by that.

Pinxi explained how helpless he had felt about the blatant interference in his affairs and his inability to protect Jackie. He was unable to show publicly any emotion or sympathy for her without reducing his macho stock (the reason for his popularity in the first place) or possibly encouraging further harassment of Jackie. This incident and its implications for individuals' freedom to act autonomously within the peer culture are later explored in depth.

The scripts at Blunkett Rise appear like a distorted and refracted Shakespearean tragedy. The social structures were not based upon family or class lines in the formal manner of the Capulets and Montagues, but the inherent power of the disapproval of the group, however that group was constituted, remained the orthodox base under the individual's 'choice' of partner.

Asynchronous attractions

Whilst exceptions like Pinxi and Boot were found to be desirable amongst girls of their own year, most of the boys were frozen out by the girls in their year as too immature to be considered as boyfriends. Generally, the boys had been extremely interested in sex from about Y8, but not usually until about late Y10 or Y11 were the few able to form sexual relationships in school with girls, and these would commonly be around a year or so younger than themselves. Despite their physical sexual development, they felt unfairly disadvantaged as desirable males because of the absence of certain masculine accoutrements such as money and a driving licence.

Many boys felt frustrated at the treatment the girls gave them due to these material deficits, and the girls would make use of such power in an indirect but effective way. This dynamic process of attraction, repulsion, desire, frustration and hostility was complex and unstable. It was also very difficult to explore in fifty minutes, but the boys here give a good account of the situation as they found it. The cycle is entered at the hostility phase, but soon works its way through.

Y10 St Joseph's boys

ND: So what sort of things might you say to girls that you wanted to upset?

CARLTON: That they're ugly, 'cos if girls, like, often put make-up on, do their hair and things, so if you say they're ugly they'd feel bad about themselves 'cos they'd spent so much time doing it, and they think they're pretty, but if you call them ugly they don't like that.

AARON: You don't just call them ugly, 'cos I mean they're *not* ugly.

ND: So you mean you'd say that . . .

CARLTON: Dog.

ND: So, you've used lots of words in describing that, but you're saying they'd know what you meant if you just said they're a dog?

CARLTON: Yeah.

AARON: Yeah.

Aaron's recognition of the objective physical beauty of the girls is the key to the boys' hostility: the girls are desirable but the boys are not. The most effective means of attacking the girls' sexuality is, therefore, not by denying their beauty, but by finding some other aspect, a negative quality which is within the power of the boys to define, then operationalising that.

Here the definition is 'dog'. The girl is too obviously attractive to other boys (and to Aaron) to be called simply 'ugly', so Aaron must attribute some other form of unattractiveness to her. Aaron's choice is to attack her sexuality because the constellation of characteristics inherent in her sexuality allows him to shift the targets if challenged. So 'dog' *might* mean ugly, or having a bad figure, or being too sexually experienced, or a bad sexual performer, or unpopular, or maybe just unappealing to Aaron. She might be good looking, but she would not make a decent girlfriend because Aaron decides she is a dog.

What *actually* makes her a dog is her propensity to make Aaron feel inadequate and threatened. Aaron feels inadequate and threatened because she is attractive to him and others, but prefers the others. She prefers the others because Aaron is immature, and so he is inadequate.

ND: What he's *(Carlton)* just said, he's said that they are always talking about older boys to make you jealous. Is that right, is that why they talk about them?

AARON: Yeah, well it seems like it. Like, they'd be talking on a table to one another and we'd be like, on the side, then one of them would turn round and say something to us. Then carry on.

ND: So you're saying they draw you in, let you know what they're talking about, so you assume that they're doing it to wind you up, to make you feel small. Is that right?

CARLTON: Yeah.

ND: So how do you feel – does that bother you?

BEN: No.

ND: Does it bother you?

Aaron: No.

ND: Does it bother you?

CARLTON: It happens all the time – I'm used to it.

ND: It happens all the time?

CARLTON: If I fancied the girl and they were talking about older boys it would bother me but I *don't* fancy them, so it doesn't bother me.

Carlton denies the possibility that, despite the girls in his class attracting older boyfriends, he is interested in them himself. The reason he gives for attacking them is not because he *is* jealous, but that *they are trying to make him jealous* through their constant references to the older boys. Carlton explains one way of hitting back is to talk in a similar way about the better-looking younger generation of girls in the year below. It is clear to these boys, however, that they are still losers in the market of sexual economy, and when this becomes explicit they admit it ruefully but with some humorous pathos.

ND: So you lot spite those girls by talking about girls that are younger than them, that you think are better looking than them. Right? And is there, these younger girls, do they go out with lads in your form then, in your year?

AARON: No!

ND: They *still* don't – oh well!

ALL: (*Laughter*)

AARON: One of them goes out with my cousin who's left school – she goes out with him.

CARLTON: *They* tend to go out with a lot older people as well.

ND: Right.

AARON: Not all of them, but some of them do.

CARLTON: Some of them just don't go out with people!

BEN: Seems like in junior schools that's probably the only time they go out with somebody in the same class.

It is this socio-sexual vacuum for boys in the middle years of secondary schooling that, unforeseen by me, became a recurring feature in the interviews. The boys who took part in the interviews in the host schools were not likely to be boys who were overlooked by girls in preference to other boys of the same age. Most were recruited for their popularity and self-confidence as well as their articulacy and perceived stable adjustment to life in school. If these boys declared such difficulties in managing their socio-sexual relations, then it would be reasonable to assume that less 'successful' pupils might be found to be in dire straits. Conversely, it may be that boys who are successful in the terms of their parents and teachers are not likely to have developed whatever is needed to be successful in competing for the interest of the opposite sex against older youths who have a quite different array of attractions.[17]

Whether these respondents were more or less prone to rejection by the girls in their year is not so important as how they perceived the situation and how they dealt with it, and the above method was commonplace. The picture is of the better-adjusted 14-year-old schoolboy learning to attack girls' sexuality as a defence against a diminished sense of masculinity. It is the fervent hope of most teachers that pupils will retain for many years what they learn in school, and if they do, there seems strong reason to worry about the incipient misogyny in the hidden curriculum.

Taking it away

By the time the boys were in their final year of school, most of their concerns about rank were resolved as Y11 generally acquired status by default even where sixth forms were in operation. Those who were interviewed were largely pupils more motivated towards achieving good exam grades, and were more in control of their identity. They felt less under pressure to prove their sexuality in the direct manner they had used a couple of years before. The masculine accoutrements of cash and cars were now well within sight and figured in their self-construct as

importantly as girlfriends. A summative expression from this time regarding relationships with girls referred to deferred gratification: 'There will be time for that
later.' It was also apparent that the socio-sexual vacuum had begun to leak, with
some considerable interest shown by the younger, but maturationally compatible
girls towards the now physically masculinised 16-year-olds.

The relationships with, and attitudes towards, the girls in their own year were
now much more convivial. Some boys were still indulging in the same anti-social
behaviours they had practised over the years, but these were regarded as highly
unimpressive by the majority of pupils. For the most part, irrespective of the
dearth of intra-year romances, the boys and girls appeared much more willing to
collaborate academically and socially where appropriate, or otherwise tolerate
the remaining differences in outlook and interests.

Summary

Sexualised interpersonal conflict amongst the pupils interviewed was high on
their list of concerns about school life. There was a definite preoccupation with
these social interactions at school, a sense of not being able to live outside the
conditions in which these practices were produced. Making an early success of
one's reputation was extremely important, and this necessitated some serious
competition both within one's own sex and with the opposite sex, and gender relations were structured around this conflict. School provided a prime venue for the
orchestration of romantic pairings conducted by the girls whilst ostensibly
engaged in schoolwork.

Clear gender differences were apparent in the forms of sexualised conflict practised amongst the pupils. Boys were subjected to a range of practices which
constituted sexual bullying by girls and by other boys, but were also subject to less
obvious forms of attack. The most prevalent form mentioned in the transcripts
generally was sexualised verbal abuse. The boys were called 'wankers' and 'dickheads' and many other casually obscene names, but those which gave most offence
were associated with homosexuality, or rather, the absence of high-status masculinity: 'poof', 'queer', 'homo', 'gay'. The ascription of such terms was seen as a
major threat to the development of a desired reputation unless one could retaliate
promptly and effectively.

Of significant importance were the transient forms of sexual bullying. These
forms, sconner-baiting for example, were always present in the school, but individual pupils quickly passed through that phase. This had the effect that no one
suffered the same forms of practice long enough to develop effective defensive
strategies against them. The power of language to define and limit was more
apparent than its power to liberate and imagine. The younger boys did not perceive these social practices as sexual bullying: they were nameless, but the boys'
recognition of their potency underlined the important part sexuality had to play
in the peer group conflict.

Younger boys were fairly oblivious to the erotic potential of their female peers:
girlfriends were seen by some as distractions from boyish interests and by others as

too difficult to manage properly at that age. Mishandling could result in disaster, not least by the intrusion of older boys into one's affairs.

Despite these disincentives, most of the boys saw it as important to court the girls' desires in order to be a popular boy. The boys often revealed a fear of being rejected by a girl to whom they had made an appeal, especially if there was a chance that it would be made public. A barrage of insults and sexual denigration would be sent up to disguise tender feelings, and the few pairings that did exist would encounter severe pressure from the male peer group. Although the boys developed increasing sexual interest in their female counterparts over the years, they seemed to undergo a commensurate emotional hardening.

Official school practices impinged heavily on the pupils' informal social systems. Around this official discourse the pupils constructed their own codes of behaviour, and this was often at variance with the school's official line, but formed from it and around it. Where the school spoke of equality but competition, value of the individual but sense of community, these sophisticated, seemingly contradictory ideologies could be misinterpreted, distorted and replayed in conflict. A recurring example of this was the championing of the 'everyone here is equal' rhetoric, whilst demonstrably favouring older pupils with privileges and informally differentiating by gender many interpersonal interactions. This contradiction was reflected in the pupils' power hierarchies amongst the age groups and enforced unofficial inequalities through bullying behaviour.

The value of the good social reputation was sometimes at extreme odds with the school's official preferences. It may be that, as a defence against feelings of failure on the school's terms, many boys felt the need to construct an alternative set of validation processes to raise their self-esteem (Ball 1981). As the school sets limits on their validation of self through competing for academic success, the boys' claims for status could emerge in the cultural form of bullying. This is not to say that there was a stream of beatings given out to weaker boys: the subcultural hierarchies were so well formed and established that such crudity was not often required. Instead there was a constant struggle for social survival which demanded a strong identity forged in that struggle and validated by that group.

2   Girl troubles

Interview climates

Each interview had a slightly unique feel in relation to the others. Some were very quiet, almost confessional, and others were lively to boisterous. Some of the groups were initially nervous and others quite confident. These differences in climate were not determined by the sex of the groups as much as by their age, although variations were evident here too.

There was no major discernible difference in the concerns expressed by girls from the four different schools but a difference in attitude did appear between the Y7 and the Y10 girls across the schools. For the Y7 girls, the boys figured as a close-up problem, but this was mixed in with the exciting challenge of coping with two new experiences: their puberty, and the general demands of 'big school'.

During the girls' interviews, the most commonly cited objectionable behaviours were perpetrated by boys, although the less structured discussions and field observations often featured other girls as an active threat to peaceful existence. The specific behaviours were being called names with a sexual connotation like 'slag', 'bitch', 'prossie', 'cow' or 'dog'. Initially, the interviewees spoke of these attacks as undifferentiated from such names as 'skinny', 'spotty', 'big-nose' and other childish epithets, but deeper discussion revealed very different meanings ascribed to this form of verbal abuse. The girls were unanimous in their dislike of this practice, but many dismissed it as juvenile and impotent. Their view was that it existed in their world like litter – ubiquitous, unpleasant and unnecessary, but usually not personal or hurtful and, in any case, too well established for them to do much about it.

Sticky labels

Y7 Blunkett Rise girls

JOAN: I hate it when they just go on and on calling you names, like.

ND: What names are the worst?

JOAN: Like when they call you a bitch, and you haven't even done anything, it's like stupid, but they always call it you, even when they aren't even mad.

LANA: Yeah . . . they say it just to be hard, just for no reason. We don't do anything to them, do we?

ND: Why do you think they do call you names?

TRISHA: Like she *(Lana)* said, they think it is hard. They want to make them big.

ND: Why do they say those particular nasty words, why do they say 'bitch' and things like that instead of, well say 'stupid' or 'stuck up' or something else, you know?

JOAN: I reckon it's just to look hard, to say something that you can't say back to them.

ND: So maybe it is to do with you being girls, they are choosing those words?

JOAN: I suppose, I don't know.

Even at this stage there was a tacit understanding of their girlhood being essentially a vulnerable area and therefore a target for the boys' name-calling. As they progressed up the years through school, an increasing use of sexualised verbal abuse was noticed by the older girls, peaking around Y9 (13–14 years of age). The boys verbally attacked girls for their femaleness using sexual terms that were seemingly irrelevant to the situation.

The language of harassment and bullying was filtered through a growing awareness of sexualised identity and emerged as a concentrate of gendered vilification. By Y10 many of the girls were looking beyond the school walls and marking time until they could leave. Already their social, cultural and sexual interests lay outside school, and they regarded their schoolboy peers as way behind in terms of maturity but an active hazard to their own development.

Collusion between some boys and some girls to attack other girls was cited, with only rare instances of mixed-sex collusion against boys.

Y10 Baker Street girls

CELIA: Sometimes it has to do with the clothes, if you are wearing a short skirt or something, they call you, or if you are always hanging around the boys they will call you a tart.

BEL: But it is the girls mainly that will say it isn't it?

ANDREA: *(Laughter)* Yeah it is.

CELIA: And the girls call the other girls slags and all stuff like that.

The boys' presence in the same classes created tension, with the two sexes in enforced close proximity but conscious of differences which prevented real integration. The girls harboured several contradictory notions about the supremacy of boys in school, simultaneously claiming they had a favoured status and were given more credit for achievement as well as dominating social relations, but despising their inadequacies, immaturity and lack of achievement.

RT: When you were in lower school did the boys in your class tend to annoy you in the same way as they do now?

BEL: They used to call you fat and ugly and stuff like that, but as you get elder *(sic)* it gets . . . worse. They get more things to say about you, because they get to know you better . . . they can think of worse things to say.

ANDREA: They find more things about you and they use it against you like, when they are not particularly in with you like.

RT: So when you were younger it was things like name-calling . . .

ANDREA: Things like name-calling, obvious things about your appearance when they see you. When they have got to know you they find more things out what to say about you.

RT: Do you think that the name-calling gets more of a sexual nature as you get older?

ANDREA, BEL, CELIA: Yes! (*Laughter*)

RT: Pretty obviously yes then! Do you think that that is because of what the girls are actually doing or what the boys think they are doing?

CELIA: What they think you are doing.

BEL: They presume.

CELIA: Yeah, they start talking about it, and then they slip up and when you correct them . . .

Ethnicity and gender: fighting on two fronts

At Baker Street School a group of four Y10 girls of Indian origin described their interactions with other ethnic groups. Cheeva and Amsa saw the smaller group of Jamaican pupils as having power beyond their numbers, and believed they were the main tormentors of Asian pupils.

Y10 Baker Street girls

RT: How many Asians are there compared to white kids . . . ?

AMSA: I think it's whites and Indians about equal really, maybe a few more whites . . . with a few Jamaican kids.

CHEEVA: But I think most people are scared of them (*Jamaicans*), that's why the Indians don't name-call anybody.

AMSA: And you get racist comments as well sometimes, don't you?

STELLA: Yeah.

AMSA: But it's not that bad really . . . you only get it when the groups of Jamaicans and the Asians are together don't you?

The abusive traits of individual boys were elaborated by the girls, and the anecdote below illustrates a combination of racist and sexist harassment apparently common in the experience of the girl respondents.

RT: Do you think it would be the same boys who would call girls both (*sexist and racist*) those sort of names?

AMSA: Yeah. (*Laughter*)

RT: You are nodding, you do?

STELLA: Yeah. (*Laughter*)

AMSA: They are mostly in our form ain't they?

STELLA: Yeah.

AMSA: I was thinking of one in particular. *(Knowing looks)*

STELLA, CHEEVA. Yeah, definitely, yeah.

AMSA: I think Mikey, Chas, and Ray, definitely.

STELLA: Chas, definitely.

AMSA: That is who I thought of!

STELLA: He is the most . . . ! We was in science today, and he kept picking on me especially, he was going . . . erm . . . I asked him about this thing, and I have got like a sort of *(white, blotchy)* rash on my arm, and he kept saying something about . . . he said 'your boyfriend has probably been coming all over your arm', and I said 'shut up', so he called me a whore, so I just smacked him one. That was it really, I can't describe him, he is just an idiot.

The content of exchanges such as these were found quite shocking when encountered by teaching staff. Many teachers saw them as perverse and abnormal, and often responded with strong disciplinary action. The pupils were much less troubled by them unless there was an added dimension of hurt such as the prolonged persecution of an individual, a publicised intimacy that struck at the core of the individual's self-esteem, or if the victim had been tenderised by other previous assaults. The girls' recognition that repetition of the hurtful names might result in cognitive change was testimony to the power of labelling and the desperation of some pupils to avoid it. In the adolescents' world, the instability of identity left one at risk of actually believing you must be what others say you are.

The girls here were relaxed about discussing their problems with the female interviewer, but reticent about making formal complaint: partly because of the feeling it would not be dealt with successfully, and partly because of the relationship between girls' and teachers' sexualities. The lack of faith in the school's official systems for dealing with sensitive complaints was not a contentious issue for the girls. They accepted it would be difficult enough to deal with bullying, but the additional sexual dimension might somehow end up with themselves being seen as the problem, and their sexuality being scrutinised as a result. Far better, then, to deal with it on a peer level or suffer in silence.

Stella's report suggests that, although she didn't welcome this kind of comment, she handled it as irritating rather than offensive, and did not credit the perpetrator with any power other than that of persistence. The boy's disgusting remarks can be seen as attempts to elicit salacious details of Stella's sex life for his own titillation, or as a direct attempt to embarrass her as he makes a mock enquiry about her skin pigmentation. If she replies at all, she must make a statement about her sex or her colour[1] that places her at a disadvantage to him, but Stella confounds this attempt by her blatant refusal to be drawn. In this instance, the difficult option of seeking help from the school's discipline system is rendered redundant by Stella's own strength and competence: she just smacks him one.

Very few pupils felt comfortable in making formal complaint about any form of peer behaviour (Tattum and Herbert 1993). Claims of personal victimisation were considered particularly hazardous due to expectations of retaliation, and sexual matters were further silenced because of embarrassment. In addition to these considerations, ethnicity created further complications.

Holland discovered significant variations among Asian, African-Caribbean and white British young women in their ability to discuss sexual matters with parents, peers and teachers. A greater number of young Asian women found parental attitudes forbidding than did the other ethnic groups, and consequently relied on peer information and school sex-education in developing their sexual knowledge.

> The Asian young women for example were subject to very particular pressures in relation to their sexuality and sexual practice emanating from culturally defined conceptions of family and religious obligation. It seemed too, that the double standard of sexual behaviour for women and men, whilst still significant for most young women in the sample, was particularly powerful for those in ethnic minority groups discussed in this study.
>
> (Holland 1993: 36)

Carnal knowledge and reputation

Girls' developing bodies were a highly vulnerable area to boys' attacks. Two modes were deployed in such attacks: the first against visible signs of puberty.

Y10 St Joseph's boys

ND: What other things, the things we have been calling sexual bullying, would upset the girls?

GRAHAM: If there is something wrong with them, like, if they have eczema or something, if they have loads of spots . . . tease them about it . . .

SPIRO: Yeah . . . we would say 'you'll never get a lad with a face like that!'

GRAHAM: If they had loads of spots 'spotted dick!' *(Laughter)*

The second form of attack was against those concealed areas of bodily development which were accessed via intimate contact and later relayed through the peer group.

ND *(laying out Q-sort 'Nicknaming Personal Attributes')*:   So . . . spotty . . .

FAZAL: Scabby, we say.

SPIRO: Hairy tits!

All: *(Extended laughter)*

ND: What?

FAZAL: Hairy tits, there is this girl who is supposed to have hairy tits.

ND: How do you know that?

NASUR: It went round for a while, it was this guy who went out with her and he started it.

SPIRO: He didn't come to this school, but it went round here mostly.

These publicised intimacies had a devastating effect on the victim's self-esteem, acknowledged by even these boys after they had sobered up. They went on to recount the war of disinformation between the sexes at school, with campaign of vilification followed by counter-campaign. Spiro noted numerous girl-to-boy attacks, usually centring on accusations of small penis size though he also complained of being called 'lanky legs'. The most hurtful attacks were against the concealed private parts which were smelly, misshapen, the wrong size or abnormal in some other way. The impossibility of refutation was the winning weapon, with the victim pinioned by his or her need to prove normality, but in doing so inviting further ridicule.

Although the older girls were generally more confident in their handling of the boys in their year, they still objected to the level of harassment they had to endure within the school system. Outside the school they were afforded whatever respect and status their appearance and behaviour merited. Teachers (especially women), in denying the girls the cultural expression of physical maturity by proscribing make-up, elaborate hairstyles, jewellery and 'immodest' clothes, damaged the girls' claims to their rightful feminine status. This status was usually on a par with boys two or three years older than themselves.

In school they felt boys' long-term knowledge of their development, and their presumption to parity because of age, resourced the boys' verbal armoury, and were constantly at hand to prevent them expressing a new adult identity through their sexuality. This intimate knowledge was especially perilous if there had been an earlier 'romance' and the boy held secrets or lies over the girl following a split.

Y10 Baker Street girls

RT: What actually might a boy do to hurt a girl about your age then?

ANDREA: Say you had been out with them. Well they might say things about you, in front of a crowd, like if you had just split up with them, they would say you were no good, to shame you up in front of your mates. They say stuff about what you had done with them and spread it all round the school so you would get a bad name.

CELIA: They would say, make it sound like they had finished with you, because you wasn't worth it and you never finished with them.

Although these were girls voicing the fear of intimate knowledge being used against them, many boys had the same worries. Spiro explained why it mattered who was thought to have been in control of the ending of the relationship.

Y10 St Joseph's boys

SPIRO: It is important 'cos it shows like if you were dumped by her she thinks 'I dumped him, I don't need him', and so she gets all the (*unclear*), everyone thinks big of her, and you, you are the lower . . .

FAZAL: Youm left low.

SPIRO: You aint popular no more, like you used to be.

Another boy was teased incessantly following an ex-girlfriend's account of his labours in unfastening the purely decorative buttons on her blouse during a 'snog'. The boy's bungling efforts were translated into the nickname 'Buttons' for the rest of his schooldays and perhaps beyond.

Ending relationships was considered to be exceptionally dangerous for girls, more so if the boy then went out with a girl who was a 'hard-case'.

Y10 St Joseph's girls

RT: When boys and girls have relationships, and then they break up, do you think that some of these things (*defamation*) happen more often then?

AMSA: When that happens they say 'slag' and that about them. They say how tight you am and things like that, but when they've had sex with them and then they say how rubbish they am. That's what normal people do anyway. They like say that about them.

BELINDA: Once the boys tell another boy, then they tell their (*new*) girlfriend, then the girl gets it back and they start arguing and everything.

The picture painted here is messy, full of contradictions and illogicalities, but whilst it is not clear or rational it does create a powerful impression of the volatility of romantic relationships in secondary school. Some girls offered reasons for the hostility, and picked up on the different motives for targeting girls.

Year 10 Patten Avenue girls

RT: Well, are the girls that would get picked on for general bullying the same ones that would probably get picked on for the sexual bullying as well?

JO: I can think of some but they would not be the same girls (*as get both sorts of hassle*).

EVA: I think . . . yeah, because the people that are going to get bullied as in name-calling, are people that they don't like, but the people that get the sexual bullying are going to be the people that they *do* like. The people that they think are pretty, so it's two different things.

JO: Yeah, they *do* like.

Signs and wonders

Younger girls concurred with this general increase in boys' sexual harassment with age and physical maturity, but described a more confused victimology, with girls being abused simply because of their advanced maturation.[2]

The effects of this attention were felt differentially according to the constitution of the girl and her social prestige at the time. Where a girl had high peer status she might acquire even greater influence, but where she was not popular or had few social skills she could feel that she was seen as just a sex object. Significantly supportive of this thesis, Thorne (1993) remarks that her group of college women recalled that social un/desirability of early maturation was dependent on whether it had been achieved by girls who were already popular. The girls below expressed their apprehension of the inevitable signs of puberty in terms of peer social response rather than the inconvenience and physical/emotional discomfort which they expected to accompany, for example, menstruation.

Y7 Baker Street girls

RT: Have you found it more difficult as you get older?

BABS: Yes.

ANGIE: As you get older people can see you are growing up, so they, do you know what I mean?

RT: Yes. You are developing into young women.

ANGIE: Yeah, well they start making stupid stories.

RT: And do you find that hard to cope with?

ANGIE: Yeah, if they say it too much, if they just said it once or twice . . .

RT: Do some girls get more of that . . . being called a lesbian or a slag or that sort of teasing?

CATHERINE: Yeah. There are some girls who are more well developed for their age.

RT: And they would get more of that?

CATHERINE: Yeah.

ANGIE: And you know that some day you are going to start your periods, and there was one girl who started her periods, and on the last day of term she had to put it (*her tampon*) in her bag. And one of the boys found it and was throwing it all round the class. That was in the juniors.

RT: Is that something that worries you as a group of girls?

ANGIE: Yeah in case any boys found out.

BABS: If I started in the middle of a lesson I'd really worry.

CATHERINE: Yeah, but the boys won't find out about our periods, 'cos we'd just tell our close friends . . .

ANGIE: . . . I'm telling no one!

The behaviour and attitudes of boys towards girls in their class beginning menstruation are very well documented (Brooks-Gunn and Ruble 1983; Weiner (ed.) 1985; Askew and Ross 1988), and reports of group bullying behaviour of this sort are perfectly consonant with the findings in the interviews and observations in these interviews. In her excellent report of a multi-method research project into girls' experiences of menstruation at school, Prendergast (1992) draws a feminist anthropological analysis from the school peer-group behaviour in her description of boys shaming girls by reworking the 'polluting' associations of menstruation. Boys were aware of the intensity of feeling attached to menstruation by the girls. They closely watched them for an opportunity to capitalise on any indiscretion, such as them taking something out of their bag when visiting the toilet or getting permission to miss PE, for example.

One incident reported by Prendergast supports not only the power of definition by labelling that is found here, but the importance of the teaching staff's response to pupil problems. 'One 5th year girl described how she had been called 'Bloody Mary' for almost two years after a humiliating incident where the teacher would not let her go to the toilet, and she had stained her skirt and the chair she had been sitting on' (1992: 64).

Shame and concealment concerning menstruation is not always the case, however. Many girls enjoy the experience on an emotional or even spiritual level if they are 'on time' and are supported and congratulated by mothers or friends (Martin 1996). In my workplace school, one 11-year-old girl called me whilst I was covering a science lesson for an absent colleague and asked for permission to go home: 'Sir, I come on this morning and I thought I'd be OK until dinner, but it's really heavy and I've started to leak. Can I go home and get some Tampax from my mum?' This detailed request was made across the room from her mixed-sex work group, with no great fuss but a little embarrassed laughter from the boys she was sitting with. Many other Blunkett Rise girls were similarly forthright about menstrual matters, with messages being passed via boy class-mates to PE staff that they were not participating today because they were 'on'. The lower-status girls were less vocal about their condition than the higher-profile girls, but the general climate was certainly less oppressive regarding the whole matter than either above-mentioned research or my own findings from other schools suggest.

This situation may have been due to the confidence and assertiveness of a number of key individuals in Blunkett Rise who had constructed a femininity that was particularly strong in announcing its sexuality. These girls asserted their status positions on a bedrock of frankness about their own bodies that snatched the initiative from boys who might otherwise abuse the information if they felt they had discovered it for themselves.

In Y7, most of the girls interviewed did not consider themselves sexually attractive or active. The development of breasts was the first publicly visible signal of sexual maturation, and this presented a number of hazards for the girls to negotiate. Many of the girls felt their sexual desirability was a threat to their safety and to their relations with parents.

The girls frequently mentioned parental warnings following their breast development, with comments about boys now being attracted to them as young women, and the need to maintain tight control of their bodies. Their courtship with boys tended to be very short-lived and characterised by merely agreeing to go out with someone, but not actually having much to do with them. Relationships were mainly kept within the same year group but, as the girls developed even more mature-looking physiques, they became attractive to boys several years older and tended to choose them rather than the boys of their own age.

Y7 Baker Street girls

RT: Can you think of any girls in your year who would get a lot of that (*name-calling*) and not be able to cope? And why is it them and not someone else?

ANGIE: Well the girl I am thinking of is really popular and pretty and that, and everybody likes her and that, and most of the boys fancy her.

RT: And yet she gets a lot of name-calling?

ANGIE: Yeah if she's going out with someone and another boy asks her out she will knock him back and he goes straight into name-calling, and says it was just a joke (*the asking out*) anyway.

RT: And who were you thinking of? Not her name . . . but how is she different?

CATHERINE: The girl I'm thinking of is developing and the boys all think she can handle it but she can't. Just because she is developing doesn't mean she can't get upset and she is still only young.

RT: So it is the physical things that would be the most upsetting to you?

ANGIE: Yes.

CATHERINE: Definitely.

RT: But you have put it at the bottom of the (*Q-sort*) list for likelihood, do you think that would change as you get older?

ANGIE: Yes.

RT: More likely?

ANGIE: Yes, you could be talking, boys and girls like, and they become more attracted to each other.

RT: So you think you are not so attracted at the moment because you are immature, physically at least.

ANGIE: Yeah.

RT: What do you think?

BABS: Same as Angie.

A substantial amount of research has been carried out on pubertal development and social context showing the importance of the dynamic relationship between these factors.[3] This research found that early maturation was a problem for girls where cultural values of petiteness and child-likeness were high, but an advantage for boys where body bulk was preferred. Late maturation for boys could result in physical abuse by older or bigger male peers and lead to behavioural difficulties in attempts to over-compensate for a diminished sense of masculinity.

The impact of culture on bodies is exemplified by two sets of research findings from the US. In ballet schools, where late maturation was advantageous to the student for lighter body weight, longer limbs and prepubertal appearance, the girls were overwhelmingly 'late' in starting their periods and changing body shape than their counterparts in a control group (Brooks-Gunn and Warren 1985). The ballet students whose menarches were 'on time' scored much higher levels on psychological tests for bulimic tendencies and exhibited lower self-esteem and poorer family relationships. These findings point to the ability of the body to adapt to cultural expectations, and the emotional cost to those whose bodies do not adapt.

Simmons et al. (1979) found that the relationship between onset of puberty and phasal transition of schooling strongly affected self-esteem and subsequent dating behaviour. Those who experienced simultaneous critical physical and socio-institutional changes fared worst. In the UK, the existence of any choice in year of transition from primary to secondary has all but disappeared, and the mass of pupils move schools when they are 11 years of age. Body image and physical attractiveness were high on the list of concerns for new secondary-school pupils, but were over-ridden by the importance of peer popularity.

In the Baker Street pupil culture, girls were just as likely to become victims whether they considered pretty or 'scutty'. As with the boys, the best deterrent against negative attention was the strength of the same-sex friendship group. In Baker Street Year 7, the girls seemed to want to have friendships with boys but were usually rejected. The feelings of the other sex confounded them.

RT: Do you think that boys are jealous of the close relationships of the girls?

BABS: I think so, because boys don't . . . girls can talk to each other, boys just keep things into themselves, they don't tell no one nothing.

ANGIE: And when girls are upset, the others will try and comfort them, but if a boy gets picked on they laugh at them.

RT: Have you got any good boy friends in your class?

ANGIE: Jack and Barry are all right.

CATHERINE: And Malcom,

BABS: He gets picked on a lot.

ANGIE: 'Cos he's got ginger hair.[4]

BABS: I think he knows how we feel a bit 'cos he gets picked on a lot. He is a bit more mature.

ANGIE: I don't think I could tell him my problems though,

CATHERINE: No.

BABS: No.

ANGIE: But you can talk to him like he was another human being. Try talking to some of them it's like youm an alien or something.

This sentiment, of some girls desiring non-threatening relationships with boys and recognising that the only way they are likely to achieve such is to befriend a boy who is rejected by the boy group, is echoed later in the hypothetical relationships with gay boys. Even in their first year of secondary school, many of the girls were aware of the dangers of being openly friendly with most of the boys, and indeed the potential existed for rumour-mongering and reputational damage where there were absolutely no grounds at all.

ANGIE: If youm talking to a boy and you hug him or something, they would go and say you . . .

RT: What would they say about it?

ANGIE: Well they, the other day Veejay, Roy and Graham came to my house and we were standing at the step and they were saying I'd been over the park in the bushes with this boy, and my mum was only in the house and if she'd heard it, it wouldn't have been very nice, all these stories they weren't true. It would upset my mum.

BABS: And if you say you like some boy just as a friend they all say to him you fancy him, so you don't say anything at all.

A bestiary of schoolgirls

Many of the girls' complaints about harassment from the boys were borne out by the boys interviewed in the same schools. The boys devoted a lot of their considerable diabolical energy into making life uncomfortable for their female class-mates, although they did not seem to have a clear or agreed motive. The casual use of sexualised swear-words to attack perfectly ordinary and uninvolved girls was very widespread, and all but the most timid of boys admitted to their use of such tactics. The prompt-scripts were used to reveal what had become an almost invisible routine for the boys. All the young people interviewed as well as the relevant teaching staff recognised this type of exchange so well they could have written the script, but its features were so well used they were taken for granted.

Y7 Baker Street boys

ND: Why do you think all these words like slag and cow have something to do with sex attached to them? (. . .) It doesn't seem to make sense. Does it?
COLIN: Naw! But most of the girls take it for a joke, don't they?
ALAN: Yeah, but the other ones they would go up and tell the teacher and we'd get in really bad trouble.
ND: So the teachers would see it not as a joke, they would be down on you?
BRIAN: Yeah.
ND: What would you say if there was a girl in your year that you really wanted to hurt ?
BRIAN: I'd call her a bitch or something.
ND: But you, and you, you said you call them a bitch anyway, and it would be just a joke. So what words would you use if you wanted to be serious? (*Pause*) Or would you say it in a different way?
ALAN: Express them . . . say them louder.
BRIAN: If there were no teachers around we'd really swear, wouldn't we?
COLIN: Yeah.
ALAN: Or write it on a wall or something.
BRIAN: Say *fucking* bitch. (*'Fucking' spoken very quietly*)
ND: But there are no other names you would use apart from the ones you also use as a joke?
BRIAN: No.

The off-the-cuff, unthinking delivery of this verbal harassment demonstrates its use by the boys as routine rather than ritual. Under questioning, they developed their sense of a continuum of potency of meaning for the same words, but the overall intent of these strategies was to position the girls lower in the pecking order than their own gender, but remain in benign dictatorship. Only when the girls tried to move from that prescribed position did the boys emphasise the underlying nastiness of their language against the girls. For the most part, the casual name-calling served to remind the girls that they were *just* girls and their value was *only* in relationship to the boys.

The fact that the boys used the same words in either hot or cold mode can be paralleled with the use of racist jokes. When the club comedian jests about Asian corner shops or laid-back Rastafarians, the language and its defining power is the same as that used in direct racist attack. Its only difference is the speaker's mood: he is not being nasty, just reminding the audience that such nastiness is available on call. The language has an integral power, but it requires skilled delivery by someone who has personal qualities of nerve and loquacity. The Baker Street boys revealed the full range of power encapsulated in the same words, but differentiated in meaning, expression and social context: cultural texts obscure to adults, but owned and understood perfectly by the peer culture.

Across all the pupil groups, the ability to define situations and people recurred as a highly important power, and one that was frequently contested amongst the pupils. Labelling a group or individual could take time depending on the object's intrinsic character, the social position and physical power of the prospective definer and the audience. The repeated attacks necessary to ratify the naming of the person, group or act were seen as very threatening. Many young people of each sex cited this repetition as a signal to fight back or else face a long-term stigma.

Y10 Patten Avenue girls

EVA: I think name-calling can hurt the most because if you have a fight with someone, sort of thing, you can just forget that, but name-calling, that can last forever, know what I mean? It can happen for ages, all the way through school . . .

RT: Do you think names stick?

JO, EVA, HELEN: Yeah.

EVA: You look at yourself and you think 'why are they doing it?' And then you start to change yourself to try to please them, and you shouldn't do that . . .

JO: And then they start to call you names even more then, just because they see they are getting to you.

EVA: You shouldn't change yourself just because they are . . . It's just stupid.

Despite reasoning that the innocent should not change themselves to accommodate the abuser, Eva identified the defining power as the over-riding force.

EVA: If they are *regarded* as a slag, no one is gonna look at them, no one is going to be nice to them, are they? They are gonna say she *is* a slag. Everyone is gonna believe it.

Cognitive change in the victim – the coming to see oneself as the degraded object defined by one's persecutors – is an effect observed by several researchers of bullying, including Bjorkquist et al. (1982). By lacing isolated incidents of disapproved behaviour (for example, acceptance of courtship) together with a simplified stereotype (for example, 'slag') the aggressors construct a negative identity for an individual. The rebuttal must be decisive: if not, the repetition of the labelling and the ineffective denials reinforce the victim's status in the eyes of other pupils. The meaning of language is defined through its use: if enough people call Eva a 'slag' then she *is* a 'slag', whatever that means, and what that means is defined by the powerful friendship cliques within the peer culture.

In this group, Eva and Jo acknowledged that the perpetrators of the abuse could be either boys or girls. In other interviews the girls thought that the worse offenders tended to be girls, with boys simply forming the audience. Whichever situation prevailed, boys were necessary for the girls as a reference for their own sexual codes. Even when the girls despised their male class-mates they needed to avoid becoming targets of their opprobrium, as the boys would seek out and exploit the vulnerable for their own sport.

Double standards

There is a widely perceived common-sense notion that a 'double standard' exists regarding sexual behaviour of boys and girls (Lees 1993; Holland et al. 1994). This perception is based upon the observation that boys increase peer status by indulging in sexual practice and publicising their exploits, whilst girls who have sexual experience are denigrated as unclean and unworthy of male attention.

Y10 Baker Street boys

ND: So are some lads called 'studs' by the girls in school?
FAZAL: Yeah.
ND: And is that a bad thing to be called?
FAZAL, GRAHAM: No. *(Laughter)*
ND: What do girls get called if they go out with lots of lads?
SPIRO, GRAHAM, FAZAL, NASUR: A slag! *(Laughter)*
FAZAL: A slut. They hate it an' all, the girls do!
ND: Is that *(being called a slag)* a bad thing?
SPIRO, GRAHAM, FAZAL, NASUR: Yeah.
NASUR: You don't know where they have been, do you?
ND: But you don't know where the stud has been either, do you?
NASUR: *(Laughter)* But that's different, because youm a boy!
FAZAL: It's a good thing for a boy . . .
ND: It's a good thing for a male?
FAZAL: Yeah.
ND: Well, I agree with you that that is the way it is, but should it be?
FAZAL: Well it's not fair . . . but . . . *(Laughter)*

Wild and Taylor (1994) found such sexual hypocrisy not only widespread but stable across cultural and ethnic boundaries. Boys as well as girls seemed to accept that this situation was unjust, but perpetuated it by colluding in the gender policing discussed below. The idea that the girl might have experience beyond the relationship between her and the potential boyfriend was repellent because it threatened the boy's control of sexual knowledge: she might have a comparator and he might not. The boy transformed her knowledge from a power to a weakness through the articulation of female sexual experience with uncleanness: 'you don't know where she has been'.

The boy's sexual worth was seen as additive: as he gained more experience it edified and strengthened. Girls' sexual value was, by contrast, subtractive, a finite resource only complete in its virginity, thereafter rapidly diminishing with age and experience. Not only was the double standard recognised as prevalent and unfair, the hypocrisy was compounded by the further exploitation of the promiscuous girls by boys seeking gratification without commitment.

ND: (. . .) What? You said you *would* go out with someone with a reputation as a slag?

NASUR: No, you wouldn't go *out* with her, you would just knock her off. She is easy, she is just easier . . . to get off with.

ND: So you would just use her . . .

NASUR, FAZAL: Yeah, skank her. *(Laughs)*

ND: What does 'skank' mean?[5]

NASUR: Use . . . skank . . . use her, skank . . . use.

SPIRO: You talk to her then you leave her out.

ND: So you mean use in a special way, skank means use badly . . .

NASUR: Misuse . . .

ND: Abuse, take what you want then dump her?

ALL: Yeah.

ND: I see . . .

In-depth discussion with Y10 boys at Blunkett Rise exposed a certain pathologising viewpoint regarding girls' sexuality. Sandra was a class-mate who was named by the boys as a girl who had had much older boyfriends since Y7. The conversation was diverted away from known individuals but later returned to Sandra as an example of aberrant sexuality:

ND: (. . .) or would you think that the (*younger*) girl was using the (*older*) boy, or the boy was taking advantage of the girl or what?

PINXI: Like I would think the lad was taking advantage of her. When Sandra goes out with a lad that is it, she will do anything, she doesn't know when to stop. She will try to do anything just to impress him.

BOOT: Hmm. Yeah.

Sandra figured here not simply as a victim of the predatory older male, but as a victim of her own female condition. She needed to impress boys, she needed to please them. This reading of Sandra's behaviour did not quite square with the consensus of the larger group of which Pinxi and Boot were vocal members. Sandra was well liked by most of her class-mates, but few of the girls wanted to be associated with her for fear of having their own reputations contaminated. Sandra was a regular victim of threats and beatings from older, harder girls. These girls tolerated the boys' abuse of Sandra, but disliked her expectations of attachment from the boys.

In her earlier years of secondary school, Sandra had provided many of the boys in her class with accounts of her sexual exploits. She simultaneously received attention from the older youths who sexually abused her, and from the less mature boys in her class who were keen on gleaning information on female sexuality and the older boys' technique. Now in Y10, Sandra had little to offer the boys in her class who were now engaged in relationships of their own; neither had she much appeal to the older boys who now preferred younger and/or less experienced girls. At 14 years of age, Sandra was seen by her peers as an example of the dangers of promiscuity.

There existed constant pressure from both boys and girls on some girls to participate in sexual activity with boys. If they did, they might lose their sexual capital, but if they didn't, they might be condemned for being frigid or a lesbian. The only success could be achieved by playing a complicated game whose rules were not explicit and constantly shifted according to the other players. This meant total involvement in the peer culture in order to keep ahead of the game.

NASUR: Frigid. *(Laughter)* We say that. They don't know what it means and all the boys start laughing and they get paranoid!

FAZAL: Fridge. *(Laughter)*

NASUR: Yeah, fridge, and they say what are you laughing at?

SPIRO: And they don't know!

ND: They don't know? Are you kidding, they are not thick! What makes you think they are paranoid?

NASUR: They go to other girls and ask them . . .

SPIRO: And they start looking at themselves . . .

FAZAL: They get mad at you and say 'what are you on about?'

NASUR: They think there is something wrong with them, they look . . .

GRAHAM, FAZAL, NASUR: *(Laughter)*

SPIRO: Or you walk up to them and you go like that . . . *(Mimes opening a fridge door and chilling his hands)*

ND: Have you done that? And would the other boys know what you were on about?

SPIRO: Yeah, all the lads would know . . .

GRAHAM: The girls, some of the girls know now too.

FAZAL: It is just something we came up with ages ago.

These boys demonstrated the game-playing possibilities of sexual reputations based on practice and knowledge: secret coding, mimicry, slang and slander were all utilised in the manoeuvring of the group. It was important for everyone to keep up with the gossip to guard against being targeted as the outsider or becoming the unwitting butt of 'in' jokes. Absences from school created opportunities for cliques to close against an individual, and in order to minimise this risk many adolescent girls seemed to play truant only if one or more of their friends accompanied them. Living outside the rules of this game became unthinkable to the majority of pupils, as non-players were flagged up as worthless but were still not left unmolested.

Hands-on experiences: sexual and sexualised assaults in school

Some girls had less resistance than others to being slagged off, and this may have increased their profile for physical abuse. Even in the small number of girls interviewed, and despite the interviews being fifty minutes of one-off group discussion with an adult stranger, a number of disclosures of sexual assault were made.

It had been made clear before, and again at the start of, each interview that personal revelations were not being sought and, should they emerge, the researcher would not offer direct intervention in any difficulties apart from referral to the appropriate person if necessary. The boys and girls were very forthcoming about some extremely personal matters. They did not seek advice or help from the researchers or ask for matters to be referred to other adults, but obviously felt better about talking things through. The Q-sort items stimulated a good deal of comment on the pupils' differentiation between physical and verbal harassment, and provoked some interesting argument over individual perceptions.

Y7 Baker Street girls

ANGIE (*ordering Q-sorts*): The boys would call us names and that but I don't think they would try to touch us. (*Pointing at 'Flicking Bra Straps etc.'*)
CATHERINE: Most of them don't know you wear a bra 'cos you've got your blazer on all the time.

Y10 Patten Avenue girls

EVA: (*ordering Q-sorts*): Look at that (*'Lifting Skirts, Pulling Bra Straps etc.'*). No one does that do they? The boys in this school are not like that, are they?
HELEN: Yes they do!
EVA: No, seriously, no one . . .
HELEN: They are, they do that!
EVA: Come on! They don't, when have you ever . . .
HELEN: I have had it, they do it . . .
EVA: No they don't . . .
JO: Yes they do. (*Laughter*)
HELEN: See, they do.
EVA: I don't think so, how many girls wear skirts in this school?
JO: (*Laughter*) Not the skirts maybe, but the bra straps.

EVA: No they don't. They don't. I've never seen it.

HELEN: *(Laughter)* They don't do it to you because they are too scared!

EVA: They don't.

HELEN: They do.

(Pause)

JO: They do.

RT: Do you talk about this sort of thing in school?

JO: No, we have talked about bullying and stuff, but not the sexual things.

The only opportunity for the pupils to talk about these issues in school, excluding informal friendship groups, was via PSE lessons. There were four disadvantages to PSE:[6]

- lessons were, for logistical reasons, most likely to be taught in full-class groups of both sexes
- PSE was regarded as a low-status subject – non-examinable, often taught by non-specialists and generally considered a burdensome appendage to the crowded 'real' curriculum
- lessons were tied to an over-prescriptive National Curriculum
- the PSE syllabus itself was a hotchpotch of disparate topics of which sexual matters formed only a small part.

Eva's lack of shared awareness with her friends on this issue was not unique. Eva presented herself as a remarkably powerful young woman, physically and mentally tough, and would be unlikely to make a soft target for anyone's sport. Though she was not a victim, it is perhaps surprising that she denied that possibility for others. She and her close friends appeared not to have discussed this highly important issue before, even though two of the group had had unpleasant experiences of that type. Some of the girls from Baker Street showed a greater awareness of physical sexual harassment at their school.

Y10 Baker Street girls

RT: Now that *(a group of boys 'raping'*[7] *or ragging a girl)* has not appeared near the top of the other pupils' lists we have already done. I'm interested in why you have chosen that one. It is as if other pupils are saying that it doesn't happen in schools . . .

STELLA: It does!

RT: Can you tell me a little about what or when . . . ?

STELLA: Well, I have had it done. Like, erm, it was in the library and they said, 'come on', 'cos there was no one there, and they just, well there was about six of them and they just jumped on me. And I know another one, who got jumped on by seven of them, and there was about three boys who jumped on another girl, and most of them got suspended . . . and that was it.

RT: And that was in the school, and in school time?

STELLA: Yeah.
RT: And where did it happen?
STELLA: Well one happened in the library . . . hallways and . . .
RT: So it tends to happen in places where perhaps . . . ?
STELLA: No teachers are about . . . and just pupils.
RT: Can I ask you when it happened to you?
STELLA: Well, last year in third year (Y9).

The male group effect

The boys produced a group dynamic that could take on a very threatening sexualised form against girls, resulting in actual sexual assault. At other times this
dynamic was limited to a highly competitive and offensive performance intended
to impress the girls. Many girls commented upon the multiplicatory effect of 'one
boy = nice company, three boys = desperate idiots'.

Many adults who work in schools – mid-day supervisors, library staff and ancil-
laries as well as teaching staff – were familiar with this type of mobbing. Both
adults and children recognised this example as its classic form. Outside the strict
supervision of teachers, a small group of boys take the opportunity to manhandle
a single girl into a defenceless position where they subject her to some form of
sexual assault. The boys are 'having a laugh', and the girl too might be laughing
whilst the incident is in progress, but she has no control over the activity, merely
a variable emotional response from laughter through to tears. This is not a con-
sensual act: it is too sudden.

Wood (1984) describes a similar practice developing into a craze amongst
pupils in a 'sin-bin' at a London school, where rough-and-tumble sex-play was
referred to as 'bundles', and consisted of boys simply diving as a group upon participating girls:

> If the girls thought the bundles a bit of a laugh it was an absolute hallmark of
> the boys' developing sexism that they completely lost sight of the girls' feel-
> ings in the matter and, once on a runaway train of their own exclusively male
> meanings, pushed for more and more. If they had succeeded in touching a
> girl's breast, they would go for her crotch.
>
> (Wood 1984: 194)

There were qualitatively different sexual acts of this type played out between boys
and girls at the schools. They were varied, but often began with a small group of
each sex engaging in verbal banter, getting to know each other and voluntarily
egging on each other's friends to go further than they would if they had been a dyad
in that situation. The physicality might come initially from either boys or girls, but
the actual physical sexual contact was less pronounced than the verbal exchange.

During these exchanges, the group effect worked differently upon boys and
girls. The girls tended to feel out their way in front of each other, checking and re-
checking their friends' approval, aiming for reinforcement and solidarity rather

than trying to dominate and lead. The boys, however, quickly reduced their morality to the lowest common denominator, with high levels of competition and devil-take-the-hindmost. In the group attacks on individual girls this group effect was very pronounced, but difficult for boys to explain after the event.

Y10 Blunkett Rise boys

VAMBO: We were just messing, just messing, and Gaz just baled on so Rob did, so I did as well. Then they all saw, and the rest jumped on too.

This frenzy was found in situations other than sexual attacks on girls. Boys would gang up on another boy to beat him up, they would join in to outdo one another in vandalising some inanimate object, or perform a daredevil act that similarly reinforced their membership of the group or their candidacy for leadership. Pikas (1989b) (regarding the mobbing of boys) suggests deconstructing the group to remove the lowest common denominator of hostility, and so raise empathy for the victim. In the case of sexualised attacks this empathy is less likely to be forthcoming if the peer group's construction of girls is founded upon a concept of otherness.

The girls regularly reported that even the most awful boys were usually OK on their own. If a group of girls were talking to a lone boy, of any age, he would chat with the girls on topics that interested them, and act pleasantly and maturely. As soon as the number of boys reached three they became noisy, competitive and usually abusive to the girls. This group effect was noted time and time again by both boys and girls in the interviews, and referred to simply as 'impressing their mates'.

Boot and Pinxi sum up this group effect:

Y10 Blunkett Rise boys

BOOT: The girls all hang about by the outside tennis courts, you can go and talk to them, but if you have your mates around there then you can't be talking to them, you start to take the mickey out of them and things like that, but you just don't talk to them. You feel obliged.
PINXI: Like when I sit next to any of them we can talk and have a laugh, but as soon as your mates arrive you cut the talking out and start to take the mickey out of them. It totally changes around.
BOOT: It's the lads . . .
ND: That's when it would change you?
BOOT: Yeah, you would become completely different . . . it's like on drink . . . when people on drink . . .
ND: *(Unclear)(Laughter)*
BOOT: It is! *(Laughs)* It is like when people are on drink. When they are on drink and they walk in a bar and only other people on drink understand them!
ND: How about the girls, what do they do? Are they different in front of their mates?
PINXI: It doesn't work that way.

Summary

This chapter has given an overview of the main problems facing girls with regard to peer group behaviour, as expressed by the pupils themselves. As with the previous chapter on the problems for boys an overlap is created by the sharing of some areas of concern, but also by my attempt to give a more fluent picture than would have been achievable by strict demarcation of the sexes.

The range of sexual bullying practices the girls endured was somewhat similar to that of the boys, but clearer forms of sexual harassment were evident against girls – particularly, boys making frequent unwanted sexual remarks or physical forays against them. Where name-calling was concerned, the boys explained the continuum of meaning that inhered in the same words and phrases and how they intensified according to important subtleties in the context of the interchange. It was important to recognise the difference between being *called* a derogatory name and being *labelled* with one. In the micro-cultural context, it was the adhesive quality of the name that presented the danger. Where the boys feared being labelled 'gay', the girls feared being labelled 'slag'. The names may appear very different, but their function is more similar than might have been acknowledged in earlier research. Both terms are defined by more socially powerful actors in the situation than the victim, and their effectiveness lies in their flexible use against core values of identity.

The language of girl-against-girl assaults was also more overtly sexual, with girls commonly referring to one another's sexual character or sexual appearance. Despite all the girls' protests at the use of the word 'slag', most were clearly unvexed at its general deployment by both sexes, although its actual mode of use was differentiated by gender and context. In heated exchanges between boys and girls it became an irrelevant auxiliary swear word, but in the closeted gossip exchange in the girls' toilets it was more incisive and damaging.

As the girls moved into their final two years of schooling, they tended to have fewer relationships with schoolboys, preferring instead to go out with young men who had already left school. This state was presented as a spiritual exodus from the school, with the mature, more popular girls evidently just marking time by attending school and studying, and with little of the thrill of social maelstrom which their earlier schooldays had provided.

As with the boys' interviews, school was presented as an important site for peer group social relations. The organisation of hundreds of young bodies engaged in inexorable change within a small physical space created conditions for an engulfing micro-culture of socio-sexual relationships. Variations in type and rate of pubertal change were noted by the peers and responded to socially through value systems and social practice.

Boys and girls were keen to gain cultural advantage by coded references and jokes that excluded those outside their circle or recruited those they wanted to join them. There was a need to keep one's finger on the pulse or lose it altogether – a feature of school life that resurfaces later in this book. To live outside these cultural practices seemed unthought of, for even marginalised pupils were drawn into the centre of attention at times to advertise the dangers of failing to perform well socially.

Girls had little faith in the effectiveness of the school discipline system regarding sexual bullying, and this was compounded if the victim was not white. In the absence of an effective official system, boys and girls were thrown back on their own mettle to resolve most of the issues of sexual bullying, with ensuing subcultural distortions and deflections. This lack of dialogue between official and unofficial discourses on sexuality points to the weakness of PSE in delivering an adequate safe forum for such discussion to take place.

3 Age differences in adolescent relationships

Standard deviations

Of all the attitudes expressed by young people throughout the research, probably the most stable view was that secondary-school girls prefer their boyfriends to be older than themselves. This trend has been noted by a number of researchers, but without exploration of its possible causes and effects. Hey describes one of her schoolgirl respondents as being purely concerned with 'older men' and the image of herself she was presenting to her school peers:

> Carol's contempt for her male peers was very vocal. Some poor undersized 13-year-old commissioned to ask her out at the behest of his first year mate had the difficult task of mediation. Carol, in a very loud voice so that the errand boy and the assembled company could hear, confirmed that she didn't usually go out with anyone under 16.
>
> (Hey 1997: 94)

As shown below, one of the attributes which girls admire in boys is a high level of 'maturity'. The girls commonly referred to a wide range of negative behaviours in boys as immature and classified virtually every obnoxious male trait under this category. This was so common a feature that it became almost a given, an understanding by every schoolgirl that every boy of the same age was functioning at a lower level of emotional development and, in most cases, that allowance had to be made for this. Whilst this was recognised in the lower school, it became a much more important issue as the girls grew older.

Y10 Blunkett Rise girls

ND: So you think that a boy at the age of 10, last year of primary school, is no different physically to a boy of 14, say?
PAT: Well his voice breaks and he is a bit taller, but you can't say much else really, can you?
(. . .)
PAT: But their brains don't mature with their bodies.
ND: You don't think so?

PAT: No, just today, they were all standing on the yard and they were throwing
       acorns at us! I mean, really! They were getting a real buzz out of it! *(Laughter)*
KIM: MARY: They were! Chucking acorns! *(Laughter)*
NATALIE: 'Ha ha! Hit you!' They are stupid!

The great majority of pupils in the UK are currently taught in age-groupings of
plus or minus one year. Occasionally, particularly in very small primary schools,
classes include a wider age-band, but where this does occur it is seen as less than
ideal. The implicit concept behind such scholastic organisation is that of the
norm. Educators have long embraced the idea of categorising children according
to age-appropriate developmental stages (Piaget 1972; Neubauer (ed.) 1976) and
normative behaviour patterns, as this provides a rational framework within which
the professional pedagogue can operate.

In some secondary schools, whilst the academic organisation is structured hor-
izontally, the benefits of mixed age contact are acknowledged by organising the
pastoral element vertically. In this system pupils are registered in form groups
constituted of five or six children from each year group but are taught in classes of
pupils of their own age. This arrangement is generally known as a house system,
and has been the topic of frequent debate in the profession.[1] Advocates point out
the familial aspects of older pupils caring for the new intake, and the beneficial
effects of peer modelling. Teachers advocating the completely horizontal system
prefer the stability of a cohort of pupils staying together as a group and moving up
through the school over the five years. Claims are made for the comparative ease
of administration of this system, and for the benefits of protecting younger children from the less desirable influences of the older pupils.

Irrespective of which pastoral system is used, pupils remain in contact with their
own age group for most of their time in school. In primary schools some general
differences are discernible between the genders, but these become much more
apparent to both the children and teachers after the first year or two in secondary
school. Despite boys' tendency to appear more physically 'busy' and robust, the
earliest-maturing, tallest and strongest children in each class are often girls.[2]

It must be remembered, however, that the variation between tallest and short-
est, lightest and heaviest in such groups is quite vast. In Blunkett Rise School, my
Y10 tutor group had a boy who measured 4′ 4″ and weighed 5 stone, and one girl
5′ 10″ tall and 11 stone in weight. There were also four boys over 6′ tall who each
weighed more than 12 stone. Many researchers have commented upon this enormous somatic variation within groups of adolescents and the psychological effects
of differential maturation rates between peers, from Jones and Bayley (1950) to
Conger (1991). However, very little, if any, research has been carried out on the
effects of earlier maturation of girls upon gender identity.

One other biological feature has an important impact upon the expectations of
status within and between the sexes around this age. The decline in age of the
menarche has been a persistent trend over the century, although some research
now claims it is levelling out (Coleman and Hendry 1990). Many girls now
experience their first periods at primary-school phase (less than 11 years old), with

the majority well used to menstruation by Y9 (13/14 years old) in secondary school. For girls, this experience may not be enjoyable – quite the reverse – but it does confer a certain seniority upon those girls who have 'achieved' this milestone, and marks the whole cohort of that sex as closer to full adulthood than could be said for the same-age boys (Prendergast 1992).

Mid-adolescent crisis

One analysis by age and sex of bullying in secondary schools (Smith 1991) shows that whilst the frequency of girls bullying others declines sharply and steadily as they go up through the school years,[3] boys' bullying decreases more slowly, with pronounced blips of regression in Y9 and Y11. It has been suggested that the Y11 phenomenon is due to a small group of disaffected boys wreaking havoc in the school in the run-up to leaving. The Y9 phenomenon is not explained other than teachers offering a general observation that they are 'always a hard year to teach'. It may be that there is a connection between the higher aggression in boys and the lower aggression in girls with the coincidence of observed sexual maturational lag, and this is discussed below.

Y7 Baker Street girls

ANGIE (*choosing a Q-Sort item*): 'Calling Boys Immature'. I do that often.
BABS: My mum says that girls grow up faster than boys.

This distinction is obscured in the early years of schooling as both boys and girls are expected to be immature, but as the distance between their development stretches out at puberty, the boys' childishness seems exaggerated, especially to the girls on the receiving end of the boys' aggression. This group of girls was interviewed just at the start of their Y10, with the experience of Y9 still fresh in their minds:

Y10 Blunkett Rise girls

ND: You are all fourth years now, can you think of the hassle you get off lads, is it worse, has it changed, are those lads who give the hassle now the same ones as always?
PAT: It is worse now. If anything they are more immature now!
ZARA: They have gone back . . .
NATALIE: They are more . . .
KIM: It's changed, they say worse now.
PAT: It used to be just names . . .
KIM: It used to be just 'you're fat', and stuff like that.
NATALIE: Now it's stuff like 'you've no tits'.
ALL: (*Laughter*)
ND: OK so that's what they say now, when did it start?
PAT: Third year (Y9). Up 'til then I could get on with the lads fine, you could say all sorts to them . . .

MARY: You could have a joke and everything.

For teachers, an important minority of boys exhibits highly disruptive and anti-social behaviour in class, particularly when they are allowed to act as groups (Mahony 1985; Lees 1987). These pupils appear in contradistinction to the more mature girls and quieter boys in the class and, often, official punitive measures are directed at the 'wild' boys that merely inflame them to further harassment outside of adult supervision. A common refrain from both boys and girls was the lack of faith they had in the efficacy of teacher involvement in peer disputes: 'If you tell a teacher, they will just get you back worse.'

Around Y8/Y9, although the boys looked and behaved much the same as they had always done, they didn't necessarily feel the same. The boys' initial pubertal development was largely unseen, but sexual desire was pronounced, and the experience of wet dreams, masturbation and crushes was very real. Gaddis and Brooks-Gunn note that, while girls frequently confide in friends and mothers about their bodies and their feelings, boys are culturally discouraged about discussing their sexual development with parents or peers.

> None of the boys had told their friends that they had had an ejaculation (whether nocturnal or by masturbation). Indeed, for over four-fifths of the boys, the study interview was the first time they had discussed this topic . . . Imagine an American boy coming down to the breakfast table and saying – Mom, guess what! I had my first wet dream last night. Now I'm a man!
>
> (Gaddis and Brooks-Gunn 1985: 333)

Older boyfriends: life after school

In the school environment where most children had most peer contact, girls became more physically attractive and desirable to the boys in their class, but this desire was not reciprocated. The boys' sexualised behaviour towards the girls merely confirmed the maturity gap, both in behaviour and appearance, and was highlighted by teachers' comparisons between the gender groups then amplified in the boys' behaviour once more. One consequence of this may have been the preference for older partners by adolescent girls shown in this and other studies.[4]

Y10 St Joseph's girls

RT: And are there many relationships between boys and girls in your year? Do girls in your year tend to go out with boys in their year, in this school, or out of school?

ALLIE: Outside of school. There aren't many relationships in the school.

CHARLOTTE: Or above, not in the same year.

RT: Because you have got a sixth form here haven't you? Do you have relationships . . . .

ALLIE: No, not really no, a few I suppose, but not very many. It's mostly out of school isn't it?

RT: Can you suggest a reason for that?

ALLIE: (*Laughter*) More mature, isn't it?

RT: So what age would you be talking about?

CHARLOTTE: 17 . . . 18.

RT: So a Y10 girl (14/15 years old) would be going out with a . . .

ALLIE: 16- or 17-year-old . . .

RT: 16- or 17-year-old.

CHARLOTTE: Some girls go out with older boys, 20, 21.

RT: And would the girls in Y10 who go out with boys 21, 22 years old, would they be more mature themselves?

ALLIE: No, more forward . . .

BRONWEN: Yeah, more forward aren't they?

RT: Is there a certain amount of status for the girls who go out with boys of that age?

ALLIE: Somebody that has a job, a car and that . . .

RT: So is it more about the outward symbols than a real relationship?

ALLIE: Yeah.

These St Joseph's girls were very conscious of the age difference and its relationship with reputation and character. Y10 girls would ideally go out with boys two or three years older than themselves, but would not normally consider boys from their sixth form who, despite being the right age, would not fit their conception of 'mature'. The theme of 'maturity', particularly as expressed by girls regarding boys, was a dominant one in most of the discussions. There seemed to be a constellation of behaviours and traits that defined maturity as a particularly male attribute, one that was an indispensable part of desired masculinity. The desirability of a male partner was rarely mentioned in the context of physicality, of superficial appearance, but always as a state of being, or a fitness for a role. This attitude is encouragingly dissonant with teenage girls' magazines that talk of desirable males almost exclusively in terms of their 'snoggability' or 'hunkiness'.

Many girls in the interviews stated clearly that they would not go out with a boy of their own age in school. One reason was that they had knowledge of the boys' limited maturity gathered over several years of close contact with them in school and the shared experience to date had, on balance, been negative: familiarity certainly bred contempt at this stage. Conversely, for the girls the experience of being treated as children by staff in front of the boys was considered humiliating and de-sexualising: it was difficult to maintain an erotic mystique with one's peers whilst a female teacher was ordering you to wash your make-up off your face and remove your jewellery to conform to school-uniform regulations.

A number of the senior girls remarked on the hypocrisy in the policing of feminine cultural expression by women staff who contravened those same regulations by wearing (what the girls read as) excessively male-attracting make-up and clothes. These women were referred to as 'tarts' or 'bitches', and were deeply resented for exerting authority over the older girls in a way that was seen as two-faced as well as demeaning to the girls' status in relation to the boys.

The upper-school girls also averred that romantic relationships needed emotional space in order to grow properly. Emotional space was in short supply in the crowded atmosphere of the comprehensive school.

Y10 Baker Street girls

RT: Are girls of your age likely to go out with sixth years, or boys out of school?

ANDREA, BEL, CELIA: *(Laughter)* Out of school!

RT: Why is that?

ANDREA: If you are going with a boy out of school, if they are not at school, you would be going out with a boy who has a job or something, it makes it seem . . .

CELIA: Like it's better to go out with someone who is not at school because they are not going to spread rumours about you all round the school.

BEL: And you have got more space. You have got space with them. Like this, if you are at school with them all the time, you would be with them all night as well, and . . .

If you were to go out with a boy in the school, you would see too much of each other, other relationships would be dragged into the mix and the romance would suffer. As boys had a propensity for using girls in relationships, dumping them, then rubbishing them amongst the peer group, it was emotionally less safe to form a relationship within the closed community of the school than with someone from the wider community.

It was also seen as desirable for partners to have differing experiences to stimulate conversation, and the urbane life of a Kwik-Fit fitter generally held more interest than mundane homework, study, assemblies and detentions. In addition to these social considerations, the physical developmental lag was so pronounced at this stage that it was unproblematically viewed as a barrier to girls' desires. Older boys also had more of the material accoutrements associated with adult masculinity, and these were seen as symbolically important. Evidence of this was found in two of the schools that had a sixth form. I had expected the Y10 and Y11 girls to be attracted by the young men they saw around school who often had fewer or no restrictions on uniform and all the other outward signs of successful maturity which the institution would allow. This was not the case. The sixth formers were generally viewed by the girls as big schoolboys: they had no jobs, they earned no money and they submitted to the school's regime for longer than they needed to. They were characterised by their conformity to the middle-class ideals which did not appeal to the majority of pupils, and they might well continue in that direction once they had left school by leaving the area and going to university.

Boys of 16–18 who were still at the same school did not have the cachet of the school leaver. Their status was that of pupil, and compared unfavourably with their peers at college, in work or even on the dole. The sixth formers were perceived by the girls to represent the less manly traits of even younger males in school. They tended to be the boys who had been 'a bit nerdy' when they were in lower school: hard working and subscribing to the academic and disciplinary ethos of the school, with little time (or social skills) for girlfriends. This view of sixth formers differs from schools that have a more middle-class intake and a stronger tradition of university destination, but the local cultures investigated here placed a remarkably low social value on that route to adulthood.

It is far more likely that young men of age 19+, out of the education system, would have more material possessions and social independence (cars or motorbikes, flats or digs) than would their younger counterparts. The type of Y10 girl who would be attracted by this would be, in the words of the interviewees, 'more forward' than they would think prudent. Interviewees described the quality of these relationships as less romantic and more shallow than their ideal, and the 'more forward' girls were considered willing collaborators in their own exploitation.

Lust, envy, fear and retribution

Y10 Blunkett Rise boys

ND: Is there any difference between the girls who choose to go out with older boys rather than boys of their own age?
BOOT: They are more the tarty ones . . .
PINXI: They tart themselves up . . .

Boys were aware of this friction between girls who kept and girls who bent the rules about age differences and, as shown later, could take advantage of this.

Y10 St Joseph's boys

ND: What are the sort of (Y10) girls that go out with those (*three or four years older*) lads then?
CARLTON: They're all right when they're on their own, but when they're all together I don't like them (. . .) really bigheads.
ND: Right, so . . .
CARLTON: They're putting all the other girls down in the class.
ND: So what do the other girls think of them?
CARLTON: Tarts.
AARON: Yeah.

The girls' practice of bragging about their personal lives out of school might have been to establish self-esteem in the face of constant attacks on their confidence by male class-mates, or it may have been simple pleasure in recounting important liaisons with their peers. However, the boys' later inference that the girls were deliberately provoking them with tales of their social or sexual contacts with older males carries some weight. For some girls, this strategy was a defence against the undesirable immature behaviour they had to endure from the boys at school. Announcing one's relationship with an older, perhaps tougher, boy was an effective deterrent against the touching up, the pushing around, the sexual teasing and the derogatory remarks commonly experienced by many girls. One way out of being sexually devalued by boys was to define oneself as the valued property of another, higher-status, boy.

Y11 Blunkett Rise boys

ADIE: The thing that gets us is when they tell you what they've been doing with other blokes. Like Dawn on the bus last night. She said to me 'I went to Flopps last night and the barman drove me home at 2 in the morning'. I thought 'what the hell are you telling me for', as if I'm interested!

ND: Why did she tell you?

ADIE: She's always telling lads about how she goes off with older blokes. I suppose she wants to get us jealous or summat.

ND: Does it work? I mean would you want to go out with her?

ADIE: No chance! Her! She's a right ugly cow! I don't know anyone who would go with her!

ND: Well the barman at Flopps sounds like he does.

ADIE: So she reckons, but she's always coming out with stuff like that. Isn't she?

CARL: Aaahh, she is. A few of them do it. It's to make her look big, but she donna impress us. She's a big mouth. Even her mates donna like her acting like that.

This preference among the girls for older boys had a profound effect on the upper-school boys. Perhaps on the grounds of their behaviour, or their earlier behaviour, the girls saw them as undesirable and immature. This reinforced the aggressiveness and feelings of rejection in the boys, which then manifested itself as further evidence of their immaturity. There was evidence of some of the boys resenting the success of older males at their expense, but as they approached that age themselves they looked likely to adopt the pattern of partnering younger girls too.

ADIE: Some of them would go out with lads their age, but a lot of the good ones are going with lads who've left school. They do it 'cos they've got cars, don't they?

CARL: All the best ones go with older lads. But some don't mind if they have a boyfriend in their year.

Some of the boys used mirror strategies to 'get their own back', but in these cases the intent seemed to be more to attract than to repel the girls' attentions. The boys' group below was obviously not so successful or experienced with girlfriends that they could counter with racy tales of their own. Instead they used younger comparators against their peers, but also deployed 'off-the-peg' stereotypes in the form of sex symbols from TV or 'page three' nudes. Occasionally they would try to provoke reaction by bringing in pornographic magazines and making comparisons between the models and the girls.

The girls were unanimous in their indifference to being shown pornography by the boys to wind them up: 'I just say "get lost", it doesn't bother you, does it, 'cos it's not you.' There was a tacit acceptance by the boys that comparison with other female bodies was not a particularly effective strategy and the girls had the edge. Even in the face of total rejection, the boys maintained the facade of being pop-ular, sought-after boyfriends. Their feelings about the predatory nature of the older boys hanging around the gates chatting up the girls in their year were con-fused and difficult.

Y10 St Joseph's boys

AARON: These people never came to our school though. These people are from Stemmingham, and they come, like, just to meet the girls but we don't really care, because the boys that they are going out with, the older ones, everybody just thinks they're really dumb anyway because they left school, and they're still going out with people who are in school.

ND: Do you look down on that then?

AARON: Yeah.

For the girls, the comparative maturity of older boys was appealing for more than one reason. Boys two or three years older were probably at a comparable level of emotional and physical development to themselves, and the seniority of their age had another bonus: at this age, 17+, one was legally entitled to a much greater degree of independence. This attraction was often mutual, as the older boys had just reached that emotional/legal stage, but had not found partners in their own age group for precisely the same reasons as outlined above.

The partnership between younger girls and older boys was by no means universal. There were many, if not the majority of, girls who were not found attractive by older boys, or who preferred to remain without observable relationships throughout their school years.[5] Also, there were a few boys who matured earlier than the majority of their female class-mates and had successful relationships of some sort with the girls. The trend, though, was for at least two or three high-profile girls in each class to fit in with the model as described, and this prevalence was sufficient to mould the per-ceptions of most pupils and fix the model as normative. A phenomenon seemed to operate where one or two key players in the peer group expressed a cultural practice and the others rapidly configured the rest of the associated practices around them. This had the effect of establishing some cultural practices as custom and, at times, raised expectations that the key players would hold to this custom, thus trapping them in a role they may not have wished to perpetuate.

The neglected or rejected boys diverted all forms of abuse towards the girls, rather than openly criticise the older boys for going out with younger girls. Verbal abuse of the girls was often twisted away from the particular and diffused into a general sexualised antagonism. This might have been due to fear of being beaten up by the older boys for defaming their girlfriends. The practice also concealed an expectation among younger boys that they might avail themselves of that same opportunity of privilege in a couple of years' time, and there would be no point in queering their own pitch by being too vocal now.

Such uncertainty and fear about one's own sexual identity and worth fuelled other destabilising features of schoolboy life. Some of these eddied around as homophobia and attacks on weak boys and are dealt with below. Some may have sedimented as misogyny, to surface later throughout adult life.

For most of the girls there was not only a dearth of fanciable boys in their own age range, but a perceived stigma about going out with anyone the same age or younger. This seems to self-perpetuate into adulthood (albeit in milder forms) with women commonly choosing partners older than themselves. Esteeming maturity as a quality in a partner appears a remarkably stable trait over time (Wellings et al. 1994).

The social as the erotic: it's good to talk

In their theorisation of teenage girls' sex-talk, Brown and Gilligan (1992) argue that the girls in their research constructed a discourse where the known reality of sexual experience was replaced by normative romantic idealisation. To these girls it was important to suppress their true feelings and responses wherever they were negative, and present themselves as participating in a perfectly harmonious emotional world.

Martin (1996) claims her interviewees held both the negative and positive aspects of their sexual experiences and aspirations in tension, and that adolescent girls' sex-talk, or 'narrative work', is a strategy for coping with disappointing and confusing experiences. These views on the meaning of girls' talk about sexual matters have a greater 'intrapsychic' dimension than this research. The emphasis in this research is on the social aspects of such talk: the micro-cultural value systems and one's place within them.

Y10 Baker Street girls

CHEEVA: There is this person that I know, a girl, and she finds this one boy attractive. But he is in the year lower than her. I asked her if she will go out with him and she said no, because he is about two years smaller (*sic*) than her. She says I think I would say no because she likes someone older than her to go out with. I thought 'well, it is up to you, but . . .'. To her it depended on age.

RT: Is it hard to go out with people younger than yourself?

AMSA: It is because of what other people would say.

BELINDA: But sometimes you don't care what other people think . . .

AMSA: Yeah, but sometimes what other people say takes out the thing that is good about the relationship, because of what they are making it into.

RT: So it makes it more difficult.

AMSA: Yeah, and you don't feel comfortable and you just want to leave it.

Two points emerge from this discussion. First, the anecdote of the girl fancying a younger boy is presented as an example of oddness: it was an unusual occurrence and therefore noteworthy. Secondly, the peer pressure to discount younger boyfriends is not only stated, it is explained in very clear terms.

Cheeva's friend's claim that she would ideally prefer an older boy may be true, but the other girls seem to feel that she is as likely to be influenced by what other people think as by her own instincts. Belinda's independent personal opinion on the matter is countered by the *reality* of the effects on the relationship of the collective opinion. Perhaps the phrase 'Yeah, but sometimes what other people say takes out the thing that is good about the relationship, because of what they are making it into' is particularly telling. From this it might be inferred that, for a girl, the good thing in a relationship was the acquisition of social status, and that this needed to be ratified by the friendship group through talk before the relationship became a 'proper' or fulfilling one.

The individual object of attraction, a younger boy, had some form of erotic appeal for the individual girl but, due to the locally prevailing gender relations, his youth reduced his social value to the girls' collective. The boy was therefore rejected as being unable to provide suitable material for all the girls' attentions. In this way the girls (and later the older boys) seemed to be eroticising the social intercourse, rather than socialising the sexual intercourse. The erotic thrill was displaced from a physical heterosexual relationship to a verbal homosocial one. The 'girlie-talk' or 'narrative work' that has been remarked on by some commentators[6] on adolescent girl culture is of central importance to gendered desires. For these girls the possibilities of the physical boy–girl encounter were brought into the friendship cliques to be discussed over and again.

Connell (1987) utilises the psychoanalytical concept of cathexis to describe processes that are similar to those in play here. The 'original' or 'natural' sexual desire for another person is strongly associated with culturally created relationships and thence with the artifacts connoted by those relationships. The pleasure and the gratification of the sexual relationship comes through the fetishised clothes, jewellery, modes of speech and gestures of the other person (or gender type), which are desired in their own right. 'Hence, most strikingly, the erotic circularities of sexual fetishism, where the symbolic markers of social categories (lace handkerchiefs, high-heeled shoes, leather jackets) or structural principles (for example, dominance) get detached from their contexts and themselves become primary objects of arousal' (Connell 1987: 115). In Cheeva's friend's case, it was the structural principle of the older boy/younger girl pairing that was taken to the group for their pleasure, the 'thing that is good about the relationship'. The peer group approval or disapproval was an essential requirement to the full and proper enjoyment of the relationship. Were approval to be withheld, all the hours of erotic chat, of comparisons and descriptions, of anecdotes and inquisitions about each other's boyfriends would be lost. The relationship would be bereft of its cultural qualities, and might not survive.

This inference is given support by the value and amount of time devoted by adolescent girls to talking about their relationships with their friends, and the column inches of the same content in teenage girls' magazines. It seems that some girls derived more pleasure from talking *about* their boyfriends than they did from talking *to* them (and, given the behaviour of many young men, that seems very reasonable). It follows, then, that this social pleasure depended entirely upon the approval of the audience. That audience may be fickle but, for all the groups interviewed, age differential between the partners in a relationship had to conform to particular formulae for it to be valued by the social group.

As well as the oral tradition, there was a prodigious quantity of 'Biro' work involved in stating one's current love interest. A trawl of pencil cases, bags and book covers[7] from any of the lower-school girls would always reveal the literal expressions of their 'hearts-and-flowers' ideology of romance. Usually it was the friends' task to adorn these accoutrements with graffiti proclaiming adoration of the chosen boy. Many lessons were spent in elaborating coded motifs, from the simple **JOO l/s BARKY** to the arcane **KAZ'N'KIPPA4EVVA2GEVVA-BCOZRLUVIZTRONG.**[8]

In the lower school particularly, girls engaged in fact-finding missions to elicit details about their heroes' biographies. It was common for girls to amass swathes of trivia on matters such as favourite colours, tastes in food (Burger King or McDonalds?), type of music and so on. Sometimes the information was collated lovingly into little dossiers or fact-files similar to magazine articles on film or pop stars; what effect these activities had on the boys' self-images can only be guessed at.

Summary

This chapter has shown how the compressed social structure of school promoted conflict at the level of pupil gender relations. The discourse of normality, that one needed to be disciplined to fit into the normative requirements of the school system, was pervasive but clouded. The developmental differences amongst boys and girls were given little thought other than an official expectation that all pupils ought to fall within vague but important norms of age-related behaviour, but the variation within the sexes was vast and, between the sexes, highly significant.

Due to heightened gendered differences in appearance at various stages, and particular cultural constructions of what constituted a successful sexuality, the girls suffered a lot of flak which took the form of sexual bullying. These critical stages were underpinned by sexual maturation being situated within a specific position in the school's hierarchy of age.

A typical scenario in Y9/Y10 was that the boys looked and behaved as they had done for the last four years: like little kids. But they didn't feel like little kids, and were intensely interested in sex. They were aware of their own physical sexuality and their arousal by the blooming physical sexuality of the girls in their close proximity, some of which was spectacularly complemented by hair, clothes, make-up and other cultural forms. The maturity/age gap between boys and girls may have appeared to adults as tiny, but it was of massive significance to those in its span.

It was apparent that boys and girls were working to rather different agendas regarding what they valued in a relationship, with the boys' groups actively deriding the girls' preferences of commitment, longevity and seriousness. The boys felt particularly aggravated by the frustration of their preferred sexual outlet and their concomitant feelings of social worthlessness. The close proximity of these two blocs of mutually antipathetic young people, wrapped together in the suffocating material of the school, benefited neither boys nor girls.

The schools' formal organisation of pupils into strict age bands condemned many to experience their pubertal development under the critical gaze of curious, unsympathetic peers whose experience was out of phase with their own. The subsequent distortion of cultural forms of courtship and their validation of desired gender identity was expressed as sexual bullying.

One of the girls' means of escape or protection was through relationships with older boys. Space in a romantic relationship was of great importance. In the compressed and adult-regulated world of classes, timetables and teacher supervision, there was a list of benefits in having an older partner out of school that included material advantages as well as spiritual ones: 'Carol's boyfriend talk always contained details of money: how much they earned and how much they had spent on her . . . She told me about their cars and their clothes. She was a genius at extracting expensive gifts and clothes from them' (Hey 1997: 95). Physically, the older boys were more mature and therefore more likely to fit the ideal picture of a 'bloke', which the girls thought desirable. With the experience of just one or two extra years, particularly over the watershed of school-leaving, the older lads were considered by the girls to be emotionally mature adults. This position gave a greater breadth of experiences: work, college, pubs, clubs, cars, holidays and the like, which were useful stimuli to the girls' interests and the subject of many lively conversations between girls about their respective blokes. These conversations were often perceived by male class-mates as attempts to provoke jealousy.

Where a boyfriend was in receipt of wage or benefit, the girl was less dependent on pocket money from parents or part-time jobs and this helped to raise the relationship into the adult league of nights out at the cinema and so on. The possession of a car or motorbike by a boyfriend bestowed even greater advantages on the relationship in both status and mobility, but the greatest asset of an older boyfriend was freedom not to be seen by him in the childish, subordinate role imposed by school. With him, a girl could construct and assert a separate identity: she could be a young woman instead of a schoolgirl.

Rather than directly express their anger at those superordinate males who were the successful competitors for the girls, the younger boys vented their frustration through anti-girl behaviour in school. This had a strong element of sexual hate even where there appeared no reason for it within the immediate context of the interaction. The distortion of sexual desire and frustration, refracted through society's contradictory and disrespectful attitudes towards women, and the powerful response of some of the girl targets, reinforced and accelerated the cycle of antagonism. Even boys outside the socio-sexual vacuum that seemed to obtain around Y9/Y10 absorbed (largely unquestioningly) attitudes and practices from the peer group culture: 'I don't know why we do it, it just seems the norm.'

4   The ideology of age seniority

Acting your age

As far as the underpinning discourses of pupil culture are concerned, the seniority of age is generally overlooked despite its indisputable pervasiveness. Even pre-school children are keenly aware of their age and its relationship with that of their peers. Infants are held aloft and asked 'Aren't you a big boy/girl, how old are you?' Siblings are told 'Susie can go to bed later than you because she is older'. Playmates are informed 'John gets to go to the park because he is older than you'. Pupils ascend the educational ladder by 'moving up' a class as they reach each chronological rung: in rare cases they talk about being 'held back a year'. Within this social organisation of difference are embedded powerful value systems of teacher control: uncooperative pupils are referred to as 'babies', and teachers often seek volunteers with the preface 'Who is grown-up enough to . . .' (Cahill 1982).

Minuscule differences in age fascinate class-mates from a very early age: most primary-school pupils can accurately rank-order by age a class consisting of thirty boys and girls whose birthdays must be only weeks apart. Position in the group's chronology does not need to match with social status, but a mismatch is often a vehicle for mockery and ridicule: 'You let him beat you and he is younger than you!' Birthdays are marked in a variety of ways according to age and local cultural traditions, from 'the bumps' to debagging, from a chorus of 'Happy Birthday to You' to an egg-and-flouring.

As the end of compulsory schooling approaches, literally thousands of markers are passed which constantly remind pupils of their position. Most of these are institutional and bureaucratic, and are at odds with the physical and emotional development of the majority of pupils. The most striking visual impact of a group of 14-year-olds is their physical variety, and this highlights the nonsense of attempts to impose a standard or norm on that age. And yet this is arguably the age when such ideal types are most aspired to in the struggle for emotional stability: as points of reference in a world which is actually shifting outside and inside their very bodies. Although boys and girls, both as genders and individuals, develop at different rates throughout their lives, the gender divisions become very apparent around puberty.

The hierarchical seniority of age was most obvious amongst the boys, with differences in their concerns split between the Y7 and Y10/Y11 groups. Whilst interviewing the younger boys for data on sexualised bullying, a great deal of discussion naturally arose around the problems faced by 'traditional' bullying, in other words older and bigger kids hurting or scaring little kids for their amusement. Research by Smith (1993) has shown that this relationship in bullying is less prevalent than originally assumed. The highest frequency of bullying interactions reported by pupils featured children in the same class, then the same year, and only then older children picking on younger ones. This finding may partly be attributed to the firm establishment of hierarchy *between* age-bands, but positional uncertainties *within* them.

Boys against boys

Even in seemingly straightforward cases of bigger, older boys bullying the Y7s, a sexualised spin could be detected in the sense of the lower-order masculinities ascribed to the victims.

Y7 St Joseph's boys

DAK: And they say 'give us your money'. Right, the other day some bigger boys said 'jump up and down' and they heard his money tinkling in his pocket, so he had to give them some money, but he didn't give them all of it. Then he came to me so I held the money in my back pocket and jumped, they didn't hear any so I got away.

BILLY: They only do it if they think they can get away with it, if them harder than you. They only pick on the softer ones and the littler ones. They don't get you so much if you are in the football team. Like me and Gaz, we are in it, Gaz is a good goalie, and me, I score a good few goals, so they leave us alone.

ND: But what about the poor lads that aren't in the football team?

BILLY: They pick on them.

ARTHUR: They call them softies 'cos they don't hang about together and that.

The dominant masculinities in this situation appeared to be physical toughness and size, allied with valued group membership earned via a sporting skill. Billy and Arthur clearly saw the advantages in belonging to the football team, although this was not a fail-safe state, as evinced by their earlier anecdote of sexual rivalry at a football match or by the experience of other Y7s in the study.

Y7 Baker Street boys

ND (*organising Q-sort*):   Now look at these words and see if you recognise them all, you mentioned kegging . . . in my school they call it kegging, here you call it debagging. Pulling someone's pants off.

ALAN: Sir, there is this fifth year, I was down the park and I was hanging on this thingy . . .

ND: . . . you were hanging on his thingy?

ALAN: No! I was hanging on this thingy . . . its like a bolt, and I was seeing how long I could hang on for, and this big boy came and pulled my trousers down, everything.

ND, BRIAN, COLIN: *(Laughter)*

ALAN *(very sadly)*:   And everyone was looking, and I couldn't get down.

ND *(sympathetically)*:   Bad news eh?

ALAN: Yeah.

BRIAN: Up near the youth club at St Thomas's where I live . . .

COLIN: Oh yeah!

BRIAN: . . . we were running around playing football, and this one kid came up behind me and pulled my trousers down.

ND: Were you upset?

BRIAN: Yeah, everyone was looking at me.

The Y7 boys were very aware of their low position in the pecking order at school. Almost anyone who had a mind to could abuse them with impunity. Their main hope of salvation was that the weakest of the weak would be sufficient sacrifice to assuage the predatory appetites of the bullies, and that they could mark themselves off from those victims by forming a group.

ND: Do you think that there are boys in the school who this *(bullying by other boys)* does affect badly?

COLIN: Yeah.

BRIAN: Some kids, they only take the mickey out of kids they know they can beat up.

ALAN: Like there is boys who just sit at the back of the room quiet like and don't mix.

Very few of the older boys brought up the subject of boys bullying other boys. It was seen as unmanly to get too involved in harassment of junior lads when there were so many other targets available. An unspoken rule seemed to be that older boys who indulged in excessive harassment of younger boys were somehow 'pervy', unless the victim could be shown as even more unmasculine, but this was not an issue which was explored here due to limitations of time.

Deference or defeat

The bigger or older boys' practice of casually physically abusing weaker boys was widely observed in Blunkett Rise and had earlier been identified as common in the three host schools (Duncan 1991). The humiliation of being overpowered, even in a 'fun' way, was a considerable source of anguish for the victims. Thorne (1993) remarks on the protection offered by high-status group membership from the 'ritual reminders' of one's inferior body: being tousled, lifted off the ground, slapped on the top of the head by passing strangers. The Y10 Blunkett Rise boys

were the only ones to raise their own experiences of being in lower school and getting harassed by older boys.

Y10 Blunkett Rise boys

ND: So the older, school-gate lads,[1] did you get any hassle from them at your previous *(secondary)* school?

PINXI: Yeah, I'd get a bit of stick off them, but nothing, you know . . . it would be
like 'oi squirt get out of the way', to you if you were second or third years, or
they'd pick you up *(physically)* and say 'do you want a fag?' Everyone is looking at you, all the first years . . . they'd sit there and do nothing wrong. Just sit
there, and know that you wouldn't do nothing like get your big brother or
that. They just impress their mates.

Boot and Pinxi identified the motivation for boys to harass others as more evidence of boys' need to continuously jockey for position within the group. Making
a strong impression on one's peers was all-important: if one didn't, one quickly
became victimised oneself. Ritual deference was expected, and if not delivered
there would follow ritual humiliation or violence.

ND: I do know of some of our lads who did get hassle, why do you think that was?
BOOT: Just to impress their mates.
PINXI: Show off to them they hang around with.
ND: The lads I know had to get on the Undervale bus, and had to wait right next
to where these older lads were hanging about. They told me they had to act
like little schoolboys, not looking at the other lads . . .
PINXI: That's exactly the same today. When you go up the town centre or any-
where, it's the same there. You go and stand in the town centre and a group
of big lads come by and, because we are younger than them, you are not
allowed to say hello to the girls that you know if they are with them, or any
of the other lads.
BOOT: Yeah, that's right.
ND: What? You are not allowed to say hello to them?
PINXI: You are not allowed to.

No one actually needed to say 'Don't talk to these girls when they are with us,
because we are older than you and we forbid it', because the occasional worked
example served as a much more powerful warning to others.

ND: What would happen if you did?
PINXI: They would threaten you.
BOOT: They would slap you . . .
PINXI: Yeah, yeah, they would get you . . .
BOOT: They would pull you out of the centre *(shopping mall)* and beat you.
ND: Boot, you come from a big hard family . . .

ALL: *(Laughter)*

ND: You do though . . . a local family everyone knows, you don't get messed around do you?

BOOT: *(Laughter)* No, not usually.

ND: But they would pick on you just the same?

BOOT: Yeah.

ND: If you set yourself up like that . . .

BOOT: Because you are younger . . . I mean there *could* be some younger than you but if there is seven or eight of them, you have no chance . . .

PINXI: They always have a young one, a small one with a big mouth who has a go.

BOOT: The mouthy one is never that hard . . . is he?

PINXI: No but if you have a go at him for giving you lip, the rest of them jump in. You see you learn to ignore them, just walk away from them. They want a fight.

The orders of masculinity exemplified in this practice were fully understood by Pinxi and Boot. Despite their own superior position in school, and all the confidence that older siblings and powerful kinship ties afforded them, when they moved into a more public arena they encountered a world constructed upon complicated interplay of male power.

Individually, the boys in the town-centre gang were not especially tough. They might be conquered in one-to-one combat by Boot or Pinxi, and they might even be the target of abuse from members of their own group. But in the territorial uncertainty of the town-centre *promenade*, and especially in the presence of that sought-after commodity, hero-worship from the girls, even the smallest and weakest boys in the dominant group became a serious threat to Pinxi and Boot's dignity. Connell describes the concept of hegemony with respect to multiple masculinities: 'Hegemonic masculinity is not a fixed character type, always and everywhere the same. It is, rather, the masculinity that occupies the hegemonic position in a given pattern of gender relations, a position that is always contestable' (Connell 1995: 76).

The conversation with Boot and Pinxi outlines three major factors in the dominant masculinity of their social milieu: age-seniority; membership of a high-status family group or friendship group with its force of numbers; and physical toughness. The older boys in the town centre may have been subordinated to another, perhaps racially or locally differentiated gang, but they maintained their own status level in relation to the younger lads by a code of violence. Many other symbolic factors were linked with the advertisement of the dominant group's supremacy: clothes, argot and gait signalled the group's position *vis-à-vis* Pinxi and Boot. Whilst this social configuration remained stable, the actors changed as they proceeded through adolescence: in three years' time Pinxi and Boot may well have assumed tenure of the hegemonic apex.

ND: If there were just lads you could go up to them?

BOOT: Yeah.

ND: And be fairly friendly? But if a girl came up to talk to . . .

PINXI: As soon as one girl comes up to them that's it, you are out of it.

ND: Do the girls, or some girls, ever do things to drop lads in it?

BOOT, PINXI: *(Laughter)* Yeah!

ND: With other lads?

PINXI: That's the girls' favourite tactic!

ND: Yeah, 'cos no one talks about this do they? Have you ever talked about it?

PINXI: No . . . *(Laughter)* . . .

BOOT: They don't. You know what's happening, but no one ever says it.

The sexualised aspects of male social relations were not something which the boys had practice at discussing. In the brief time available to them they covered a lot of ground and requested, as many others did, to reconvene for further discussion. What began as a very difficult and nervous interview soon became an enjoyable opportunity for the boys to explore their own identities and social practice.

Not every older boy was socially dominant over every younger boy and anomalies were ever-present within the school system, but very few boys would stand up and challenge their older counterparts. The only occasions when this seemed to happen was when a younger 'mascot' of a gang would be groomed and set against an older boy who was a social isolate or member of another gang. Mascots of this type were not uncommon. Often they would be an established gang member's exceptionally tough younger relative and the discourse would include references to showing off the family's aggressive pedigree. Kinship ties featured importantly in the levels of confidence expressed by many pupils, both boys and girls.

It was unusual for adults, or rather householders, to be involved in directly attacking juveniles but common for them to warn off other parents from involving the police during disputes, pressuring them to 'let the kids sort it out' no matter how unfairly. The most important matter in this type of situation was that the power remained with the group of older boys who were mentoring the mascot, and ownership of the mascot reinforced the reputation of the group or family.

The gangs used mascots to wrong-foot 'difficult' non-members of their group. A challenge would be made via a mascot with little chance of a fight actually ensuing, but with a well-publicised refusal from the outsider. The mascot was often eager to please his older mentors, and knew that if he fought and won he would be fêted. If he lost, he would be hurt but would not lose face, as he was the official underdog in any case. The outsider had much more to lose. If he won the actual fight he would gain no better reputation for beating a younger boy and might be set upon later by the gang for an unfair match. If he lost he would be humiliated as well as physically beaten. If he walked away, he would be a coward.

Deano

Around the time of the above interview with the Y10 Blunkett Rise boys, events developed within the peer group that forced a reconsideration of the strength of the social hierarchy based on seniority of age. A situation arose in Blunkett Rise that gave a different view of these customs following the arrival of a Y10 boy who had transferred from another school.

Blunkett Rise had suffered declining numbers on roll for some years, and was obliged by law to admit any pupil wishing to transfer, up to the limit set by the 'standard number'.[2] Pupils transferring schools during their penultimate year of schooling generally do so for one or both of two reasons: they have moved from another locality and/or they have been excluded from their previous school. Four pupils, two boys and two girls, arrived in the space of a couple of weeks, all known to each other, and all excluded from at least one of their previous placements. These new pupils quickly formed a power bloc within the peer group, and became the focus for socio-sexual structuring across the whole school.

One of these boys, Deano, was the embodiment of all the dominant masculinities available to schoolboys at Blunkett Rise. He was good-looking in a male pin-up way, and attracted from the girls comparisons with contemporary male icons. He displayed a calculating hardness in his interactions with both staff and pupils and was particularly stylish in his unnerving public chivalry: he could hold open a door for a teacher with a flourish that was at once courteous and threatening. He was bright enough to be placed in the top set for all subjects, studiously underachieving in all of them, and he was a black belt in free-style karate. His aggression was not confined to the sport, however, and had caused him to be excluded from four previous schools, two of them primary schools.

Deano was a formidable character. He waited quietly for some months after his arrival, keeping a low profile as far as discipline was concerned. He avoided the cultivation of a hard reputation as there was still a full cohort of Y11 boys in the school, many of whom would have been pleased to put Deano in his place as a newcomer bereft of indigenous support. During this time Deano earned further male status as heartbreaker of the many girls in his year, who saw him as exceptionally attractive. Although younger than ideal, his youth was compensated by his association out of school with young men of substantially greater age with whom he had served his time as a mascot.

Hierarchical reformation

Amid rumours that she was already pregnant to a Y11 boy, Roza began going out with Deano as soon as he had established himself as the main man in Y10. Roza was already firmly established as the hardest girl in Y10 and the linchpin of a clique that I had observed over four years. This liaison was the equivalent of a royal wedding, for Roza had befriended the two tough girl newcomers, and one of those was now going out with Deano's lieutenant, Tig. The foursome of Roza and Deano, Helen and Tig made its presence around the school felt by attracting an entourage of lower-order courtiers who managed to pair up in every possible permutation. This group split up into two factions following events described later, with Helen spreading rumours about Deano to Roza, and involving a new boyfriend in the trouble. The underlying causes of the next sequence of events are unclear, but the actions and their consequences were very evident.

Helen's new boyfriend and his mate, both ex-pupils now in their twenties, came onto the campus looking for Deano. The word was carried that they were there to teach him a lesson for slagging off Helen. Both young men were armed, one with a baseball bat, the other with a pool-cue, and were waiting for Deano with a crowd of Y11 spectators. When Deano turned up, he disarmed Helen's boyfriend in seconds, then beat him senseless with his own weapon. A large group of Y10 boys was there to watch, but then joined in the rout by giving both visitors a real beating. Y11 boys, who were there in expectation of the upstart getting his just desserts, were amazed at Deano's fighting skill. Even the younger brother of one of the defeated pair admitted to me that the fight was spectacularly efficient, with the captured weapons used to break the dispossessed lads' wrists leaving them defenceless and humiliated whilst the younger boys vented their pack fury.

The school was an 'interesting' place to teach in for the rest of that day and for several days after. The air of triumphalism was everywhere amongst the Y10 boys and girls. Most fell into line quickly along the Roza/Deano axis. The outgoing Y11 pupils were very subdued in public, but eager to talk when in lessons. They were astonished that anyone could act as such a catalyst. Although they had no great enthusiasm for outsiders beating up pupils at the school, neither could they stomach the overwhelming success of Deano, as he was both a newcomer from a different area of town and a year too young for the mantle of hardest kid in Blunkett Rise. The situation was even more uncomfortable for the Y11 lads, as the summer term was passing and they were on the verge of leaving school themselves, most of their hard boys were no longer frequent attenders and the remainder were preoccupied with exams.

The situation was regarded with grave concern by the staff of the school. This had been yet another in a long line of forays onto school premises by violent young adults; Deano himself had been the target on two previous occasions. The fight had caused serious disruption to the running of the school day with rumour and counter-rumour abounding, and keeping Y10 pupils to task was becoming even more difficult than before. In assemblies, senior staff called for calm and restraint, proclaiming that the excitement was over and the school should get back to normal. These exhortations and expectations for resumption of mundanity were premature, for the heat had not left the situation.

Attempts at restitution

Visits to the school by older youths intent on punishing one of the pupils were a common occurrence, and one that rarely needed to be repeated for the victim. During the period described above there were several visits, some by males, some by females, mostly centred on Deano but with no overtly declared connection with each other. The response by older local youths to this pretentious upstart had been almost organic: a rejection of his intrusion into their communal body. To them, the most objectionable thing of which Deano was guilty was his gate-crashing of the unofficial leavers' party.

Traditionally, on the last day before officially leaving school in the summer term[3] the remaining Y11 pupils would ritually destroy their school uniform, get staff and pupils to graffiti their blue shirts then head for the local park at lunch-time. In the park they would collect stashes of booze and cavort about the bandstand getting drunk. Sometimes a few older youths would meet up with them, usually to be with their girlfriends, but never were any younger pupils invited or allowed to take part. Staff annually tried to think of ways to circumvent or prohibit the more extreme activities, but they were never successful. That year, however, Deano and Tig went along in their dinner hour, allegedly selling cannabis and then soaking some of the revellers with a garden hose. This was not considered funny by some of the boys who had not attended school for some time due to exclusions or truancy and therefore had never met Deano or Tig. These boys would have acted as a natural deterrent to any Y10's challenge for peer-leadership amongst the boys, but had been absent during Deano's ascendancy. Some of the ex-pupils present at that occasion were particularly outraged at Deano's impertinence in gate-crashing an exclusive rite of passage, encroaching on the cannabis trade and then trying to spoil the fun by taking over as master of ceremonies.

A couple of weeks later, two 18-year-old ex-pupils, Gary and Robert, came onto the campus looking for Deano. These two were infamously involved in drug dealing and had been excluded permanently three years earlier. Reports were telegraphed around school that they were armed with knives and, although no reason was given for this, the pupils assumed that this was in retribution for Deano's *braggadocio* and interference with their drugs business.

Senior staff had warned Deano after the last occasion that, although he was obviously not the initial aggressor, he certainly was doing something serious to encourage so many outsiders to seek him out at school and attack him. They instructed him to remain with staff should further trouble arise. The staff were less than delighted at this role, but when Gary and Robert appeared outside the class window challenging Deano to step outside, the teacher insisted that he remain indoors. This was ignored: Deano left the room and ran out to where the two were waiting in the street and faced them off. Gary and Robert were then shocked to see about thirty Y10 boys surge through the school gates with sticks and stones and begin to run directly at them. Deano, thus encouraged and already only a few yards from them, ran at them too. A posse of staff and less-involved pupils brought up the rear, and the neighbourhood was treated to the spectacle of several dozens of pupils in school uniform chasing a couple of young men right around a third of the school's boundary, to where they escaped into a waiting car.

The incident ended in a bloodless victory for Deano and his cohorts, but the situation was deemed to have gone too far. The decision was made to permanently exclude Deano for disobeying clear instructions about remaining on site. The irony was not lost on his friends that he, who had sparked off so much violence but remained unbloodied, was being excluded because the school could not guarantee his safety. The details of these incidents were impossible for teachers to fully comprehend as they happened. In general, only one or two facts were known to any one person, and only I was in a position to collate these in order to see a wider picture.

Special conditions

The uniquely significant feature of this episode was the precocity of Deano's role as top dog. Many pupils arrived with hard reputations and were keen to establish a role commensurate with their social expectations. Mostly, these expectations remained firmly within the year group to which they belonged, and the collective interest of the most senior year limited the Young Turks' progress. One means of extending a reputation upwards was through association with the senior boys to become accepted as one of their lower ranks, whilst continuing to show due deference to the very hardest boys' seniority.

In Deano's case, he managed to make a quantum leap from low-profile newcomer to outrageously successful tough-guy, seemingly skipping a year of cadetship. The reasons for this included his undoubted fighting skill, his aggressive attitude, his intelligence, his physical attractiveness to girls and his social skills in grouping other pupils around him. Other pupils had previously possessed similar attributes but had not risen so far, so fast. Through a combination of luck and judgement, Deano had been in the right place at the right time to fully exploit his situation. Under normal circumstances the Y11 boys would never have tolerated Deano's behaviour and popularity in school. But at the time when Deano vanquished the interlopers with the baseball bat, the outgoing cohort was depleted – troublemakers having been weeded out by exclusion over the year. The pressure of final examinations and college/job interviews had also engendered a more adult approach among the remaining leavers, so there was little or no restraint on Deano.

Deano's case demonstrates the structuring of social relations by the formal organisation of the school, predicated upon the seniority of age. If it were not for the vagaries of the academic calendar, Deano's opportunities would have been restricted to his own year group and, quite probably, he would not have provoked the reaction of the older boys in such a violent manner. By becoming the hardest boy in the school a year early, so to speak, Deano seriously disrupted the normal peer group gender relations. His pairing with Roza was remarkable enough, as she would previously have been thought too high-status to go out with any boy in her own year. The situation was made all the more remarkable by the myths and rumours surrounding her finishing with her Y11 boyfriend.

The amount of open conflict between many groups of boys and girls seemed out of proportion to the mini-saga of this small clique. In discussion with my own form group it became clear that the usual brisk trade in pairings had been disrupted, virtually halted, due to uncertainties in the market. No one seemed to know who was eligible for whom and there was fear that any overtures might inflame one or another group's claims on friendship, thereby provoking a beating. Roza was identified as being responsible for this situation. Only her exceptionally strong character and solid support from other tough girls, including a tight and daunting kinship group, enabled her to ride the suppressed tide of disapproval amongst the girls at Blunkett Rise.

Just after his permanent exclusion from Blunkett Rise, Roza became pregnant to Deano. This enabled Roza's remaining supporters at Blunkett Rise to point to the natural resolution of true love: a wanted baby. A few months later, Roza herself left the school on medical advice regarding her pregnancy. Roza's story regarding these events is presented in the following chapter. The resumption of business as usual in respect of older boy/younger girl pairings was remarkably rapid.

School-gate gallants

A common feature of the pupils' sexual world was the small crowd of youths who congregated around the school gates at home-time and often at lunch break too. These boys were generally no longer pupils, although they sometimes included truants or excludees. They might be of school age and subject to an exclusion from another school, but usually they were a few years older and either ex-pupils or complete strangers to the school. The reason for their appearance at these times was to meet schoolgirls. In most cases there were relationships in progress, but some boys were accompanying friends who had girlfriends in school and were speculating on their own chances. The phenomenon was well recognised by the pupils participating in our research, irrespective of the school or year group. My own teaching school provided opportunity to probe deeper into the backgrounds of one set of these boys and, given the comparative interview data, I have no reason to believe it differs much from the conditions at other similar schools.

These gallants obviously had free time when many others of their age were at school, college or work. They appeared to operate as groups rather than singly in their courtship, and they often deployed 'props' in the form of an attractant forbidden to the schoolboys: a ghettoblaster; a car; a motorbike; cigarettes; booze; drugs, and so on. Their choice of clothes represented the extremes of teenage fashion, almost invariably a 'hard' look that was discouraged by the school for its own pupils. At the time of writing, the favoured look was a boxy half-length leather coat, rather Gestapo-like, and cropped hair with a longer fringe gelled and combed severely down over the forehead. In inclement weather, however, the coat could be exchanged for a long baggy T-shirt and canvas trainers. This symbolic inversion of conventionally appropriate attire marked the youths off from sensible, 'tame' dressers in the most superficial way possible.

Those gallants who were recognised by current boys and staff at the school were not remembered for academic excellence nor for their impressive social behaviour. Significantly, they were seen as abject failures in the delinquency stakes as well. In their time in lower school they had been the butt of some humour and targets for bullying. Later, in upper school, they had graduated into bullies themselves and had been regarded with disdain by their peers. They constituted what Besag (1989) describes as 'bully-victims', boys immersed in a bleak cycle of low self-esteem from years of victimisation, now replaying the abuse with themselves in the power position but receiving only fear and loathing rather than respect in return. This low status among both staff and peers did not prevent them from having a high profile. They were 'dickheads'.

I was at the school long enough to see a cohort of these gallants graduate to the school-gate role and could confirm their status as expressed by those who knew them. It is important to note that no one, neither staff nor pupil, could recall any of these boys having girlfriends at school, but some figured prominently, sometimes seriously, in incidents of sexual harassment against girls. Now that they had left the school, they had somehow acquired a social status that some schoolgirls evidently found irresistible. The general practice was for some girls who had just begun to show outward signs of physical maturity, usually ahead of their peers, to suddenly begin grooming themselves, and to express their sexuality in a spectacular way. Sometimes the transformation occurred, literally, overnight. Hair was coloured and styled in a way that needed constant attention during lessons. Faces were made up, with sophistication giving way to enthusiasm. Ears were ringed, noses studded, skirts tightened or shortened, white blouses contrasted with black bras. Friends were bewildered, schoolboys amazed, teachers mortified and trysts commenced at the school gate.

The boys who shared classes with such girls were generally aware of the girls' activities without fully comprehending them (as this usually happened around Y8), but the other girls in the group recognised the situation as variously exciting, dangerous or disgusting. It didn't take too long before the girls' reputations were made, voiced first by older girls within the school, then by girls in their own year as they realised the implications of such a choice of image. The proportion of girls to whom this description might apply appeared to be about 1 per cent, but it was pivotal in the balance of peer-group sexual relations. Boys, however, remained muted. This was in part due to their own developmental lag, but more especially because of the threat, or potential threat, from the school-gate gallants. It was common for younger boys to be harassed as they passed the gates simply as a matter of course. Parents sometimes contacted school to complain that their sons had been jostled, jeered, spat on or actually attacked by the youths. Staff on bus duty were also threatened by ex-pupils who had old scores to settle and were now enjoying the immunity of a school-free life.

It is unsurprising that the schoolboys were careful with what they said about the gallants' paramours: as the boys had to run the gauntlet of these bullies at hometime anyway, the additional threat of being singled out by their girlfriend was a very real one. This form of girl power continued throughout the boys' school careers. Even the older, tougher boys at school would avoid open criticism of the girls, and the rippling effect of silent resentment against the youths and girls involved broke out in distorted ways. Although no direct or open criticism would be expressed, girls in general were slagged off with particular girl groups being given public exception. This, by process of elimination, focused on the offending girls. The boys pushed the limits and sometimes exceeded them, but to protect themselves from the responses of older boyfriends they linked their misogyny with that of the gallants, citing their approval of the exploitative nature of the relationships.[4]

The schoolboys had a low opinion of the gallants, but still feared them and kept on superficially good terms with their girlfriends. These girls were seen by the schoolboys as 'slags', but a good laugh, and sexually stimulating and informative. The girls were likely to be only too happy to discuss their sexual exploits in graphic detail. For many boys this provided their first intimate contact with the opposite sex, and the experience was formative, if vicarious. The girls might be used for sex if the opportunity arose, but not for a 'relationship'.

The girls were seen as being exploited by the older boys. Pinxi and Boot even expressed pity for a particular class-mate, Sandra, who was used by large numbers of older lads. Sandra's sex drive was seen to be faulty, compelling her to take whatever risks it took to please boys. Her male class-mates were sympathetic to her plight but saw no role in protecting her or challenging her exploiters.

Odious comparisons

Another ideological feature concomitant with the above-mentioned misogyny was homophobia. The boys were aware of the bodily difference between themselves and the girls in their year group, but less aware of the developmental lag. They saw only other boys as yardsticks, and didn't compare themselves with the girls' sexual maturity. The lack of ability or opportunity for boys to relate to one another about their emotional and physical development has been remarked on above.[5] Their body hair, body odour, acne and change of vocal register reinforced their feelings of lack of control over change and of inferiority to boys who had passed through that stage.

When they compared themselves to older boys, the hierarchy of age seniority was reinforced by their obvious physical differences to older boys, and these differences were not read simply as differences but as comparators, with their own positions marked as inferior. The majority of boys would not countenance an attempt to usurp this 'natural order'. Very few older boys would put themselves in jeopardy of being beaten in a fight, or risk any other status disadvantage with younger boys. Even quite timid boys, way down the pecking order of their own year, would take strong action to avoid the loss of face that would ensue if a younger boy tried to outrank them.

Boys very rarely expressed admiration for the appearance or physique of another male in the same way that girls referred to their friends as being 'really pretty', looking 'really nice in those clothes', or having 'a good figure', for example. The modes of appreciation for males were always mediated through sporting references ('He's the fastest runner in our year'), or dismemberment ('He's got massive pecs (pectoral muscles))', or fetishised accessories ('He has a smart pair of trainers'). In fact, the older male body was hardly ever viewed by boys as attractive, but as repellent, as a threat.

Playboys of the playground

The previously low status of the school-gate gallants when they were still schoolboys was quickly forgotten, if known at all, by the pupil cohort, but my schoolboy respondents at Blunkett Rise were able to offer predictions on which boys in their year would turn out to be school-gate gallants. The boys gave four nominations, two who were familiar to me and two that I did not know well. The two that I knew fitted the bill very well as socially unimpressive low-profile bullies; one of them was the only known drug dealer in the year at that time, a role that featured amongst the petty criminality of the older gallants.

In one of many similar incidents at the schools, staff were called to the front gates to disperse a gang of youths who were behaving offensively to the mid-day supervisors. As the head teacher was asking the pupils to come back inside the gates he was met with catcalls and verbal challenges from the gallants. One recently excluded boy repeatedly called out 'suck my cock' to each of his requests.

This sort of abuse gave a clear message to current pupils on the limits of the school's authority. It was interpreted by anti-school pupils as encouraging, but to those pupils seeking the school's protection it was frightening.

The fatal stabbing of headmaster Philip Lawrence outside his school in Maida Vale in 1996 occurred in much the same conditions, and illustrates the fragility of the physical, moral, legal and professional boundaries maintained by schools. On occasions when school-gate activities really got out of hand, such as the open passing of drugs to pupils, or stolen cars being raced around the playground to deliberately provoke official reaction, the police were slow to respond, if they responded at all.[6]

The influence of the gallants intruded into the school's discipline in a very subtle way, with occasional incidents seen in isolation. As several of the schools were open-access campuses within large council-housing estates, many pupils lived within a ten-minute walk from the school, as did the gallants. If the latter wished to visit their girlfriends, they could easily mix with the pupils at break or lunch-times without official regulation. Since the teachers' industrial actions of the mid-1980s, no teaching staff need carry out lunchtime supervisory duties. This role was performed by mid-day supervisors, 'dinner ladies', who patrolled the pupil access areas for an hour a day. At these times, as one moved about the school site, it was not unusual to see schoolgirls in an amorous clinch with their older boyfriends. Most staff turned a blind eye unless they were actually offended by what they saw, and most pupils played the game of 'acceptable limits' so actionable incidents were not too frequent, perhaps a couple of times per year. When limits were breached, usually by the girl returning late to afternoon lessons rather than by being too publicly sexual, staff attempted to assert their authority. Again, this mostly passed without incident, with the teacher focusing on punctuality and the girl accepting punishment for that aspect of her behaviour. At other times teachers expressed their disapproval of the sexual aspects of her behaviour, moral outrage at indecency and so on. This could prompt a reaction, perhaps not from the girl at the time, but from an irate boyfriend who might later appear outside the classroom window making threats and demanding satisfaction.

The above type of occasional incident was absorbed into pupil mythology and helped curb some teachers' excesses. It is easy for staff to be seduced into assuming omnipotence whilst monarch of the classroom. Expectations from both above and below constantly reinforce the need for teachers to maintain classroom control, but such control relies on fragile psychological contracts. In such conditions many teachers take the line of personal infallibility and rarely or grudgingly admit they may have got things wrong. Often the more insecure the teacher, the more offensive the discipline and the more crushing the reversal of fortune.

Contriving to be overheard by their target staff, pupils were able to remind each other of occasions when such staff were shown to be out of their depth. This could be achieved by merely invoking the name of a gallant, perhaps mentioning his presence on the school site. It would not be every pupil who would do this – indeed many pupils were very disturbed by the usurping of teacher authority, afraid of the incipient anarchy and the implications for themselves. Both male and female teachers were subject to the power of non-pupils and their effects on the relationship between themselves and their current pupils, but their treatment at the hands of the non-pupils was significantly gendered. Male staff were much more likely to be threatened with physical aggression for their efforts in exerting control in these situations, with their *de facto* authority called into question. Female staff were more likely to be ignored or dismissed by the gallants as a spent force. Disempowered by their lack of *de jure* authority in their attempts to control behaviour outside of their remit, female staff were disrespected, often in a sexualised mode, but rarely threatened physically.[7]

The acme of executive discipline in the schools was founded upon a particular form of masculine power: a mixture of age seniority and concealed physical threat, delivered via a professional male individual. Attempts to extend teacher authority beyond its official boundaries exposed the artificiality and hollowness of that power. Across the line of the school gate, all three elements of it evaporated. The individual professional appeared isolated in an environment inhabited and controlled by groups of youths. These groups presented a physical superiority which did not respect age when dissociated from virility, but despised it. The male teachers were trapped in a no-win situation where they could not respond in kind without fear of defeat or legal action, but if they were to retreat or evade they would be diminished as men. The disavowal of pupil sexuality enabled certain forms of discipline and control to function in the school's favour, but it still existed beneath almost every social exchange, ready to disrupt and distort honest relationships within the institution.

Summary

The ideology of age seniority is a crucial element in the understanding of sexual bullying. Schools play an important role in such bullying by amplifying the importance of age differences between pupils to such an extent that, even years after leaving school, adults can remember other contemporaries' ages relative to their own: 'Oh yes, she was in the year above me.'

The examples of inter-male conflict illustrate the degree to which the struggle to assert a desired sexual reputation permeated ostensibly gender-free cultural practice amongst the young men, and the part age-ranking played within it. The prohibition of Pinxi and Boot's platonic friendliness with female class-mates in the

public arena can be read as a direct response to the potential testing of the masculinity of the older boys.

Older boys had a strong expectation of obeisance from their younger fellows,
more so than was evident in the girls' groups. When this status system was threatened, retaliation to restore order was rapid: the sudden eruption of violence in
these situations was real and frequent. The young men in the interviews knew
what was happening but found it difficult to talk about, partly because the concepts were intricate and not fully formed in language, and partly because they
probed the core values of their shaky identity.

One of the ways that this structure of peer relations reinforced itself was
through the transient tenure older boys had on their age rank. Most of the boys in
the dominant position had only a year or two at most before they moved on to
other pursuits. Those who didn't were the less socially mature individuals –
'retards', stuck in an age-inappropriate role. As the older boys moved on from
hanging about in gangs in the town centre to pubs, work or prison, new blood like
Boot and Pinxi would fill the gap. The rapid rate of phasal change gave this
social structure gyroscopic stability: no one was in either position, senior or junior,
long enough to analyse or change the structure. This phenomenon has great
durability but, despite its prevalence, is largely overlooked by commentators on,
and practitioners in, education.

Deano's rise and fall sheds some light upon the organisation of pupil affairs as
structured by the school's official regimen. Had the timing been slightly different,
Deano would not have emerged as such a precocious threat to the established
order. His exceptional personal characteristics prompted him to challenge the old
guard rather than wait his time until they left. It would have been far less likely
that, had he made it into the final year, he would have been excluded, as the
school expects a Y11 boy to hold the title of hardest kid, and an unpleasant order
is easier to control than an unpleasant disorder.

Not only did the official practices of the school modify and condition the
sexual expression of its pupils, the practices of the pupils modified the school's
stance on discipline. The sporadic intrusions of gallants and older boyfriends into
school areas gave substance to the very real sense of a 'bottom line' to teacher control. The gallants offered an alternative and apparently successful, if only
short-term, role model for masculinity that fed less ambitious forms of resistance
by the pupils against the staff.

In the staffroom one evening, a male teacher approaching early retirement
from Blunkett Rise asked a younger colleague to move his car from one car park
to another at the far end of the campus. I was intrigued by this request and asked
him why. His purpose was to avoid passing a senior girls' hockey match where he
expected to encounter abuse from spectating boyfriends whom he had taught in
the past: 'It's just not worth it. If I get called a bald cunt one more time I'm going
to crack up.'

5 The culture of feminine violence

Hard girls

A powerful set of social attitudes exists towards female aggression and violence. Many parents are more strict in controlling their daughters' physicality than they are their sons', and are especially sensitive to public display of their daughters' aggression, forbidding it in the street whilst tolerating it in the home (Newson and Newson 1978). Amongst the middle classes the phenomenon of girls fighting other girls is rarely encountered, but working-class females are more familiar with such incidents. In some circles girl fights have such a mystique that this practice has become quite eroticised, with (predominantly) men paying high prices to watch females box or mud-wrestle.

In my introduction I stated that my intention was to explore the mid-field players of gender relations in school and to leave the better-known extremes of youth subculture to those who have an interest in deviancy. The common experiences of the majority do, however, need the extremes of pupil behaviour to mark out their own sense of normality. The exceptional violence in the cases of Deano and Roza illustrate the 'normal' state of affairs by their disruption of them during that particular summer term, and illuminate the structural strength of the hierarchies of masculinities and femininities which created the conditions for sexual bullying.

During that term at Blunkett Rise there occurred a series of incidents that combined to create a very special climate for pupil relationships. This chapter describes some of these incidents in the form of a case study. The study attempts to explore the change in gender relations across the whole peer group as affected by one or two unusual events sparked off by one or two unusual individuals. The principal themes and characters have been introduced in earlier chapters; their re-presentation here is to give narrative context to some of the important events that are interpreted as critical in the production and reproduction of gender orders at Blunkett Rise.

For some years I had observed one particular pupil cohort's struggles for sexual reputation (and the ensuing bullying) as I had special pastoral responsibility for that group. The patterns of these struggles, some of which have been discussed above, included, for boys, the promotion of a hyper-masculinity for successful relationships with girls and status amongst boys, and the relegation of all other forms of masculinity to subordination and persecution. Relationships with girls were most valued in the form of serial conquests without commitment.

For most of the girls the ideal was an older, more mature male partner who had access to symbols of adult success, such as independence from other adults (teachers/parents) and experience in the social world of pubs, clubs and cash. The most valued relationships were long-lasting and 'serious', with evidence of commitment from the boy. But certainly in Blunkett Rise, and probably in the other schools too, the counterparts of the aggressive, hyper-masculine sexualities were evident in the subcultures of some of the 'hard' girls' cliques. These girls were involved in a great deal of threatened, and executed, interpersonal violence which they deployed to gain status and control over the affairs of boys and girls with whom they appeared to have little connection. Unlike the middle-of-the-road girls who were the subjects of my interviews, these hard girls were sexually aggressive and often dominant in their relationships with boys, seeing nothing wrong in short-term relationships where quantity replaced the quality esteemed by the majority of the girls.

Love hurts

In the four schools in this study, the perception of physical violence was predominantly of boys fighting or threatening other boys. Fights between girls seemed much rarer on the surface, but were more frequent than supposed. Whilst teachers condemned outright any fighting in school, they were less surprised by the violent acts of boys than of girls, seeing the latter as not only unruly and uncivilised, but also more deviant from supposed feminine codes. When girls did fight they attracted just as much of an audience, and were just as violent as the boys. The sexes were equally represented as spectators, irrespective of which sex was fighting, and equally vociferous in their encouragement of the combatants.

The preliminaries of the fights, however, were profoundly differentiated by gender. Boys' fights were often flash-points which erupted and were completed in a break-time with little or no prior warning. There was often intimidation by the favourite's friends, but rarely did this affect the outcome of the fight. With girls the situation was quite different. The confrontations were more planned, with messages and warnings being carried by runners sometimes for days in advance. The same cliques who organised the courtship pairings were generally involved in organising the fights between girls. Teachers in tune with their pupil groups observed dramatic changes in friendship groups, alliances being created and broken, and support being canvassed by the organisers, who were rarely the combatants themselves. There were often one or more false starts to a fight and frequently there was a resolution without actual violence. On the other hand, the hate and fear could smoulder on for weeks or months.

In each of the research schools the interviewees often reported the occasional physical violence of girls against others, and linked these occasions with the sexual rivalry between the girls – a motive never attributed to fights amongst boys:

Y7 St Joseph's boys

ND: Have you ever seen a fight between a boy and a girl?

ARTHUR, BILLY, CIARAN, DAK: No.

ARTHUR: Only like arguments.

ND: Ever seen a fight between girls?

CIARAN, DAK: Yeah. *(Laughter)*

ND: Often?

ARTHUR: Not as often as boys.

CIARAN: No, not very often.

ND: What do you think girls fight about?

CIARAN: Calling names.

Billy: Well if one girl is nicer looking than another girl, then that girl will call the nice looking one slut or slag or something.

CIARAN: Whore.

ARTHUR: Or if one girl knows that a girl fancies a boy and she has gone out of her way to ask this boy out and the girl fancies him as well, well that might cause friction.

ND: So jealousy of boyfriends, stuff like that?

ARTHUR: Yeah.

ND: Or the way they look?

ARTHUR: Yeah.

ND: What do you think boys fight about then?

ARTHUR: 'You call me names so I will batter you!'

This type of gendered differentiation of violence was also found by Davies, where her 'wenches' claimed as much physical aggression as boys, and teachers and both sexes of pupils saw 'girls' fighting as resulting from jealousies over boys, while boys fought over football teams' (Davies 1984: 10). The bullying amongst girls was usually over a longer period compared to the boys, and more intractable for staff to deal with. In general, Davies found that boys and girls both thought that boys fought more frequently, but when girls did fight they were nastier to one another and more people were involved.

In Blunkett Rise the Y10 cohort of girls had been fairly settled for a long time. One or two key individuals had been permanently excluded in the previous year for seriously bullying girls in the same year group. Since then there had been an easily recognised hierarchy, at the top of which was Roza. By Y10 Roza had managed to blend beauty and terror seamlessly into her image. Other girls admired and coveted her long black hair and flawless complexion, but when she shaved her head and acquired prominent tattoos she seemed to become even more attractive. Her choice of clothes was similarly extreme but perfectly suited to her. The rapidity with which Roza changed her image was blinding, and left many imposters trailing in her wake. It was not, however, only in superficial matters that Roza excercised dominance.

The school disco: breaking tradition

The school disco had become an important tradition in the Blunkett Rise pupil culture. It represented a unique opportunity for the pupils to present themselves *en masse* out of uniform and in a relaxed situation. During the disco boys and girls would spend the most time outside the doors or in the toilets, arranging and re-arranging pairings and generally enjoying the social buzz. One of the most popular girls amongst both sexes in my tutor group, Gina, made it known to me that she would not be going that year.

GINA: It's always crap but I would go for the laugh, but it won't be the same this time, all the fourth years *(Y10)* are going out with each other and it's just hassle.

ND: What's wrong with that?

GINA: Normally, you know, all the girls in our year and fifth year *(Y11)* have older boyfriends and we can go to the disco and talk about them, and have a laugh with the lads in our class. We don't fancy them, just have a laugh. It's a girls' night out. But this year all the lads are going out with our-year girls and it just won't be a laugh.

A range of femininities was in evidence through the experiences of the Blunkett Rise girls. Gina's feminine identity was not as dominant as that of Roza and her clique, although its wider currency in society outside of school meant that she and her friends were given a good deal of respect from Roza. Gina was more academically successful, more conforming to school rules and very much less aggressive than Roza. Her expression of femininity was that which would likely take the hegemonic position in many other schools where there was greater academic competition amongst the pupils, and street-wise wit and style were valued more than raw power.

Ball (1981) describes such a femininity in the upper-band girls at Beachside Comprehensive. Whilst retaining an identifiable style not wholly conforming with the school's preferences, these girls were able to adapt the straight style to their own values. In so doing they showed the lower-band girls up as trying just too hard, and appearing forced and awkward instead of cool and nonchalant.[1]

For Gina and the other more mature girls, one of the enjoyments of the 'crap' school disco was its freedom from girls' rivalry for the attentions of the immature boys. The real objects of desire would probably be down the pub or similar, whilst the girls could have a dance and a chat and socialise on a platonic level with the 'almost fanciable' older schoolboys without any competitive atmosphere. Now that the boys in Y10 were going out with the girls in Y10, the situation would be too intense. Roza and Deano's example had brought together a highly compacted set of boy–girl relationships which was bound to affect everyone else in the year. The emotional and social space claimed above to be needed by the girls were no longer available even in the relatively free cultural space of the school disco.

It was these conditions that created the following situation for one of the boys in Gina's class. Pinxi was a very popular Y10 boy at Blunkett Rise. His short-term relationship with Anna, a fringe member of Roza's clique, had been ended for some time, but at the school disco the clique were determined to exert their influence on the pupil group, and messages were sent to Pinxi's prospective Y9 girlfriend, Jackie, to back off. Anna told me later that she had no desire to fight Jackie, but was so pressured by Roza and her friends to preserve the reputation of the group that she felt she had no choice. Jackie had continued with her overtures to Pinxi, and was later assaulted outside the disco by Anna surrounded by six of Anna's mates. Jackie was a quiet girl, physically and emotionally mature for her age, but inexperienced with boys. She had fancied Pinxi for some time but had not moved in while she thought Anna was still interested in him. She had assumed that, as Pinxi had had another girlfriend in between Anna and herself, the pro-tocols had been observed, so the assault was a complete surprise. Jackie spent the next school day's breaks under the protection of staff in the Special Needs centre. She told me she was scared but wouldn't back down whilst Pinxi still wanted her. She hoped the girls would move on to some other amusement and leave them alone.

Pinxi's view of the episode was confused. He had finished with Anna amicably a while back and had not expected her to interfere in his affairs as he had had sev-eral brief liaisons since then, all with girls in his own year. The mutual attraction between him and Jackie had been noted and was frowned upon by girls of his own year. Pinxi had heard the warnings at the disco and encouraged Jackie to leave with him. He did not want to stay as he was out of his depth with the hard girls' clique (and their boyfriends) and thought that leaving was the only option. Jackie wanted to stay at the disco with her friends, and so they parted.

PINXI: Well my ex punched her, but Jackie couldn't do anything because there were six others who would have got her.
BOOT: That's the problem, it's bitchiness.
PINXI: It hasn't changed how I feel, she wants me back, but I don't want to go out with her again. Jackie was shouted over to her and all her (*Anna's*) mates were there, she (*Jackie*) wouldn't have stood a chance Sir, if she'd tried the others would have jumped in. I was really cut up about it when I saw her this morning. I told her to come away but she didn't. I was really cut up about it, I was.[2]

This form of sexual bullying – girls attacking, or scaring off, rivals for contested boyfriends – has also been noted by Davies (1984). In this case the beating up was done not directly because Anna perceived a grievance against Jackie, but because Roza and the rest of her clique felt they needed to preserve the integrity of the group: a liberty taken against one was a slight against all. In this matter the feelings of Pinxi, Anna and Jackie were all subservient to the subcultural law.

The hard girls justified their use of violence by mirroring the boys' chivalric codes in a feminine mode, defending the honour of a jilted friend. Prospective paramours were sometimes told that they should not go out with a certain boy because another girl had a claim on him. Even if the boy did not agree, the clique would maintain that he was doing one of their friends an injustice and any girl who broke the embargo would suffer accordingly. This sinister form of sisterhood was well recognised by the girls, but often played down because of the far-reaching power of some of the hardest girls who blended raw coercion with friendliness to give carrot, as well as stick, to those under their sovereignty.

Under normal circumstances this problem would not have occurred, as Anna's attachment to Pinxi would have not encroached upon the pool of lads eligible for, or desirable to, the Y10 hard girls. The opening up of this unexploited male resource had only come about with the advent of Deano and Tig, and had created a ripple effect of increased social status amongst the other Y10 boys. Jackie had been taken by surprise at the value conferred upon her choice of partner, Pinxi, by his female class-mates, but she was socially skilled enough to recognise this new development in the peer group's gender relations and to adapt to it quickly. She acknowledged the authority of Roza's clique, and after a suitable period of keeping her deferential distance, she made appropriately friendly contact with that group, eventually being accepted on its fringes.

Roza: dominant femininity

Roza was a member of a well-known family. Their extended kinship could be found throughout the community where they were perceived to be 'a right lot' by other, more law-abiding families and were treated with caution in any dispute. Roza had no males in her household,[3] although there were plenty of uncles and cousins close at hand. All four of her older sisters had attended Blunkett Rise; one was still in Y11. Roza was considered brighter than average, as were all her sisters, and had followed the pattern of working very well in Y7 then doing the bare minimum whilst she concentrated on administering her social domain. From her arrival at Blunkett Rise, Roza was never without a boyfriend and constantly ran the gauntlet of staff disapproval for her extreme dress style. On more than one occasion she was sent home to replace a micro skirt or see-through blouse.

Roza was recognised by many staff as a threat to both boys and girls who did not comply with her needs and wishes, but she was also a formidable opponent to teachers and very few staff could cope easily with her influence in class. I found Roza to be very bright company; her verbal swipes at teachers' characteristics were blisteringly accurate, and I was on the receiving end of her stinging humour on many occasions. I was lucky in that I did not have to teach her directly, only as a support teacher to her class, and so could engage with her on a more sociable plane. For those she considered owing her liege, she could turn her prolix talents to more vicious ends and quickly resort to physical engagement should she feel the need.

Sovereignty in the classroom

Roza could express boredom with a lesson and immediately other pupils would take care not to show any enthusiasm: fewer hands would be raised in answer to the teacher's questions, books would be grudgingly handed out and class discipline would seep away from the teacher to Roza. She would organise seating plans, go-slows and works-to-rule; she would scare kids into truancy and teachers into not setting homework; she would ridicule any praise given for effort or compliance. But she knew precisely how far to push her resistance to the school's authority, and although she often deliberately went too far she never made the ultimate sacrifice of getting herself excluded. She had it sussed.

Such power resident in one pupil was not comprehended as a whole-school problem but was experienced in discrete doses, by busy teaching staff whose work-load consisted primarily of delivering the curriculum and fulfilling administrative demands. Compounding this was the very human reluctance to disclose one's personal difficulties by seeking help in dealing with a single adolescent girl. When the picture could be reviewed globally and with more time to consider the social life of the institution, Roza could be discerned as not an independent agent in this system. Over the years she had shown the mental and physical toughness required in a dominating person. She had, however, been supported and manipulated by other girls for whom the crown was too heavy but who desired the privileges of court. Roza was perceived by most of the girls as a good laugh, not oppressive and not a thug unless someone attempted to usurp her.

The gender relations within the year group had been dominated by Roza's clique for some years. Her preferences had conformed to the pattern outlined as prevailing in all the other schools: the higher-status girls all went out with older males who had left school. Very few newcomers to the year group had made any impact on this arrangement until the arrival of Deano and his friend Tig, followed closely by two girls, Helen and Tammy. All these new pupils had been excluded from schools on the other side of town following violent behaviour, and knew one another well.[4] As they had arrived, each one had been assimilated into Roza's clique alongside the most influential boys and girls in the year.

Deano and Roza emerged as the outstanding couple, each with an array of attractions that seemed to give them semi-mythical status amongst the other pupils. Had it been any other boy but Deano, Roza would probably not have considered a same-age boyfriend. But Deano really was something special. On his arrival, Deano's effortlessly muscled physique, teen pin-up looks and casually expensive style combined to create an arresting image. Many staff queried his age, as his appearance and carriage gave the impression more of an 18-year-old than a 15-year-old.

If Roza had passed up on Deano there would have been no shortage of Y9 girls keen on partnering him, with herself stuck with a lesser man despite any age seniority. With the pairing up of Roza and Deano breaking the mould of the older boy–younger girl pattern, Roza's influence gave sanction to more same-age part-nerships amongst Tig, Helen and her other friends, thus establishing the nucleus of a new order.

Caroline: ineffective submission

Every boy and girl had a different tolerance or resistance to the pressure of the group. Some pupils were robust enough to withstand appalling torment and abuse from their peers. Jackie was not physically tough, but handled herself effectively enough in the aftermath of her beating to prevent the quality of her life suffering more than temporarily. Other pupils were deeply affected by just witnessing harsh social treatment meted out to others (Duncan 1991). The arrival of another Y10 girl into the group, Caroline, who had transferred to Blunkett Rise from Patten Avenue, illustrated the intricacy of the forces of hegemonic masculinity and hegemonic femininity within the year group.

Caroline's form tutor raised with her the possible problems of settling into an established group. She alluded to 'new girls sometimes getting hassle off some of the tougher girls', and indicated that support was at hand via the pastoral system for that and other potential difficulties. Caroline was a strikingly good-looking girl in conventional terms, and was of above average academic ability. She seemed to take great care to be fashionable but modest, and she attracted a lot of interest from the boys in her year that she handled without fuss.

Caroline had been one of the cohort that I had interviewed at Patten Avenue, although she had not been one of the actual interviewees. According to the data received from that group, Caroline would have been used to associating with the boys in her year without any romantic expectations. Like most of the popular girls in her year she would have been likely to look outside the school for older partners, and not expect resentment from other Y10 girls over her platonic friendliness to Y10 boys.

As was customary at Blunkett Rise, a pupil 'buddy' was chosen to help the newcomer find her way around for the first few weeks. Lindsey had been selected by the head of year for the job as she was reliable, hard-working and conventional. In discussion with Caroline it emerged that her pairing with Lindsey had prompted Caroline to give signals to other pupils that she was not as 'goody-goody' as Lindsey, and should not be treated as such. These signals had provoked Lindsey into giving minimum support and alerted the harder girls of a potential challenger for senior status in their year.

Almost immediately it became apparent that Caroline was having problems. She rarely sat more than once with the same companions in lessons, and staff reported that she spent all her break-times alone. Caroline was offered the option of having lunch with the Special Needs staff in their working area, which she accepted eagerly. Over the next weeks Caroline slowly revealed an eating disorder, and this problem was tackled by the special needs staff in liaison with her parents. A suspicious pattern of absence was also emerging, and Caroline had approached one of her teachers with a request to be moved from the top set to a lower ability group despite her obvious academic strength.

Across the timetable Caroline was having all sorts of difficulties, and giving different reasons to different staff. Rumours from the girls in her class circled around her becoming the object of Roza's jealousy because Deano now fancied Caroline.

Despite direct inquiries by staff regarding this rumour, Caroline dismissed any problem of that nature, claiming instead that she felt friendless as she moved around the classes in the school. Although each individual pupil was pleasant enough she could not gel properly with any of them. The situation was so bad she now wanted to leave Blunkett Rise and transfer to yet another new secondary school.

Social embargo

In a meeting with parents and pastoral staff, Caroline was pressed to convince the adults why a third secondary school would be a sensible resolution to her relationship difficulties. Under this pressure Caroline eventually explained that her early days at Blunkett Rise had been promising. She had been accepted as one of the group fairly easily, but had shown interest in Deano as he was also new to Blunkett Rise, and she had met him during his brief time at Patten Avenue. In a brush with Roza over a trivial matter she had backed down but Deano had come to her assistance 'as a friend'. She had been surprised at someone of Roza's status going out with someone in her own year, but had quickly adapted to this relationship. Nevertheless, Roza had orchestrated a campaign of persecution against Caroline to establish her as a social non-entity in the school. Due to the power axis between Roza and Deano, this scheme had been remarkably effective in turning boys and girls away from Caroline for fear of upsetting either of these two peer leaders. Caroline described how she could enjoy friendly relations only in certain conditions within her tutor group. Initially, Roza sought out girls with whom Caroline appeared friendly and spread rumours about her: if Caroline showed any response Roza would draw her clique together in a show of physical strength. Later she consolidated her power and kept up the pressure by less blatant methods, such as making provocative comments within earshot and pressing the others to laugh with her against Caroline.

Caroline had miscalculated her entry into the social establishment, then compounded her mistake by backing off submissively at the first sign of hostility. Over the following weeks Caroline could never become part of a social group without causing a tension between the others. No one wanted to be seen to befriend Caroline and risk Roza's disapproval. When pressed on the totality of this social exclusion, Caroline explained that Roza did not need to establish control over everyone in school, but only to pick out key pupils when Caroline appeared to be receiving succour from them. Yes, there were many pupils who were not directly influenced by Roza, but they were not the natural attractions for Caroline either and, if they became so, Roza had made it her business to move against them too.

Roza's influence reached into classes where she was not present. She could establish such a strong grip on specific girls that they would act as her agents to enforce the embargo in her absence. This was a superbly refined strategy, with an effect close to a double bind. If no girls were willing to sit or talk with Caroline, it left her physically isolated other than from the attentions of the boys. If she was then seen to accept the attentions of the boys, and there were usually plenty of offers from the less popular lads, then she was further confirmed as a 'slag'. If she rejected them, she would be regarded as frigid as well as friendless.

Early staff suspicions of bullying had been well founded, but Caroline had strenuously blocked help for fear of publicising her victimisation. The pastoral staff had offered to surreptitiously manipulate pupil groupings and social situations to her advantage, but Caroline had thought that this would be detected by her peers and expose her weaknesses. Every suggestion of tackling the problem had been rejected and she was now locked up in her own feelings of inadequacy and helplessness. She was terrified that an adult might be seen acting on her behalf for such a deeply personal issue. The staff would not act without Caroline's express agreement, and this was not forthcoming.

Caroline's parents were incredulous. They imagined that she was suffering from some form of advanced paranoia, and linked other aspects of her recent behaviour with her present inability to cope with her current situation. In tears and gasps, Caroline begged to be removed from the school for another fresh start. She felt she had messed things up and blamed herself for not standing up to Roza on the first occasion. She also regretted spurning Lindsey's friendship as that group of popular, but less exciting, girls had turned away from her in pride. This had given Roza the psychological advantage and, although Caroline could rationalise that she might well win in a physical encounter, the emotional stakes were too high and the social disadvantage she now found herself in was too great to turn around.

There seemed to be a conflict between Caroline's affective needs and her objective interests. It was resolved that Caroline should talk privately to her family and decide whether to leave the school for another, to confront the issue with or without adult help or to transfer to a different academic grouping within the school where Roza's influence was thought to be weaker. This last option was decided upon – with little gusto from anyone, but at least it achieved a short-term solution.

Both Caroline and Jackie were victims of a turbulence in a usually stable set of gender relations. Caroline, intelligent and popular amongst the boys, had not expected to walk into a new school where the boys in her class were esteemed as boyfriends by the other girls in the class. She had misjudged her response and paid the price of prolonged psychological and social freezing which hurt her deeply and wrecked her erstwhile confidence. Her reduced status on the social periphery became her fixed identity whilst in school, although her social life outside school in her own neighbourhood retained something of its former glory.

Close relationships: Deano and Roza

As major investors in the sexual economy of Blunkett Rise, Deano and Roza stood to lose most if the market went against them, but, in organising the gender relations on a different basis, away from one which had evolved around the school's official structure, they came adrift. The difficulty of living, loving, fighting and working in such close proximity with one another and all their friends proved too much to cope with. One can gauge the pressure of this

emotional volatility by reflecting on the well-known advice to stable adult part-
nerships considering working, as well as living, together: don't. The unusual rota
of same-age partners in the same classes created unbearable friction and jealousy.
This confusion of multiple and sequential immature relationships, all compressed within the disciplinary structure of a school day, soon reached critical
mass.

Roza and Deano were each regarded as the best looking, toughest and best
bloodstocked of the year. Both had big families with big reputations, and they were
intelligent and socially skilled enough to make full use of these attributes. Now
that Roza's clique had grown too large but too intimate for her to maintain complete control, Roza's toughest ally, Helen, was growing disaffected. As a newcomer,
Helen had never quite acquired the status of Roza, who was now further edified by
her relationship with Deano. Helen broke ranks and resumed dating much older
youths from outside the school. She then approached Roza with some news of
Deano's infidelity with her aunt.

The polarisation of girls within this group was very sudden, and crystallised
during one lunch-time at school. Roza's response to Helen's warning of infidelity
was to accuse her of 'stirring it' between herself and Deano; Helen reacted angrily
and, instead of pursuing what had been ostensibly a sisterly line, she now ridiculed
Roza's trust in Deano and publicised the embellished story throughout the school.
During the early stages of her romance with Deano, it had been whispered that
Roza had terminated a pregnancy arising from an earlier relationship with a Y11
boy previously excluded from Blunkett Rise. In a grotesque act of defamation, graffiti began to appear in the girls' toilets that made reference to this and other
sensitive areas of Roza's biography. From the Queen of the May to the slag of the
school, Roza's descent into a hate figure needed arresting promptly. A fight was
arranged for after school, but the elaborate organisation requires some
explanation.

After hubris, nemesis

Helen was physically and mentally tough, not only taller and fitter than Roza,
but with at least as much moral support from acolytes outside the school. Her
family was immersed in crime culture locally: three older brothers had recently
been in the national press for football hooliganism and their reputation was
fearsome throughout the town. Helen had no fear of Roza, and was determined
to oust her from her pedestal over this issue. She was also angry at Deano for his
casual manipulation of events. He had caused a great deal of trouble but
remained unrepentant and still in credit. Helen arranged for a very public punishment beating for Deano, courtesy of her older boyfriend and one of his
cronies. This was supposed to be in response to Deano's slandering of Helen, but
was seen by most of the pupils for what it truly was: a challenge to Roza's leadership. In the event, Deano trounced the two older boys (the fight is recounted
in Chapter 4).

During that same lunch-time, but in a different area of the campus, Helen and her aide, Tammy, challenged Roza to a fight. Roza declined, saying that Deano forbade her to fight as it was unseemly, but that her friend Mary would be happy to act as champion. Mary was a very strongly built and aggressive girl, with no following in the school other than one close friend. She was now thrust into a situation way beyond her social skills, and so she simply attacked Helen at the next provocative remark, leaving her, then Tammy, battered and bleeding within moments. The violence of this fight was underscored by Mary ripping out Helen's earrings for trophies.

This spectacular explosion of violence within a restricted social group had an electrifying effect upon the whole school. The Y10 boys behaved in a fairly uncomplicated way, with a couple of days of celebration, recounting over and again the events and Deano's victory. There were no further incursions to fuel the excitement and, as no other boys were involved from within the school, only the winning side was evident, and the thrill died away over a couple of weeks. The girls' situation was somewhat more volatile. The overt aggression shown by the two new girls, Helen and Tammy, was enough to have both excluded for a week. Many staff had been aware of the bullying by all the main parties in this episode (it was they who had beaten up Pinxi's girlfriend) and were glad to be able to confront them with a concrete contravention of the school's discipline code.

In the absence of Helen and Tammy, the fêting of Mary, the new-found champion and defender of the faith, was allowed to proceed unhindered and with the added piquancy of an imminent return to school of the other combatants. One or two girls who had been closely involved with Roza, but felt aggrieved about the years of her aggression and domination, had sided with Helen at the showdown. These girls were not the toughest nor most popular girls, and were now persecuted and harassed by Roza and her gang. I heard the inside story from Helen's best friend, Julie, who was one of my own tutor group.

ND: Why did Helen stir things up with Roza about Deano and Stacia (*Deano's other lover*)?
JULIE: 'Cos it's not right, they were mates, and she knew he'd been two-timing her.
ND: But how come all the girls have fallen out with each other, but Deano is still talking to everyone? Isn't it all his fault?
JULIE: It's Roza's fault, she's a slag.
ND: She used to be your mate!
JULIE: Yeah, well she was a slag then as well.
ND: So why are you not friends now?
JULIE: 'Cos Helen is my friend, I am not breaking friends with her. I want to move schools. I know Roza will try to get me if she can't get Helen.

There was much talk of stabbings and gang beatings arranged for outside school. Those who were not with one side must be actively supporting the other, and so would be issued with threats as well. This small group needed protection from Roza's gang, and this was supplied as effectively as possible by the teaching staff, who were under extreme pressure from the victims' parents to punish any girls involved in the dispute, with the exception of their own daughters.

This situation continued for more than two weeks, confused and inflamed by sporadic absences by each of the main players. Julie was particularly worried, as she was seen by Roza as a traitor and easy meat for her or any of her sergeants. Julie had been chased out of school by one of Roza's older friends who had been waiting at the classroom door allegedly to stab her. The same young woman, about 20 years old, was seen regularly hanging around at the end of the school day, but little could be done by staff other than to accompany Julie and the others wherever possible. As the days passed and the situation remained unresolved, Julie, Helen and their splinter group missed more and more school.

The deadlock between Helen and Roza was at last broken by Deano's permanent exclusion from the school following another violent incident with local youths. One result of this exclusion was another lurch in the power equation between Helen and Roza, this time in Helen's favour. Helen took the opportunity of Roza's reduced circumstances to call an informal truce, operationalising the anti-school ethos that prevailed due to the loss of friends from both camps through exclusions: the common enemy was now the institution. Shortly after this episode, Roza left school to have Deano's baby.[5]

The ascendancy of Roza's highly aggressive 'masculinised' femininity had not lasted for long, burned out by its own intensity. Not everyone was directly involved in this dispute, but the whole system of gender relations was affected, and the disruption highlighted the cultural continuities which normally prevailed.

Summary

These events demonstrate the violent potential of the girls, normally restricted to behind-the-scenes organising of affairs, with more evidence that virtually all important social interactions contain elements of sexualised gender conflict. The cultural expressions of violence by the girls were differentiated from those of the boys by their perceived motivation for conflict. Lads battered lads over just about anything except girls, but girls fought almost exclusively over boys, because boys are culturally valued in ways that girls are not. The notion of the asexuality of lads' aggression has been shown to be a fallacy, however – its sexual core masked by a sheath of masculine pride, separate and aloof from public concerns about girls.

The importance of the school's formal organisaton *vis-à-vis* age banding again made itself felt in the realm of pupil culture. Although the girls did not make explicit the connection between the school's age groupings and their emotional space, Gina's reasoning on the effects of same-age partners spoiling the girls' fun at the disco matches earlier comments from other girls. The girls' usual popular choice of older boyfriends outside the tight compound of the school had acted as a pressure-release valve in the past, and had yielded the emotional space that many girls claimed was necessary for a sound relationship. With that space denied, the stress of managing the complex and volatile pairings (as well as the shortage of emotionally mature boy partners in their class) erupted into flaming rows and physical violence in a venue where all the official pressures of conduct and productive work inflamed matters further.

The school's enclosure of informal social systems intensified the anti-social effects of competition for desired socio-sexual status. Pupils like Roza were expert at subverting the formal classroom practices and directing their energy into making life hell for peers who crossed them. Social systems such as families, schools, army units and prisons vary in their degree of closure, but the victims of bullying within these systems share the misery of not being able to see beyond the emotional reach of their tormentors. Caroline was wholly occupied during her waking hours with avoiding or minimising the destruction of her self-esteem, and could only imagine escape through leaving the school for good.

It would be unfair to say that schools breed this behaviour but reasonable to suggest that they provide fertile conditions for its growth. Some pupils exploited the system to its limits without detection, so densely compacted were the layers of interpersonal interactions that were always buried beneath a surface of academic activity. It was of the utmost importance to the pupils to win and keep a desired socio-sexual reputation. The social ranking was evidently based upon how well one achieved culturally constructed ideals of gender type, and where one's position was located in the hierarchical structure. To be traduced by those in power meant one could eventually become a non-person, a non-entity who would be used as a cipher for any negative quality and excluded from the group. The toughness and social skills necessary to successfully avoid or survive this snare were exhibited by Gina and Jackie, but not by Caroline, who was further confounded by the unusual relationships she had stumbled into at Blunkett Rise.

Sexual bullying, driven by jealousy and the desire for social status, had been present in Blunkett Rise for as long as anyone could remember, but the climate of fear and violence that prevailed during that summer term was quite unprecedented. There were many factors at work here: the admission of violent expellees who all knew each other and had arrived at a critical time in the school calendar; the exceptionally tough personal qualities of some of the main actors and the ineffective reaction of the 'rightful' title-holders in Y11 and their friends in the locality. The factor most destabilising to the peer group's customary gender relations, however, was the unusually high level of compression of socio-sexual pairings within the year group.

6 Homophobias: intra-gender policing

Homosocial heterosexuals

Chapter 5 examined some of the range of feminine identities available to girls, and their inter-relationship in Blunkett Rise School. This chapter looks at some of the ways in which boys policed the boundaries of acceptable gender identities in school by aggressive enforcement of specific forms of heterosexuality, and the underlying motives of these practices. It also demonstrates some of the unintended effects on sexual bullying of the school's formal and informal roles in forming masculine gender identities.

The interviews and Q-sort results showed that the most prevalent and hurtful accusation levelled at boys by both sexes was to be called 'gay'. Like its counterpart 'slag', the accusation was virtually impossible to refute without a dramatic change in social behaviour and it could be deployed on a continuum of severity or seriousness, from throwaway jocularity to ultimate degradation of the victim, whether true or not.

Y7 Baker Street boys

ND: What else would they call you? What is the worst thing they could call you?
BRIAN: Gay.
ALAN: Gay.
BRIAN: Pervert, or poof.

Y10 St Joseph's boys

NASUR: I don't mind it if they say 'gay' just once, but if they keep saying it and start spreading it, that does your head in.
GRAHAM: Yeah, but that ain't true though, 'cos you have already gone out with a girl and that proves it.

All the boys interviewed had the same dual understanding of the term: first as someone who should be rejected as a pariah whether homosexual or not, then as a homosexual male. The commonest usage by far was that of low-status male, someone who did not merit the term 'boy' other than by biological default. The boys were worried about the situation of being seen as 'gay' or having to cope with a 'gay' friend. The older boys, particularly, were violently opposed to making any concessions towards tolerating that form of masculinity.

Carl and Adie were incredulous about the actual existence of real homosexuals in their world. They freely used the terms 'gay' or 'poof' in their derogatory sense, but had some difficulty in handling the concept of homosexual identity. To them a 'gay' was a boy who did not meet with even the lowest acceptable standards of 'laddishness', someone whom they felt they had the right (or perhaps a duty) to beat up and abuse for being an apology for the male sex. There was nothing personal in this, as Adie magnanimously pointed out, but if you were not a wimp/gay, and you didn't take advantage of those who were, then you might end up being treated like one yourself. The positive attributes of the hegemonic masculinity must be contrasted with those traits that were absent from it: caring, sensitivity, emotional accessibility, empathy, compliance and tolerance. But even boys with these traits were not considered *homosexual*; that would be ridiculous.

Y11 Blunkett Rise boys

CARL: Most of the lads in our year are OK except the wimps, we donna have anything to do with them.

ND: Why not?

CARL: We get on with them all really, except for the gays.

ND: What gays?

ADIE: 'cos they are wimps, most of them we've battered in lower school, when we were younger like, and they wouldn't want to be mates with us anyway. I've got nothing against them, like.

ND: You said gays, do you really think there are some gay kids in school?

ADIE: No, not proper homos, like. They are *gays*, you know?

ND: I'm not sure.

ADIE: I mean there's no proper gays here, we just call them that 'cos they act like it. They don't mess with us lot.

ND: You mean they don't fight you?

CARL: Jesus. No. They don't mess, play . . . well not play. They don't mess about for a laugh. They keep to themselves . . .

ADIE: . . . they are stiff, they are gay, man.

ND: Right, but do you think they are actually homosexuals?

ADIE: No, no way!

ND: But that is what gay means isn't it?

ADIE: Well . . . no, not here.

ND: You mean that there are no real homosexuals in our school?

ADIE: There aren't, are there?

CARL: No there aren't. (*To ND*) Do *you* think there are, like?

For researchers as well as others, defining people on the basis of their sexual orientation is best avoided, and terms like 'lesbian', 'gay' and 'homosexual' should perhaps be left to those who identify as such to define for themselves. Not surprisingly, no pupils identified themselves as gay in these interviews and so there was no opportunity to listen to their point of view: 'By the time I was 15, I led two lives: at school I was a 'straight guy' (I was occasionally bullied by those who saw me as sissie and were upset by it) who liked drama not football, while outside school I spent hours cruising cottages' (Humphries 1992: 151). The definitions imposed upon 'gay' pupils by peers were often incoherent, and were infected by the language of oppression that they reserved for the alien. Nearly all the boys had knowledge of the existence of homosexuality but could not relate this knowledge to their school experience or people whom they might one day meet. The boys' assumption was that to be gay meant belonging to another world far removed from their own everyday existence. To stimulate thought in this area the pupils were asked to consider some possibilities based on statistical probability.

The Fifth Column: the beasts inside

A large-scale questionnaire survey by Wellings et al. (1994) puts at 6 per cent for males and 3.4 per cent for females the incidence of self-reported homosexual behaviour. As with all such studies, there are widely varying percentages offered by researchers using different methodologies and definitions. From a practitioner's perspective, Harris reckons: 'One in every ten of the students whom we teach is lesbian or gay. There are likely to be 100 of them in a school of 1000. It is reasonable to presume that they do not fare well in our schools, which present in microcosm society's homophobia' (Harris 1990: 19).

In some of the interviews I referred to the claim that 10 per cent of the general population might be homosexual and suggested that this number might be reflected in the school population. This was by no means an attempt to impart 'factual information'. It was an initially impromptu remark that stimulated discussion so effectively that it was used in several successive groups. The possibility of male homosexuals in school provoked a variety of responses. Who were the gays? How many were there? Were they always gay or, if not, how did they become gay? I asked groups of boys, and of girls, what they would do if their best friend confided in them that they were gay. The older boys responded with frightening alacrity that they would attack them, even if they had been close friends up to that point.

Y11 Blunkett Rise boys

CARL: There is no way I'd be mates with a poof.

ND: What about you?

CARL: If he was a queer? I'd slap him, I would. I would not have him coming near me.

ADIE: It's right. I would do the same, not hit him, but tell our mates and we'd probably all get him. Let him know.

ND: Really, you would have your best mate beaten up because he is gay?

ADIE: But like you say, it's what we would do but we're not gay. We're not gay.

CARL: If there was gay kids in this school I would have moved schools.

ND: Where to?

CARL: To another school where there were none . . . like Stanley Grove.

This level of homophobia may be comical in its ignorance, but it presented a hideous threat to boys who could not, or would not, achieve the narrow stratum of successful masculinity set by these, the arbiters of masculinity in the school. The possibility of gay kids' presence in school was loathed far more strongly by the boys than by the girls, and perhaps it was only their incredulity that prevented a witch-hunt.

The Y10 boys were doubtful that gays would keep to themselves. Gays would either outrage 'normal' kids by their antics, or would not be able to control their lust for normal boys. Such wild shenanigans would not be tolerated by the huge mass of 'normal' kids and the gays would be purged. As this had obviously not happened, it followed that there must be no homosexual boys at their school.

Y10 Patten Avenue boys

ARKHTAR (*responding to the 10 per cent suggestion*): That would be forty lads, forty gays, that's like two classes!

ND: Well if there are that many in your school they must be doing a good job of not bothering anyone for no one to notice any of them.

For girls, the prospect was just as surprising; reactions were mixed but somewhat more humane and moderate than those of the boys. Here, confusion reigned regarding the number and identity of possible gays and the girls handled their own muddledness with humour.

Y10 Blunkett Rise girls

ANNETTE: There can't be that many, they definitely aren't in our school. They must go somewhere else.

ND: Would that mean because there are none in Blunkett Rise, there must be extra in another school?

BIX: Yeah!

ANNETTE: Of course! (*Laughter*)

SUE: Sure that makes sense!

ALL: (*Laughter*)

Like the girls, the younger boys were less reactive than the older boys.

Y7 Baker Street boys

ND: Do you think there are any gay people in the school?

ALAN: A few.

BRIAN: You can't really tell,

ALAN: You don't know though.

BRIAN: It's like, you don't really know.

ALAN: It's like they look gay, but you can't judge a book by its covers.

BRIAN: What?

ALAN: You can't judge a book by its covers.

ND: That's very wise words!

How to spot a gay in one easy lesson

These same Y7 boys had a surprising collective view of how they might detect gay activity. The following transcript shows an incipient 'contamination theory', how one might become gay by contact, even unwitting or unwilling, with a real homosexual. The boys described a scene where an innocent boy is seduced by a homosexual teacher abusing his authority in a clandestine way. The teacher chooses a hard-working and well-behaved boy, not one of the more masculine examples amongst which they included themselves, and asks him to remain behind after class.

Y7 Baker Street boys

BRIAN: Say he hasn't done nothing (*naughty*) in class, and the teacher says 'stay behind the class'. To us that would give it away . . .

COLIN: It'd be suspicious.

ND: Why?

BRIAN: 'Cos he ain't done nothing, so we'd spy.

COLIN: Say he's working away, right, and he's just doing his work, and the teacher says 'you can stay behind', right.

BRIAN: All the boys go and all the girls go, if it's just the teacher and him in the class when he hasn't done nothing, and they go 'hmm'.

COLIN: 'Hmm'. (*Raises one eyebrow knowingly*)

ND: So what do you think the real reason is? Are you saying that might mean they might be gay?

COLIN: To chat you up. Youm a perv.

ND: That the teacher might be a perv?

BRIAN: Yeah.

COLIN: That's just an example.

This is not a situation teachers would usually imagine could put their sexual reputation at risk.[1] Such interactions with pupils take place many times in schools each day, but for these pupils it would signal some impropriety on the part of the teacher, and a dangerous situation for the boy. The important feature of this encounter, the factor that turns it from innocence into perversion, is the otherwise unattributable motive of a male teacher wanting to talk to an individual boy outside a disciplinary confrontation. Being friendly and serious with a male pupil just didn't figure. To be friendly with a boy, a teacher would have to play to the group, exert his masculine power and 'have a laugh'. In a remarkable reversal of pupils' reading of teachers' actions, the same group later went on to laud a different male teacher for hitting the boys in their class.

ND: Who is your favourite teacher?

COLIN: Mr Kerry.

BRIAN: Yeah.

ND: Why is he so good?

BRIAN: He beats everyone up . . .

ALAN: . . . say you've been naughty, he just jokes and punches you like that . . . (*Gives Brian a slow-motion punch to the bicep*)

BRIAN: . . . but the naughty kids he'll do it quite hard won't he?

ALAN: He punches them on the nerve like that and gives them dead arms and everything.

ND: (*Laughter*) He sounds a great sort of a bloke! I'm glad you all like him so much!

ALAN: (*Laughter*) He only does it really to the really naughty kids though.

The physical horseplay by Mr Kerry with his 11-year-old boys was seen by them as a wholly positive trait. Motives for his behaviour were attributed to his quest for good pupil order in his class on his terms. These terms were not the inflexibility of some other staff, or the seriousness of teachers earnestly trying to make working-class boys into academic successes: he had a blokishness with the boys ('he just jokes'); he was a bigger one of them. Whether or not they were aware of it, he was using his gender to succeed with the paid work of teaching. Mr Kerry was playing out the role of the sexual bully, and the boys accepted this more easily than they would accept another adult male wanting a private chat with a well-behaved boy (Beynon 1989).

Underlying this seemingly contradictory attitude is the notion of *knowing the person*. Mr Kerry was OK because he was around every day. He was seen as normal within the school context, even though certain aspects of his teaching or pupil-management techniques were unique in the boys' experience. Mr Kerry appeared to have articulated his own idiosyncrasies with a fundamentally sound set of teacherly practices and created a successful and accepted whole. He was a man of parts, but he was greater than the sum of his parts. The hypothetical predatory gay teacher that the boys invented to work through their thoughts on homosexuality in school was not a man of parts. As an heuristic device he was conceived of only on one dimension: his 'gayness'. Despite an infinite number of possibilities, many of which might be prompted by the school setting, he was attributed no further motivation for wanting a young boy alone other than to gratify his perversion, because he was simply and unproblematically 'gay', and the quiet boy pupil was his prey.

As Davies (1984), Wolpe (1988) and others found, male teachers often exerted a physical power over their unruly boy pupils that acted as an intermediate stage before formal corporal punishment. This form of physical strength was predicated upon the sanctioned use of casual violence to control pupils, a situation which is no longer part of the experience of pupils but lingers on in the techniques of staff who were fluent in its use until the last decade.[2] The expression of a similar form of male physical power persisted in the guise of comic threats, or minor assaults such as ear-twisting or hair-tugging, which boys had to play along with if they wanted to be seen as 'big enough to have a laugh'.

The same group of boys also detailed the activities of one of their class-mates whom they thought might be liable to charges of being 'gay' by those who didn't know him.

ALAN: Yeah. And there is one boy, Fulton, in our class, he licks you and every-thing.
ND: You what?
ALAN: He licks you, no no, licks your face.
ND: He licks your face?
ALAN: He licks your ear and that, he does it for a laugh.
COLIN: I don't like it.
ND: I'm sure you don't.
BRIAN: But he only does it for a joke and a laugh.
ALAN: He comes up and bites you. He bites you on your shoulder.
ALAN, COLIN: *(Laughter)*
BRIAN: He's funny though, he only does it for a laugh.
COLIN: If he gets out of hand we'd tell . . . We'd call him names and that.

Fulton's behaviour would appear very bizarre to an outsider, but to these boys he did not pose a threat. In fact, Fulton was just one of many pupils present in the mainstream system who had a statement of special educational needs for behavioural difficulties, and his excessive behaviour was seen by staff in that context, although other pupils would not have been party to that information.

Fulton's situation fits the 'Leroy Syndrome' as described by Troyna and Hatcher (1992), amongst others. In his case the social prejudice was against his bizarre behaviour rather than his skin colour, but the effect was the same: although he was a 'nutter' he was a known quantity. The boys didn't necessarily enjoy or approve of his attentions, but tolerated them because they knew him as a person, and they liked the diversion of someone having a laugh at school. They also knew his limits: he would only go so far with them otherwise they would tell on him if he 'got out of hand'. Despite his actually licking their ears and faces, the boys didn't attribute any homosexual motive to the actions: it was just Fulton, and he was just doing it for a laugh. A strong parallel can be drawn between Fulton's face-licking and Mr Kerry's arm-punching. Both are superficially anti-social and would be proscribed by the school. But somehow the behaviour is accepted through the redemptive power of 'the laugh'. The laugh here is the playing out of outrageous behaviour in the safe knowledge that Fulton can be grassed on if he 'gets out of hand', and that Mr Kerry only really means to hurt the really naughty kids.

Fulton's acting-out provided more than entertainment. By watching the reactions of others around him, the boys could vicariously test out the tolerance levels of their social world. His name cropped up again in this interview, but he was also mentioned by the girls' group, and later by the head of lower school in less affectionate terms, for his overt sexual harassment of girls. The interviewed boys were aware of the serious potential of Fulton's misdemeanours and were very interested in the way they were handled by the school staff.

Fulton operated on the very margins of the official tolerance of difference. He was perceived as being 'mad' rather than 'bad', and this long-term intimate knowledge enabled his schoolmates to cope with him because they knew his behaviour was abnormal enough for them to seek staff protection. Other forms of offensive peer behaviour were less manageable for the boys. The sexual bullying which they endured from some older boys was more difficult to fend off as it was normal, pervasive, systemic and covert. Although Brian, Alan and Colin relished the details of Fulton's outrageous exploits and could measure up the school's responses to them, they were not inclined to emulate him. What Fulton gained in exciting notoriety, he lost in terms of membership of status group: he was a loner with an unstable identity and his capacity for sexual bullying could cut both ways.

Jake the square peg: intolerance of difference

In all the schools where this research was carried out and beyond, into other workplaces and in friendship groups, a common feature of schoolboy life was the myth of monsters. These individuals had some form of physical, sexual abnormality, a bodily aberration that fascinated peers. That no one around had actually ever seen these features mattered little; the important thing was to recount the hearsay over and again.

Y10 St Joseph's boys

ND: Well, in all the schools I have been in, there is always a rumour of someone with, say, a really small willie . . .

ALL: (*Uproarious laughter*) Ian Liversidge!!

ND: But surely it can't be that in every class of a dozen or so lads, one has a really small willie, or a huge willie, or one ball?

FAZAL: There has to be one to take the pee out of (*sic*), don't they?

The main reason Fulton's behaviour was tolerated by his peers was that he was very much a unique, isolated and known quantity (he had moved up from the same feeder primary school as many of the other boys and girls). In Blunkett Rise, another boy with special needs encountered a very different set of reactions from his peers. The gender policing of older boys proved much harder on newcomers than the Baker Street Y7 boys' methods of 'telling the teacher if he got out of hand'.

Jake arrived in Blunkett Rise School near the end of Y9. He had been attending a rural school in another LEA and had been permanently excluded after years of behavioural difficulties, culminating in a siege where he used a crossbow to hold off his social worker and an armed police unit. Jake had been raised by two uncles with little knowledge or interest in his development (for example, despite being an only child, he had never had a bed to himself). He was taken into care some weeks before his school exclusion and relocated to Blunkett Rise's catchment area. He was 13 years old at that time.

Jake's sexuality had been the subject of some professional concern for years. He was an early developer of unusual physical dimensions. On transfer, at 13 years of age, he was over 6′ tall and very powerfully built. Coarse blond chin-stubble and an 'agricultural' haircut presented him as a big, fully grown man. Indeed Jake had been living the life of such, with weekends in the village pub, paid labour on the local farms and afternoons in the bookmakers. Having been used to a lifestyle almost unfettered by officialdom or age-related expectations, Jake took badly to the state's intervention and, unsurprisingly, was reluctant to transfer to a new school where the comparatively metropolitan culture was a disorientating shock.

Jake found difficulty assimilating into the peer group but, realising the permanency of the arrangement, he made strenuous efforts to do so. He had been by far the biggest boy in his own village school group, but in his new class he was by no means the dominating figure he had once been. One strategy he deployed to make friends was by founding a colourful sexual reputation. Soon after arrival he was in trouble with girls in his teaching group, who reported him to the head of year for propositioning one girl by means of a note. In this note he claimed tender and undying love to Trish, and closed with 'I would really like to fuck you as well'. In this enterprise he was encouraged by some of the boys in his group. Several girls, including Trish herself, admitted 'setting him up'. Jake's clumsiness in matters of the heart had been too much to resist, and she had led him on to the point of finally being scared of his reaction. This knockback clearly upset Jake. He sought help and guidance from pastoral staff on the issue, but he did not drop the idea of establishing his identity in the group through his sexuality – he merely tried another strategy.

Having been thwarted in direct attempts to establish himself sexually with the girls, Jake then encountered trouble with a boys-only group. He was enjoying a chat on the playing field with the smokers' collective, who were talking about pornographic magazines, when he made an ill-advised statement about his own masturbatory practice. Several boys had admitted buying such magazines, but no one had confessed to actual masturbation with them. Jake, in the time-honoured manner of one-upmanship, told in detail how he regularly visited a much older male friend on Sunday afternoons. On these occasions they would put on a blue video and sit together on the settee wearing condoms. A masturbation race would then take place, with the winner ejaculating over the other.

Jake's schoolboy audience listened in prurient silence. Then, having gauged the mood of the others, they turned on him for being a disgusting pervert. Jake suffered humiliating name-calling and was publicly denounced for several days until he absconded during school hours. When he was returned by his social worker it was apparent that he had inflicted several nasty wounds to his own forearms and face. He then sought support from me, as his form tutor. I interviewed the boys involved in the persecution individually to gain multiple accounts. The opinion of the boys was that Jake had gone too far in two respects. First, he had exceeded the limits of appropriate self-disclosure as a newcomer. He should have added to the conversation piecemeal, tested the temperature of the group at each stage and only continued if it was safe to do so. Other boys might well make self-disclosures, but only incrementally. Irrespective of the subject being discussed, to boast recklessly of any exploit without a feeling for the probable audience response was just stupid and invited attack.

The second offence was the level of sexual depravity detailed in the disclosure. Jake obviously viewed the practice he had described as one of the highlights of his week. Whereas most of the lads would tacitly admit to solitary masturbation, they would do so with the qualifier that it was a poor, but necessary, substitute for sex with a girl. They would also be careful not to give the impression that they were stimulated by anything other than conventionally attractive naked young women. Jake had described to them a scenario of sexual activity which was far removed from their ideal, and had presented it as a valid sexual experience in its own right, and one which he felt should gain him kudos for his participation.

As form tutor to most of the boys involved, and as the teacher responsible for Jake's integration into the school, I had to repair the damage as best I could. I adapted the approach recommended by Pikas (1989a) and tried to deconstruct the group dynamic against Jake's sexual identity and increase levels of empathy on a series of individual bases. In individual sessions with each of the principal tormentors, I focused on the breach of the code of disclosure, minimising the details peculiar to Jake's case. The boys all agreed that these were mistakes caused by naivety, and that their 'sophisticated culture' (sic) at Blunkett Rise was alien to Jake. They graciously agreed to draw a line under that matter. The sexual detail of the disclosure was rather more awkward, both for them and myself. Most thought the practice was 'pervy', and that Jake deserved any punishment coming to him in the form of verbal abuse or ridicule. In the end, my poor best was to accept their distaste but remind them that Jake had done them no harm and that we all had secrets that we would not like publicised. They were also warned that if they continued to harass him they would be causing disruption to the smooth running of the school and would be punished accordingly. This fallback invocation of teacher authority and punitive power did not sit comfortably with my personal ethics, but time to deal with such matters was limited in a busy school day, and effective alternatives were in short supply. The official response was a blunt instrument, training and motivation were both low in the area of peer group sexual conflict, and I was constantly aware that I might be doing more harm than good.

Over the next few weeks I checked on the situation with each of the boys involved. Jake was relieved that the teasing had abated, and I was able to pass on my personal approval to the others that they had resisted, with decency, the temptation to make capital out of the incident. Some months later, however, the name-calling resurfaced, due to the most immature member of the group falling out with Jake and spreading the gossip amongst other boys and girls. Jake was now the owner of a nickname (not revealed here, for reasons of anonymity) referring directly to his confession, and was now openly labelled thus by pupils who had taken no part in the original episode.

Jake was horrified by this resurgence and blamed me for not quelling it effectively. While I was dealing with this second phase, one of the original group initiated a long and deep discussion with me to satisfy his own curiosity. Larry wanted to know why I had not allowed Jake to be abused by the group for his transgression. Why had I intervened in such an unusual way? Why was I so protective of Jake? Wasn't I disgusted by his revelations? If I really wanted to do something for him, why not get him to see a psychiatrist? Larry had not been involved in the second phase of bullying, but admitted he was tempted. He was not sure, however, what succumbing to that temptation would have made him.

Larry's puzzlement pointed out the rarity of staff involvement of this sort in peer group sexual policing. To him, the only way to resolve issues of this sort was to let the macho boys persecute and ridicule Jake. The consequence of not doing so might be the unthinkable: a signal to other boys that a sexuality such as Jake enjoyed was normal and acceptable. Larry's comment about taking Jake to see a psychiatrist was especially telling. Larry had absorbed the official discourse on the tolerance of difference: the medicalisation of the cultural deviant, the pathologisation of the victim.

In a strange parallel, retelling the story of Charles Jouy, a simple-minded nineteenth-century farm hand who was apprehended by villagers for having a young girl masturbate him, Foucault asks:

> What is the significant thing about this story? The pettiness of it all: the fact that this everyday occurrence in the life of village sexuality, these inconsequential bucolic pleasures could become, from a certain time, the object of not only collective intolerance but of a judicial action, a medical intervention, a careful clinical examination, and an entire theoretical elaboration.
>
> (Foucault 1990: 31)

In responding to Jake's problems by approaching the peer group's attitudes rather than focusing on Jake's deviancy, I was working against two forces. The invisible professional pressure to take an authoritarian line just to keep the peace, to preserve the order despite injustice, had been powerful. The pressure from the peer pack, with its drive to expel deviancy and punish on its own terms, had been quelled by my intervention – and the pupils accepted this up to a point. But my follow-up was challenged by the pupils because I did not invoke the official pathologisation of deviancy to continue the purge from the point where the vigilantes were forced to stop.

The symbiotic relationship between the official and unofficial responses to individual sexuality in schools meant there was no hiding place for Jake. The conflation of sexual deviancy and moral order built up too great a pressure for him to survive, and he was transferred to another school for a 'fresh start' yet again.

Growing up the 'hard' way

Sexual orientation notwithstanding, the abusive term 'gay' was much more commonly used to attack boys who did not conform to or did not achieve the group's standards of masculinity. Some Y10 boys had difficulties explaining the circumstances in which a boy might be labelled 'gay' through the 'wrong type' of heterosexual activity.

Y10 St Joseph's boys

CARLTON: If the boy was really popular with all the girls and he used to really hang around and talk to them all the time, he'd be called a poof or something.
ND: 'Cos he's going out with loads of girls?
BEN: It depends . . .
AARON: Not in my case it doesn't. Well, it depends if he's hanging around with loads of girls *all* the time, then I suppose he would be.
ND: What, because he was just friends with them?
AARON: Yeah.
CARLTON: Yeah.
ND: Right, I see. What you're saying then is that if a lad wasn't trying to go out, like boyfriend and girlfriend, but was friendly and nice to girls, and being able to talk to them about things they liked, have a laugh with them and sat with them in class, that he might be called a poof by the rest of the lads?
CARLTON: Yeah.
AARON: Yeah.

Singer points out the connection between schooling processes and the emotional hardening of boys: 'boys are taught not to pay attention to what we are feeling: competitive work situations demand that we don't feel what we are doing to others . . . or we might begin to sympathize with those we are supposed to beat' (Singer 1992: 55). If a boy attempted to make genuine friends with a girl or several girls, without obvious exploitation, he would come under suspicion from his peers. If he were to reduce his contact correspondingly with his mates, he would then become a reject. The male group would not allow its integrity to suffer a passenger or a free agent. To police their group's integrity the boys called into question the masculinity of the transgressor. It had to be his sexuality that was attacked, because that was the perceived dividing principle between boys and girls as well as the basis of the girls' attraction to boys. To preserve that attraction in a form that the boys' group could both understand and control, the deviant had his sexual core impugned. No real boy would actually want to engage emotionally with girls. He must have something wrong with him: he is too un-male, too feminine. He must be 'a gay'.

Surely, an observer might remark, any boy, no matter how heterosexual, could find pleasure in the company of girls without wanting to exploit them as outlets for sex? Seemingly not. Only if they came from another culture where such liaisons are an accepted part of boy–girl relationships, or if they had no interest in belonging to the dominant male group as it actually existed and formed their immediate socio-sexual experience. With the long historical investment in male dominance over females rewarding the boys' continuation of these social conditions, the number of boys who actually challenged the code of schoolboy masculinity was very low. Added to the loss of privilege that would ensue was the odium of the betrayed friends. There was just no incentive to change (Mahony 1985). Adie and Carl gave their opinion.

Y11 Blunkett Rise boys

ADIE: You can't be the same with a girl when you are on your own as when you are with your mates. You know, if she was asking you for something you would creep to them wouldn't you? You would say 'yes love that's OK'. But if she tried it on in front of your mates you wouldn't have any, you'd say 'get up the road'.

CARL: Yes, you couldn't be shown up. If she started on you, and your mates were there, you'd put her straight. 'Get up the road.'

ND: Why is it different when your mates are there?

ADIE: You don't want them to see you creeping. They'd take the piss and say you were under the thumb.

ND: Why would that matter?

CARL: Well if your mates thought you were a crawler they wouldn't want you as a mate. They wouldn't bother with you so you wouldn't have any mates left.

ND: So mates are that important, are they?

CARL: Of course . . . your mates are always there aren't they? Your girlfriend might finish with you and then you'd have no one.

ND: So, are you saying that the reason you sometimes, or lads you know, put girls or girlfriends down in company is because you are impressing the other lads?

CARL: Well, you've had your mates for years, and you don't know how long you'll have your girlfriend. Mates are much more important than a wench.

In one sense this exchange displays the monolithic nature of male solidarity, the total denial of genuine emotional bonding of a male with a female partner. Carl and Adie's beliefs were manifestly of the same kidney as those that have been the source of so much feminist struggle amongst working-class women down the generations. Carl's voice resonated with echoes of pub culture or the factory floor: 'Well if your mates thought you were a crawler they wouldn't want you as a mate. (. . .) Mates are much more important than a wench.'

In another sense, there may be detected a glimpse of what Mac An Ghaill (1994) sees as the fragility of working-class hegemonic masculinity in schools. Carl and Adie were at a critical time in their lives. They had the desires and aspirations of their older male models, they were in their last throes of school-boyhood and within a matter of months fully expected to complete a journey towards a role of husband and breadwinner where they would remain for the rest of their lives. This was their 'best-case scenario', and even this would have to be fought for.

The only support the boys expected to sustain them was that of their mates, the same mates they grew up with, who constantly confirmed their individual identities as referenced by the male friendship group. The *group* craved status through its popularity ranking amongst other groups of boys. If the group was successful it would be over-subscribed, and an informal waiting list would form. If seen to have members quitting it for the attractions of a girl, then it would lose its status. Defectors from the group were punished by social opprobrium focusing on their lack of manliness in allowing a partner to lure them away. This strategy ensured not only that the defector was slighted, but that his girlfriend's success in 'catching a real man' was also devalued, for if a lad got a reputation for being not man enough to keep his girl in order, the girl also lost face amongst her friends. The lose/lose nature of the girl's predicament in this case is depressingly circular.

A pressure existed, either internally or externally, for the boys to engage emotionally with their partners, but the only proper place for this was in the home, certainly not in public. The boys knew that such pressure needed careful negotiation with friends and partners or else one or both might be lost. In Carl and Adie's case the priority was to maintain the old relationships with mates.

ND: It sounds like you expect to go courting just for a short time until you are married then back out with your mates again like in school, is that right?

CARL: Ahh.

ADIE: Ahh. That's it, ahh.

CARL: Me and him will still be doing all this when we're wed, won't we?

ADIE: Ahh. Course.

ND: Would you tell each other all your problems then, really confide in one another?

CARL: What do you mean?

ADIE: Secrets and that, that's it. Aaah.

ND: Yeah, more or less, let the other one know what you really worried about?

ADIE: Well I suppose we have got secrets, but I wouldn't tell him what I was worried about. Would you?

CARL: I'm not worried about nothing.

ND: But if you were?

CARL: But I donna worry about anything.

ADIE: Aaah. He donna, that's true.

This almost psychopathic reluctance to own any feelings that might be shared even by one's closest friend widens the picture regarding Carl's attitude towards girls. His objection to getting emotionally close was not limited to sexual matters with girls, but to any crack in the defence of his identity as a true man. The intimate bullying pressure on mates to stay as mates was immense, but rarely shown. The dominance of this form of distorted masculine expression was matched by the bluntly sexist destiny of domestic bondage for their girl partners.

School traditions of masculine power

Unlike the other boys interviewed in this study, Carl and Adie were not chosen for their nondescript middle-ground status in the school, but were simply a convenient entry-point for the research in its early stages. Carl and Adie did have a reputation amongst both staff and pupils for being peer group leaders. They held the highest office amongst the peer group of being hard but quiet. They achieved high status by occasional assertion of their toughness in beating people up, but were normally no problem unless challenged by upstarts.

One set of such upstarts was the procession of new teachers throughout their school career. The ritual of new staff having to win their authority over a long period of time was well established, and Carl and Adie would have been names burned into the memories of many students, probationers and their supervisors. The strategies of pupils contesting teacher authority are well documented elsewhere and survival guides for new teachers are plentiful,[3] but less work is available on the motivation behind the energy expended by pupils in their quest to mentally break down new staff.

Generally speaking, Carl and Adie were not disruptive in class (many others were more overt), but when faced with new figures of authority they were certainly the most intractable. Carl's rationale for this was that (male) teachers 'tried it on' with him, they 'acted hard' to get him to do what they wanted but they had no right. He didn't owe them anything, but they had expectations of his subordination. Most of them bore a strong resemblance in one or more respect to the 'gays' in school: they wore similarly 'dweeby' clothes, took schoolwork too seriously and were obviously desirous of their supervisors' approval, and this in turn emphasised Carl's position at the bottom of the official heap. Often the young male teachers/students were the same age as his older mates or brothers, and the contrasts in their cultural expressions of masculinity were very obvious. Carl particularly criticised the appearance of Mr Armstrong.

CARL: Have you seen him? He wears that suit like a manager at Comet. If he came round our way he'd get sent to bed. I know he's only a student but they want to tell him, like. He's too cocky.

Mr Armstrong represented too closely those subordinate masculine forms that the boys customarily dealt with violently whenever they encountered them in other pupils. These criticisms appear to be located in trivial dislikes, but can be better understood in the context of which teachers these boys do and do not accept. As with mates, the greatest quality in a teacher is longevity.

CARL: He's been here for ages, he taught my Dad when he came here, he did! He's all right is Mr Trent.

Mr Trent would possibly not have recognised this approval in his day-to-day interactions with Carl and Adie, but would certainly have noticed it if it was ever withdrawn.

Along with longevity came familiarity and a mutual knowledge of the other as a part of the same whole. This was often expressed in accounts of past experiences that marked milestones in the school life of the pupils.

ADIE: On that (*school*) camp Mr Walter and Mrs Hindforth went down the pub with us lot and we knew he fancied her so we kept walking with them, just to annoy him, like. He kept saying things like 'you go on and see how far it is' and I said 'but Sir, you said we shouldn't get lost'. It was only a main road like, but he couldn't say anything.

Special credit was given to any protective role assumed by the teacher in defence of his own charges against irate members of the public on school outings, or in this case against a pupil from another school.

CARL: Mr Johnson was reffing that match, do you remember, and Collier got his head split by that High Bank fifth year. So Johnson gets this kid and he says 'I won't just *show* you this red card, I'll shove it where the sun don't shine.'

The highly gendered interactions between male staff and others appealed to many of the boys witnessing them. Physically powerful, authoritative and noble, the masculinity dominant in these images was digested by the pupil culture and its forms replayed in general social relations. Authority was most palatable when something was owed to the teacher, some unspoken debt, or an accumulation of shared experiences which retrospectively helped to form the biography of the pupil. By this process subtle male bonding transpired, but the essential nature of this positive relationship, this safe shared environment, was its integrity and its separateness from females and outsiders. New teachers, new pupils and new ideas were not welcome, and resistance provided a test of the home culture's strength. Women teachers were denied access to this mode of pupil management and, should Mr Kerry have started work at Blunkett Rise, his strategies of playful but painful punching of Baker Street Y7 pupils could not have been transplanted to Blunkett Rise's Y11 without the likelihood of a retaliatory brawl.

Gays and girls

The friendship bonds between the boys were powerful, but not indissoluble. Discussion revealed that leaving the locality usually meant losing touch. A major revelation or character change might put paid to a friendship. Some breaches even of the strongest codes – 'grassing', doing well economically or academically were disliked but seemed not to strain friendships too much. But, apart from 'being under the thumb of the wench', it was coming out as gay that provoked by far the strongest response. That would definitely necessitate a severing of the friendship bond. The thought of males having a homosexual relationship was considered much more perverse and revolting than of girls doing the same thing.

Y10 Patten Avenue boys

ND: Is that something that would bother you, if a girl was a lesbian?
TODD: Well! It wouldn't bother me like. Only if I fancied them!
IAN: I'd ask if I could watch!
ALL: *(Laughter)*
ND: It's funny you say that because that isn't what you said about gay lads.
IAN: Well I wouldn't really, it was just a joke.
ND: Would you have made the same sort of joke about watching two blokes?
IAN: Get lost! No way!
JOHN: If you did you'd get called a perv.
IAN: *(Laughter)* I wouldn't. It was only a joke about the girl anyway.

The older boys appeared to accept friendship with lesbians more easily than friendship with gay boys. Perhaps it seemed less threatening because it was unlikely to 'contaminate' their reputation, and it also fitted well with the notions of weakness and passivity that they attributed to femininity. With the commodification of the female body so prevalent in the wider culture, it is unsurprising that the boys saw more erotic promise in lesbian activity than they did in male homosexuality.

The girls themselves found less revulsion in either sexuality than the boys did, but some could not cope with the group's liberal attitudes.

Y10 Blunkett Rise girls (group of seven)

PAT: It wouldn't bother me because she had already been my friend, so you would know she wouldn't be interested in you.
ND: OK.
KIM: It would sort of bother me, you know, you wouldn't want them to come and sit next to you or anything, she could be leaning over you and you would think . . .
PAT: Yeah, that would bother you.
KIM: *(Unclear)*
ND: What Kim, you would give them a kicking?
KIM: Not kicking, maybe hit them and that.
MARY: Sir, I have two friends who are gay. They only became gay because one was married to this man who used to treat her really badly. He hurt her in some way, so she became gay.
ND: If a boy told you that he was gay, would you feel the same about him as you would a gay girl?

TRACY: You would feel safer.

PAT: Yeah. You would feel closer to them. If they had told you the secret, you would trust them more.

ZARA: You would be able to say 'ooh, *he* is good looking, and *he* is good looking'.

ALL: (*Laughter*)

Despite Kim's disgust, this group of seven girls presented a much more liberal attitude to homosexuality, male or female, and tallied with the other girl-group interviews. Some expressed worry at their reputation being tarnished through contact with known gay girls,[4] but not to anything like the extent of the boys interviewed. They were more unsure of the interpersonal handling of the relationship if the girl made a pass at them, but even here they were more level-headed than most of the boys. A positive feature of a hetero–gay relationship for some of the girls was the great measure of confidence it permitted for the sharing of secrets and emotions. This contrasts powerfully with Carl and Adie's fears of closeness followed by betrayal and rejection.

One large group of Y10 Blunkett Rise girls discussed in depth with me several aspects of homosexuality. Two girls claimed to know older women who were in lesbian relationships that were friendly and otherwise unremarkable, and another offered an anecdote about an encounter with an aggressive lesbian in the shop where she worked. Most of the girls contributed to a debate on social attitudes towards homosexuality and 'coming out' where their total knowledge was formulated around a number of soap-opera characters faced with that dilemma. Being called a lesbian as a form of sexual bullying was no longer a threat to these girls, although they all agreed that it had been so in lower school.

Girls in the younger groups were still in a phase where they were commonly called lesbians by the boys in their class, but their accounts are congruent with the general picture of greater tolerance of homosexuality wherever it was found, than that shown by the boys.

Y7 Baker Street girls (working on a Q-sort)

ANGIE: (*Puts 'Calling A Girl Lesbian' at top*)

RT: Why do you think they call girls lesbians?

ANGIE: 'Cos I hang about with Susan, like, 'cos we talk about different things, and if you don't let the boys hear, like if they can't hear they think that we're lesbians. Like the other day I was upset and Susan put her arm round me just to comfort me, like, and they thought she was hugging me like.

RT: The boys did?

ANGIE: Yeah.

RT: What did they do?

ANGIE: They tell everyone that I'm a lesbian.

CATHERINE: I just ignore them.

Angie's preference for her girl friend's company offended some of the boys in her

class, and they attempted to divide the relationship. There was no serious impli-
cation that she and her friend were lesbians, but this didn't figure in the boys'
reasoning, it was simply an insult that could be fired off like a heat-seeking mis-
sile, sure to hit its target because it applied to any two girls closer to each other
than to the boys.

The girls displayed a strong resistance to this type of insult, even in the event
of the accusation being true. In these younger groups the boys were not in any
direct danger of their friendships disintegrating due to the lure of other Y7 girls.
In this context the boys were operating in a very different mode to the older boys
above. Where the older boys were strenuously trying to prevent boys defecting
from their group, these younger boys were actively smashing the girls' friendship
groups with defamatory accusations of homosexuality.

RT: Do you think that boys are jealous of the close relationships of the girls?
BABS: I think so, because boys don't . . . girls can talk to each other, boys just keep
      things in to themselves, they don't tell no one nothing.
ANGIE: And when girls are upset, the others will try and comfort them, but if a
      boy gets picked on they laugh at them.
RT: If you found out later on that one of your friends *was* a lesbian how would
      that be?
CATHERINE: Well I'd think she was still my friend whatever she is 'cos she hasn't
      changed . . .
ANGIE: You never knew she was a lesbian in the first place, so . . . (*indistinct*).
RT: So it wouldn't necessarily change your friendship?
CATHERINE: They would have to be quite close friends for them to tell you in the
      first place, its hardly the sort of thing you'd tell everyone.

It was just this strength and quality of relationship between girls, even in the lower
school, that was absent amongst the boys and came under continuous attack from
them. Signs of incipient emotional sharing between boys were always shut down
quickly, degraded to the lower orders of the gender and pushed out beyond the
margin. The affective need for an outlet of love between boys only surfaced in the
culturally acceptable form of the codes of 'not grassing on your mates' and 'lads
have to stick together'. The tight support available through friendship groups
soon became emotional straitjackets, confining boys to a thin and impoverished
range of expression for their feelings.

Summary

The discourse of homosexuality, as a mode of policing gender identities, was
deployed most fervently by the older boys but reverbated throughout the whole
pupil social system. The schools' informal discipline codes were also implicated in
those practices. Actual homosexual activity was found incomprehensible by the
majority, and some of the boys were so appalled at its existence they baulked at
defaming even 'gays' with that level of alien depravity. Even the instance of Jake's

masturbatory practices was seen as perverse but not gay, despite the involvement of an older male in the game. However, the case of Fulton exemplified the breadth of possible peer perspectives and responses on unusual sexualised behaviour, with bizarre interpersonal acts being tolerated due to specific local circumstances.

The forms of sexual bullying practised against subordinate masculinities – and potentially femininities – by their own sex again comprised both verbal and physical abuse. There was an important difference in the degree of homophobia expressed by age and sex groups, with the older boys far and away the most violently opposed to (male) homosexuality. Such findings suggest that boys' unpreparedness for heterosexual, or indeed any human, relationships, combined with their discharge from the familiar compact social world of their school, made them more callous in their general social attitudes.

It seems the emotional hardening of boys occurred as the male friendship group was threatened simultaneously by the boys' growing attractiveness to girls and the diaspora entailed in school-leaving. Boys met the fear of possible entrapment and isolation with a girlfriend/wife by objectifying women and by hardline policing their groups' hyper-masculinities. The sexual bullying and oppression of young women and weaker males was an attempt to destroy the qualities on offer in alternative socio-sexual arrangements and retain the freedom and power position which the tougher boys had fought for and enjoyed throughout their schooldays.

Many boys, especially the younger ones, fused the sexuality connoted by 'gay' with niceness to girls: even the heterosexual act of kissing girls, rather than relieving their more carnal urges upon them, was considered 'gay'.[5] The younger boys and all the girls also tended to feel it was not desirable or advisable to claim or confess a homosexual orientation, but without the heat evidenced by the older boys. The girls were quite sanguine about their hypothetical friendship with gay boys, and saw possibly the best type of inter-sex platonic friendship in this combination. There was some evidence of younger boys attacking friendships between girls by using the lesbian tag, but older boys were more intrigued by variations of female sexuality than disgusted by them.

The pervasiveness of certain forms of masculinity as a means of controlling boys in school created unintended and perhaps unnoticed consequences. This chapter has shown how some male teachers still used heavy physical contact with some types of unruly boy in an informal, jokey way to control their classroom behaviour. Other practices included the articulation of masculine interests of domination, partisan support for the group, and heterosexuality in an inter-generational, cross-class discourse of male solidarity. Those teachers' survival techniques were never acknowledged as a form of sexual bullying, but essentially that is what they were. Male teachers could reinforce (unwittingly?) the persecution of subdominant masculinities by demonstrating male-to-male dominance in the classroom through an 'I can take it, not everyone can' mentality within the macho boys' group. The naughty boys were dealt with roughly, but in fun. Although this form of control was accepted as such by both its 'victims' and the 'ordinary' boys in the audience, it actually boosted the status of the macho boys for allowing the teacher to use this method without official complaint, as well as reinforcing age seniority. This made it all the more difficult for staff to criticise the bullying of 'gay' boys when the bullies could respond with 'we were only playing, Sir, they just can't take a joke'.

In school, masculinities were seen in terms of their hierarchies within the staff structure too, and young male teachers were given a lot of stick for expectations of instant kudos. If the boys detected similarities between the masculinities of the young male students or teachers and those of the 'gay' lads in the school, resistance to their authority could be intense. The 'old-guard' males were often successful with the boys as they posed little threat to their machismo. They formed part of the schools' function of combining individual biography with collective mythology in a condensed form. Many staff had taught members of the boys' families consecutively for three decades. In some of these cases the older male teachers had been given a status akin to that of tribal elder, their idiosyncrasies and eccentricities reported by the boys with reverence: 'He doesn't half do you for nothing, but he's a dead good teacher.'

Many of the most extreme cases of obdurate masculinity were represented by young men who had grown up in the absence of a father in the home.[6] For some, the male teachers represented important, though not always comfortable, gender role models, with many more hours spent in contact with them than with any other men. This situation was not appreciated or acknowledged by the schools, and if it had been, it might have threatened to undermine many of the working strategies of school discipline.[7] The arm's-length policy of male contact, apart from in dominating horseplay, continued to recycle the macho ethic, and an attempt to relate on a more emotional level would certainly have been read as unnatural, possibly perverse.

It would appear, then, that as boys and girls proceeded through their secondary-school careers, their sexualities developing apace, a virulent homophobia was created within the older boys' pupil culture, formed from a confluence of wider cultural beliefs and personal practice in the struggle for sexual reputation and status. The factors influencing this development were complex and unclear, but they included a dynamic between family and community experience, modes of official masculine control in school, and physical pubertal change.

Individual practitioners attempting to work with unruly boys seemed unaware of these processes, preoccupied as they were by the formal workload as well as the tremendous pressures of pupil management. With the overview of whole-school discipline, the senior staff did not recognise the importance of sexuality as a motor for disruptive behaviour, perhaps due to other distractions, or perhaps as a defence against the radical changes demanded by them.

The schools' 'hands-off' policies (in both senses) relating to pupils' sexuality were necessary due to external pressures as well as to staff apprehension and lack of resources. With the compression of so many young people undergoing puberty within the architecture of an institution that excommunicates the sexual, inside a parental society that exalts it, psychic agitation can only be expected to discharge through antagonistic cultural practice.

7 Summary of findings: the importance of being gendered

The continuum of sexual bullying

In its deconstruction of bullying, this study has assembled new ethnographic data informed by cultural- and gender-studies perspectives. I have attempted to re-draw a range of anti-social pupil behaviour as a manifestation of gender conflict in the pursuit of a desired sexual identity. The resulting focus on sexual identity formation within the formal organisation of the secondary school has highlighted the important but unintended consequences of schooling, as distinct from the official aims of education.

Once schooling has been stripped of its many official and traditional connotations, one can see it as the processing (both in the sense of passing through and of modifying) of boys and girls through their early adolescence by a system of formal practices which ignores or displaces their sexualities. This skinning of the educational discourse of schools enables a concentration on the relationships between the individual, the micro-cultural value systems of pupils and the organisational architecture they inhabit.

Many distinctive socio-cultural practices were found at the sites of sexualised gender conflict in the schools. The practices took a number of forms which included: sexualised name-calling and verbal abuse; rubbishing sexual performance; ridiculing physical appearance; criticising sexual behaviour; spreading rumours; aggressive propositioning; threatening behaviour; unwanted touching and physical assault. Two features of these practices raised them from a simple taxonomy of anti-social behaviours. First, they could be seen to be not discrete, but linked and melded as a continuum of socio-cultural practices ranging from non-focused verbal banter to violent assault. Second, they were clearly not uni-directional from bullying boys to victimised girls: distinctively differentiated forms of masculinities and femininities were evident in a variety of active and passive roles and relationships. Rather than publish a list of deviant behaviours definable as sexual bullying, I have presented patterns of practices that, within specific socio-cultural situations, were considered by the actors to be examples of interpersonal sexualised, gendered conflict. I have also presented a range of situations, conditions and incidents that, from the special standpoint of the researcher, I believe constitute sexual bullying in schools.

By reading back from the most extreme forms of sexual bullying – the violent physical assaults reported in the interviews and observed in schools – I have been able to expose the noxious aspects of the less dramatic practices that mark the boundaries of gendered power domains. At the outset of my project I considered some observations of sexualised verbal abuse, and asked 'what was going on here'? The answer is not simple, but the purpose behind the seemingly inconsequential sexualised remarks and references, during what would otherwise be civilised exchanges, is the marking out of gendered role limits: reminders that relationships are ultimately structured by power and that power is gendered.

By incessantly expressing the expectation that boys should be served and provided for by girls, the boys knock back any advances by the girls to assert their personhood as independent of masculine supervision. So, when a girl is called a 'bitch' for not giving up her spare pencil to a demanding boy, invisible links are made between female autonomy and sexual perversity. This connection is not a theoretical conceit but a social and physical reality: the ratchet of male response clicks up from trivial name-calling to denigration of sexual worth due to non-compliance, and thence, ultimately, to a state of social non-being.

The extreme practice of rape is rare amongst school-age children and does not feature in any of the data presented here.[1] But it is not so rare that it does not feature as a possibility for those girls who do not conform at some point to male demands. Rape may be (comparatively) rare, but physical and sexual assault are not, and the lower range of conflictual sexualised gender practices keeps that threat alive on a daily basis.

Boys v. girls (re-match)

A clear assertion by the research into bullying has it that boys bully physically and girls bully emotionally. Little explanation is offered regarding why it should be so, but it is claimed that boys use their physical power to hurt and dominate both sexes, whilst girls use rumour and withdrawal of friendship for the same ends – but almost exclusively within their own sex. I feel there is strong evidence to dispute this view. Boys and girls are very obviously not homogeneous groupings, and hard girls emerge as dominating even some hard boys. Fear of losing face by coming second in a straight fight with a girl causes many boys to make all sorts of avoiding manoeuvres, including enforcement of an ersatz chivalric code in which one is too noble to retaliate against girls physically, and accommodation of the excesses of some girls despite obvious discomfort on the part of the boys.

The senior boys were very aware of the real social power of the hard girls in their school. These girls were connected throughout the school years by sisters, brothers and cousins as well as beyond school with older boyfriends and in-laws. This culture was very working-class in its expression of kinship but held enough sway over the more professional-class pupils to influence gender relations amongst pupils right across the school.

From the outset it was girls who took the lead in organising romantic affairs. Cliques quickly formed amongst the girls where schoolwork was rushed off in order to concentrate upon the real business of sorting out who should go out with whom. Where the physical force of boys was greater than the physical force of girls, the hidden feminine industry of romance-management operated coercion by reducing the number of girlfriends available to any particular boy by physically threatening or punishing girls who acted outside the cliques' influence.

Another significant finding was the multi-directional flow of sexual bullying: to boys from boys and girls and to girls from girls and boys, with examples of collusion between sexes in some cases. These data contest assumptions found in some other research that all boys are beneficiaries of an exploitative and abusive gender system in schools. Instead they suggest that, whilst there is a set of general advantages to be gained from being a boy, only a few boys dominate proceedings with any degree of comfort and that many girls win their own space in which to develop socio-cultural power.

Frequently, the interviewees noted boys' change of attitude towards girls when they were joined by other males. Although all the interviewees (male and female) recognised it, they had not talked it through before and could not rationalise it other than as 'lads impressing their mates'. Indeed, that is all that seems to lie behind this behaviour: a form of masculine group consolidation, a public pledge of a lowest-common-denominator attitude towards the girls. The reduction of individuality and empathy was interpreted as strengthening the known and avoiding emotional risk. The lads' competitive behaviour in front of girls was to display their trustworthiness to their friends: *they* wouldn't be the first to break rank and give up the comfort of simple-minded mate-hood.

The inadequate aspects of masculinity, and the puissance of much femininity, are illustrated by this desperation of boys to control and disrupt inter-female relationships whilst struggling with their own competitive inter-male friendships. Girls' friendship groups were constantly under attack for their prospective autonomy from boys, and boys who did not attain the standard set by the dominant group (and, by definition, most could not) were reviled and denigrated to mark them as alien to their superordinates.

The assumption in previous studies, that boys enjoy a secure and comfortable dominance over girls, is further undermined by the deployment of language as a sexualised, gendered weapon. In a great deal of earlier research on sexual harassment in schools, much was made of the power of female-hating words that had no equivalent forms for males. The power of these hate-words is attested to in this study, but boys too revealed themselves vulnerable to many slanders and slurs on their sexuality. The term 'gay' was the most used, and was effective in summing up a sense of non-boyness and therefore of non-entity-ness. This was a fearsome hardship for boys to bear, as the term was impossible to refute without recourse to violence and the tormentors did not use it where violence was an option for their victim.

The 'masculinisation' of girls' sexual style could be detected in the language used to ascribe active and passive sexual roles. Avant-garde comedians and comediennes[2] and media 'personalities' now commonly refer to 'girls shagging blokes', and some of the girls (and boys) used this expression in the schools studied. The power of language as a tool in shaping sexualised gender identities is immeasurable. Boys and girls verbally attacked both boys and girls by persistently jabbing away in the hope of finding a weak spot. The notion that boys bully mainly by physical force appeared to be nonsense.

Another important finding was the change in practices at different age bands within the school. Some bullying research (Smith and Sharp (eds) 1994) recognises the change of frequency of some modes of bullying with age, but does not link these changes with development of sexual or gender identity. I found, however, that boys and girls exchanged vague gendered unpleasantries in the lower years, with boys assuming supremacy over same-age girls and fearing only older boys. As they underwent pubertal change the boys became more interested in the girls in their class and insults became more sexualised and funnelled through two modes of expression: misogyny and homophobia. This was mirrored by the majority of girls becoming less interested in friendships with same-age boys. Some of the harder girls sexually bullied some boys by attacking their lack of masculine maturity (drawing on older boys as comparators); they also punished other girls whom they deemed guilty of some feminine malfeasance.

Love is all around

I had originally imagined that, in the investigation of sexual bullying, I would be examining overt acts between boys and girls. Much of what practitioners see as the hard face of sexual bullying is attributed to testosterone-induced lust: the boys feel sexy so they make a play for the girls in a crude and direct way. Closer observation and analysis found sexual bullying in schools to be deeper and more pervasive than superficial slagging off and touching up. It soon became evident that a great deal of what is called 'ordinary bullying' (in other words boys hitting boys, or girls shunning other girls) was sexually structured. At risk of succumbing to 'red-beetle syndrome',[3] it seems adolescent sexuality erupts in so many forms that it must underscore even seemingly non-sexual behaviours in schools.

Both boys and girls constructed visible group identities based upon a gendered set of friendships and these affected many other aspects of school life: potential inter-sex friendships; attitudes to academic work and school discipline; sporting associations; fashion styles and subcultural affiliations. For much of the time these friendship groups were at peace with themselves and one another, but the dynamic nature of personal development during adolescence generated conflict through change and instability, and disruptions were commonplace.

These disruptions formed a range in type and severity. At one extreme were the disputes over commonplace trivia that are pandemic in secondary schools and have nothing directly to do with pupil sexuality but are overtly sex-referenced:

> Lend me your ruler.
> No.
> You tight bitch, fucking slag.

Attacks of this kind were so widespread that their origin was obscured and their impact diluted, sometimes completely ignored. When the pupils were asked to analyse their choice of insults and look closely at the sexual content of what they were saying, they found it hard to rationalise it. The sexual content of verbal abuse went similarly unrecognised by teachers. When it came to their attention, they usually perceived it simply as obscene and irrational abusiveness that could be dealt with through the usual disciplinary channels without the need to enter into the unfathomable depths of adolescent sexuality.

At the other extreme were conflicts that were not overtly sex-referenced but were forged in sexual rivalry. One example of a sexual undercurrent beneath ostensibly non-sexual intercourse was offered by the 14-year-old boys who felt comfortable talking to the girls in their class and were happy to associate with the 17-year-old lads in their community out of school. But when they encountered those youths accompanying the girls in the town centre the wise thing to do was to nod deferentially and walk by. Any attempt at friendliness or parity would be seen as impudent and result in a physical response: they would be cramping the older boys' style by presumptuous association. The girls were aware of their effect on male group dynamics, and sometimes deliberately compromised the subordinate boys for amusement. Such cultural practices disguised their sexual content even from the actors/actresses themselves: 'everyone knows it's happening, but no one ever talks about it'.

The data supported earlier findings regarding female violence (Davies 1984). Where the reason given for girls fighting other girls was usually sexual jealousy, the reasons given for boys fighting their own sex were fudged and varied. From the researcher's vantage point, however, many of the fights were discerned as combats over masculine identity and status; they might manifest themselves as disputes over anything from football teams to TV programmes, but the bottom line was a perceived challenge to some aspect of masculine authority or status.

Another, somewhat astonishing, sexualised reading of non-sexual intercourse was made by the 11-year-old boys regarding the ulterior motivation of a male teacher's non-disciplinary interest in a boy pupil. Despite its hypothetical nature, the threat of discomfort and tarnish of reputation inflicted on a boy as a result of friendly adult male contact, suggests many implications for other interactions not detected by this study. When pre-pubescent boys proscribe such liaisons within an academic institution as being beyond comfortable limits of sexual decency then the entire warp and weft of schooling itself must be seen as sexualised.

Do you know who I am?

Individually, sexual bullying practices are manifestations of sexual power struggles. Collectively they signify the production and maintenance of a value system based on gendered identity, continually rank-ordering individuals according to values measured by sexual reputation. These cultural value systems were so powerful that isolation and exclusion were feared, and there was a rush for inclusion within a high-status friendship group. There needed to be only one or two high-profile 'first movers' to start this rush before everyone was caught up in the stampede.

From an early age, children in contact with groups of others understand the socio-material benefits of being popular with one's peers. This peer popularity is heavily gendered, with separate leagues for boys and girls. If one becomes a star, one is offered more material and experiential choices of fun, greater personal security from harassment or hurt, and the warmth of increased self-esteem. The logic of popularity is that not everyone can be a star, not everyone can be the centre of positive attention, and so a popularity contest ensues amongst peers. Such competition is not necessarily unhealthy unless the resources being contested are the sole carriers of essential emotional well-being to the runners-up. As individuals enter adolescence and their bodies begin pubertal change, however, the sense of both self and of other is destabilised, creating new threats as well as new opportunities. The already gendered self must now become hetero-sexualised too, creating a new erotic dimension to social relations.

The boys and girls became aware of the socio-cultural values bestowed upon sexual reputation in the secondary school and its enhancement of life-advantages through exalted status. This status was formed in hierarchical relation to lower orders of the same gender and in opposition to the other gender. The wider power relations between the hierarchies of masculinities and femininities were asymmetrical, with some masculinities prevailing. Competition to attain or maintain high status within the hierarchies created inter- and intra-gender interpersonal sexualised conflict. Sexual bullying appeared as the most sharpened form of the discourse of reputational struggle. The words and gestures, fights and threats, shunnings and shamings were all simultaneously factors and products of the competition for a desirable social identity. The timing and diacritical marking of a handful of key words and phrases were imbued with a significance which accomplished most of what was needed in the restricted codes of sexual bullying.

The boys and girls were clear that one's reputation is set soon after arrival at secondary school and, although it can be damaged or destroyed during one's school career, it is unlikely that it will be improved. The mission, therefore, is to make a claim to being a dominant, popular, desirable person as early as possible and hope that alliances can be formed with similarly important peers which will protect that reputation by defining others as inferior. The fear of being cast by the peer group as a loser, one of the negatively valued others, struck many pupils interviewed. If you are called a name once with impunity, OK. If you are called it again you must react violently to avoid the label. As a result, classrooms and corridors echoed to the sound of petty name-calling, the small-arms fire of sexual skirmish, the perpetual testing of defences and the barrage of decoys from weak spots.

Not all interpersonal or inter-group power struggles are fuelled by the imperative of achieving social status through sexual reputation. At the adolescent stage, however, and within the cultural architecture of the secondary school, this aim does appear to predominate in gender relations with the collateral impact described above on seemingly non-sexual practices.

Finely graded and vacuum-packed

After the family, schools are the most powerful socialising influence in our society and arguably the most normalising. Where families take on a multitude of shapes, and create unique conditions in which the child can develop, schools are the only sites in our lives where we meet as age cohorts to such a structured and uniform degree. The vast majority of boys and girls in the UK are educated in institutions that are remarkably similar to one another, directed to be so by state order.

Four aspects of the formal organisation of secondary schools contributed to the pupil subculture's value system as regards the formation of sexualised gender identity: the compression of bodies; the promotion of normality and competition; the seniority of age; the disavowal of sexuality.

Compression

The compression of bodies in a controlled space was a feature of each of the secondary schools.[4] Y6 pupils had been the big fish in their primary schools, but with the confluence of streams of boys and girls from many tributary primary schools, all running into an ocean already populated with bigger, older pupils, they found themselves needing to assert an identity based upon superficial image. This profound need is eloquently described by John Walsh, whose daughter was to begin (private) secondary school the next day. Sophie affirmed that walking out into the playground for the first morning break would establish who would be the style dictator, and who the style victim, for the rest of her schooldays – perhaps for her life:

> 'But sweetheart', I said, 'you'll all be wearing school uniform'. 'Daddy', she said, 'that isn't the point. Everyone will be looking to see who seems nice, who laughs too much, who looks cool, and who looks as though they might be friendly, and who looks like a complete dork. You've got about 30 seconds to make an impression.'
>
> (*Independent*, 4 Sept. 1998)

The pupils in each of the schools in this study knew this too. It only took a few high-profile competitors in each year group to initiate a power struggle for social dominance before large blocs fell into the configuration. As the numbers involved in playing the game swelled there became less and less space for outsiders to manoeuvre in, and soon the majority were preoccupied with avoiding being negatively defined by those with the power and the interest to do so. Visible exemplars of social failures floated dead in the water as constant reminders of the importance of winning and holding social success.

The struggle for an identity to buoy one up in these turbulent waters became a preoccupying concern. The obvious strategy was to set course for those beacons visible at the end of the school experience – the high status of the most respected Y11 pupils. The flow was tidal, back and forward from youth to maturity, with the lived experience of gender relations at school influenced by the apparent success or otherwise of specific masculinities and femininities in the wider social frame and, in turn, influencing the next generation of young adults.

Young people experienced this formal reorganisation of their school life simultaneously with the reorganisation of their physical appearance and their emotional constitution. The getting of a new body and its concomitant difficulties and delights was associated emotionally with the burgeoning social experiences now possible. Boys and girls were thrown together in these institutions at a time when sexuality was the critical variable in their changing social status. The close-up magnification of every facet of this new set of identities is hard to over-state.

Normality and competition

A basic organising principle within schooling is that of the norm: the underpinning belief that boys and girls should reach certain developmental stages at specific times. Immense batteries of tests are marshalled to ensure that any deviation from normal academic attainment is noted and action can be instigated. Schools' expectations of standards of pupil behaviour are also very prescribed and are constantly an issue in pupil control. The strikingly effective power of teachers to control large numbers of pupils often rests on appeals to normality. Deviant behaviour is framed as undesirable egocentricity: 'It is a pity for the majority to be disrupted by a few individuals.'

Cultural expressions of adolescent gender identity were often found in emblematic form such as clothes and hairstyles. In all four schools these expressions were controlled and proscribed, to varying degrees, by official discourses of normality and uniformity. The more socially articulate pupils of either sex found subtle methods of circumventing these restrictions, or were well-enough adjusted to comply during school time. For the less socially able there ensued considerable conflict between staff and pupil, for where symbolic expression of sexuality was denied, acting-out became more important, and sexual bullying was a primary mode.

Whilst exhorting tolerance of difference, the schools constantly underlined the need for conformity with discourse geared to age norms: 'You should be able to cope with that at your age.' Being measured always against a set of norms, frequently without their criteria being made explicit, constructed a myriad of interlocking hierarchies in which pupils were constantly weighing up their values relative to those of others. This resulted in the strengthening of competition for a desired social identity. The competitive ethos and drive to succeed were necessary means of covert social control by the school authorities. They represented a direction in which all must head, an orientation that occluded alternatives and so obtained the compliance of pupils in the effort to achieve a corporate aim.

Seniority of age

Owing to the emphasis schooling places upon age-related norms, its administration is easier to manage if pupils are banded in distinct age groups throughout their formal education. This study has demonstrated the importance of relative age for hierarchies of peer social status and the power of the secondary school as a site for the enforcement of this system of value and privilege.

The secondary school represents a very special venue for the transformative process from childhood to adulthood, reflecting in its structure and discourse the accretion of social status (and hence self-worth) directly related to age and maturity. Pupils arrive from primary school already gendered and sensitised to age seniority, but it is in secondary school that most experience the physical changes of puberty and that gender becomes fully sexualised. However, the banding of children in narrow age-related groups takes no account of the earlier sexual maturation of many girls or of the social problems that such arrangements produce.

The interviews consistently threw up difficulties encountered by girls being harassed by less emotionally mature boys with whom they were obliged to spend five formative years in close proximity. The spurt of emotional/physical growth that many boys had in their last year of schooling came too late to benefit either sex in terms of their mutual regard. Many boys were set to leave school with a sexual identity disfigured by years of homophobic and misogynist training, and many girls with years of sexual denigration and low self-esteem.

Disavowal of sexuality

Schools openly control and order, manage and measure just about every other aspect of their pupils' experience but sexuality. Any human quality can be glorified and commended by praise from the assembly-hall podium: honesty; diligence; sporting and academic success; but not sexuality. The official silence surrounding the topic is deathly, with curricular remit halting at procreation and AIDS awareness; 'relationships' being discussed only fleetingly in PSE lessons.

Schools assume (or hope) that their pupils will mature into sexually well-adjusted adults irrespective of what they do, and so attempt neutrality or, at least, minimal impact. There is no doubt that the enormous and increasing workload of schools discourages closer engagement with this important area of child development or that current cultural sensitivities present further hazards. But, despite the official disavowal of pupil sexuality, the regime does not accept a *laissez-faire* approach. Instead it displaces sexuality for moral order, officially sanctioned as discreet and controlled heterosexual romance (Wolpe 1988). Within this void, the peer group wrestles with the problem itself.

The conflict and pain that this study observed continues. Because the phenomena are embedded in the state apparatus of the schooling system they remain a constant but permanently hidden feature, as those damaged by them continue their slow progress up the ladder towards socio-sexual maturity and uncertain acquisition of a culturally valued masculinity or femininity. As secondary school-ing and early adolescence are largely coincidental, the individual cannot distinguish the effects of either from the other and, whilst subject to them, ado-lescents are disempowered from recognising or dealing with the salient problems.

The rate at which young people pass through the education system, and the lack of time or encouragement for personal supportive contact from trained and caring adults, prevents those casualties most in need of help from getting it. Once damaged in such a way, as adults themselves, they are rarely in a position to make or suggest changes to the system that did not serve them well. This hidden grad-uation through socio-sexual frustration cannot be imagined to encourage healthy attitudes towards sexuality, gender and the celebration of difference.

8 Analysis, discussion and wild speculation

Female hegemony

Connell claims that there is no global structural version of feminine hegemony, that 'no pressure is set up to negate or subordinate other forms of femininity in the way hegemonic masculinity must negate other masculinities' (Connell 1987: 187). The perceived cultural transgressions of toyboy-users, home-breakers, incompetent (working-class, single) mothers, adoptive lesbian couples, career women and whores powerfully counter this view. Whilst there is a global subordination of women by men there can still exist a hierarchy of femininities which exerts dominance over some masculinities some of the time, as well as oppressing other forms of femininity. Connell argues that only in the face-to-face relationships, such as mother and daughter, can intra-feminine power conflict be institutionalised to the same degree of intensity that is found elsewhere in intramasculine conflict. He does, however, concede that some institutionalised relationships have a 'muted' form of intra-feminine conflict and names schools as venues for such.

The data from this study dispute the view that feminine practices of sexual bullying are always muted. Their form is different from the usual masculine modes of sexual bullying, but physical violence is still at hand ready to cut in when required. Misrecognition of feminine modes of bullying says more about ignorance and evasion on the part of patriarchal authority than it does about girls' subcultures. The apparent fact that boys resort to fighting amongst themselves more readily actually reinforces the argument that the hierarchy of feminine power rests on winning consent through the articulation of ideology with social practice rather than open coercion – a *sine qua non* of hegemony.

Although the concept of hegemony is useful it is not entirely satisfactory in its applications outside class relations, as the idea of cultural capital requires development before application to this field of research. Nevertheless, hegemony does offer an interesting analytical framework through which to view the gender relations in this project.

The status hierarchies of boys and girls stood apart but in relation to one another, and each afforded some mobility within its structure. The boys', however, was augmented by the macro-social advantages of masculine power and retained a blurred and fading ideology of global male supremacy which the girls' did not.

The boys' social system was proactive, and the girls' system appeared to be constructed around responses to it. This relationship cannot run on empty forever, and changes were already detectable in the forms of sexual bullying practised by the hard girls at Blunkett Rise.

The girls showed that their sense of place in the subcultural order was just as important as that of the boys. The dominant femininity, especially in the last couple of years at school, stood higher in relation to their male age-peers' dominant masculinity but was predicated on asymmetrical pairing with older boys outside the school system. The gender order within the school was not fully in the control of boys. Even though many boys would graduate to positions of superordinance in the wider society, the school remained a site of fragmented and contested gender power relations.

Let's get physical

Whilst not referring specifically to the physical phenomena of puberty, Connell has contributed a great deal to this study through his theorisation of body-reflexivity. His belief is that the body is inescapable throughout our lives: we can transform it to create and play out our vast social repertoires upon it, but we cannot ignore it. This notion could be of central importance in understanding better the intercourse between the school as institution and the palpable sexualities of its pupils. The schools' construction of a delusive form of purdah around maturing boys and girls does nothing but harm to their emotional health, it merely confirms the system's inadequacy in dealing with real people.

There is a wider dimension to these concerns regarding the sexualised, gendered body, as bodies may be attaining a greater significance in social identity than they have for a long time (Shilling 1993). This study supports the idea that the emphasis on sexual reputation as a core element of identity may have become heightened in recent years through the macro-societal changes evident in the strongly working-class communities where this research was carried out. Generally, the young people seemed to have a dwindling reserve of community identity signifiers that enabled accurate and settled positions within the subcultural status system. Gone are the old certainties by which, only a generation ago, young people could be known. In their place, the body, particularly the changing and changeable body, has increased its value and importance as an heraldic shield upon which to announce one's position. Although these thoughts are at the speculative end of theorisation, they may provide some basis on which to consider the contradictions and fractures in the union between micro-cultural and macro-social theories of gender.

Increasing fragmentation of family identities and roles has left a vacuum. There is less certainty of trade or occupational identity for either young people's parents as heads of household or themselves as school-leavers. Trade-union and political affiliations for young people, which once provided a medium in which identity could be formed, have also declined in availability and sphere of influence. Education's old status-symbolic gradings of streaming, tripartism and elite college/university destination have become more fluid and less emblematic, thereby closing down opportunities for either belonging *to* something, or even separating *from* something, identifiable.

With the atrophy of such social and community referents, and with the wider cultural exaltation of the personal and individual self, the primary signifier of who or what one is may have become an engorged sense of importance of the body. More now than ever, the body is associated with the individual's identity: pierced; tanned; tattooed; carved; depilated; shaved; coloured; pumped and sucked into shape; irrigated; fed and starved in ever more refined techniques and with widening participation by class, age, ethnicity and sex. This tightening focus of attention on the body-self in our modern western adult culture has led to even pre-adolescents becoming vulnerable to somatopsychotic pressure.[1]

Between bodies are the power relationships that exist in every social group. The adolescent subcultural value system – influenced by these societal values in dynamic relation with the agency of the participating individuals on a local level, and constrained yet intensified by the schooling process – is one of reputational status based on peer group approval of gender identity. The sexualisation of this gender identity during pubertal growth promotes a cathectic relationship with social status, a sexualised fetish of personal reputation: sex and self are conflated.[2]

> And when I lie on my pillow at night
> I dream I could fight like David Watts,
> Lead the school team to victory,
> Take my exams and pass the lot.
> (The Kinks)

The target of desire becomes detached from the person and projected onto the status position. The aim, the life project at this stage, is the achievement of a desirable, very gendered, sexual reputation. As this is won in competition there must be a gold standard embodied in another pupil, real and corporeal: a fetishised identity. There needs to be a superlative image that talks and walks amongst the common people. It must be composed of a combination of traits and attributes that, in their discrete states, are attainable by the majority but, in their complete consolidation, represent the apogee of desired adolescent identity: a locally produced hegemonic masculinity and femininity.

The hegemony is not a simple coercive leadership where physical power is used without challenge and inferiors are in constant oppression. The most senior positions in the gender order are actively supported by the majority of subordinates, despite their own unilateral interests, but those interests must be balanced against the hazard of disturbing the order and thereby risking one's relegation or banishment. Even acolytes closest to the throne, who may possess all the attributes they need to seize it, continue to pay allegiance if they perceive an accompanying poison chalice. The combinations and exclusions that constitute the hegemonic identity are infinitely subtle and eternally altering, but always a senior boy and girl become the role models for other pupils' identity. The active ingredients consist of a core (of body power, mental toughness and a prowess for social management) and cluster (of specific stylistic accessories).

At school, success in achieving the valued goals of peer popularity, sexual partners and respect from older youths is signalled back down the age cohorts, mediated along the way by incipient pretenders in each of the year groups. Those who achieve high rank are emulated in dress and taste and style of speech as well as behaviour in socio-sexual relations, edifying their status and developing a tradition.

> If I could only be
> The Queen of Popularity,
> What I would do
> . . . if I were you.
>
> (k.d. lang)

The singular force of the hegemonic identity is apparent in its vitiation of counterfeit. If the top girl wears a black bra beneath a white blouse she makes it OK. One or two close mates might emulate the style with approval, but if a weak pretender attempts the same she becomes a figure of fun, mocked not only by her superordinates but by her own-level peers. If she persists, the top girl moves on to another, more exclusive, signifier.

Although the external purchasable image is important, it is not sufficient in itself to achieve status: secure upward mobility needs careful social management. Here and there in the study, examples were encountered of bad errors of judgement. Looking too sexy, too hard, or too cool could lead to a rapid and painful fall. Progress needed to be made incrementally and cautiously, style developed conservatively; and self-disclosure and opinions needed to be tested in tight friendship groups.

This struggle for improved status did not express itself in articulate speech with abstract concepts and out-references. The effective means of self-expression on identity formation was through lived texts of concrete signs: haircuts and training shoes; fashion labels; slaps and tickles; sweaty clinches and sexual and physical conquest. Language was stilted and often inchoate when discussing important ideas in the clinical environment of the interview room, but bursting with tricks when switched to confrontational dialogue mode in the corridors or playground.

The pupils showed that they had a fierce preoccupation with acquiring a status within the peer group necessary to their self-esteem. Sexual reputation was an organising principle in the peer group during adolescence, and this identity was formed in praxis from the lived experiences of boys and girls mediated through the official discourses and formal organisation of the school. Secondary schools do not produce sexualised individuals from unsexualised raw materials, but they do impact strongly on young people at a critical period in their lives by exerting powerful influences on the conditions in which pupil cultures produce their sexual value systems. Gender plays such a central role in education that, when institutions do not engage with sexuality as a vital part of pupil identity, its potential for conflict is realised as cumulative processes that have damaging effects on social relations generally.

Triggered by the feminist action of the 1970s and subsequent equal-opportunities initiatives, LEAs have sought to address the underachievement of girls and improve the quality of their experience in schools. Such improvement has been long overdue, particularly in the areas of curriculum access and GCSE performance.[3] Whilst recent gains are neither secure nor complete, it would be churlish not to view these achievements as progressive and optimistic. Girls are now acknowledged to have a different set of needs due to gender imbalance in our society; the disadvantages they face are given some special consideration. However, a significant pattern has emerged over the past four or five years that reveals male fortunes in schools to be rapidly declining. This is evident in the over-representation of boys considered in need of specialist education provision; the exclusion rate of boys (Garner 1994); the unequal distribution of boys in 'difficult' class groups; and their second best to girls on exam results (Power et al. 1998). Outside schools, the sharp increase and huge male over-representation in suicides[4] amongst 11–18-year-olds and their higher rate of criminal offending suggest a multi-systemic failure to meet the needs of young males in our society.

The effects of these changes, combined with the macro-economic reality of male unemployment, have produced a discernible weakening of schools as masculinised institutions where patriarchal privilege can be expected. The current experience for many boys is that schools are unfriendly places,[5] with higher exclusion rates, lower academic achievement rates and fewer job opportunities than for girls. The commonly espoused belief that, as a homogeneous grouping, boys see themselves as superior may need to be re-thought now, and a more sensitive understanding formulated of their differentiation from men and from one another. For schools to continue their evasion of pupils' sexual identities as an issue for support and guidance will result in further systematic production of abusive and exploitative relationships and social failure.

Despite the advances towards a better understanding of gender, progress and interest have lurched from one sex to the other, with the relationship between femininities and masculinities constantly strained in the process. It is time for the interstices to be addressed: for an exploration of the spaces between, and within, the gendered lives we live.

Possibilities for further research

It is customary to end books such as this with a call for further work to be done in the field. I continue that tradition by offering two planes along which further work might be useful: looking outward at the wider picture, and looking deeper into some of the more interesting findings.

One obvious line out from this research would be to study schools other than mainstream, co-educational comprehensives. Having began my career teaching in residential special schools, I have experience and data that is illuminating, but unfortunately difficult to assimilate into this study. The fluidity and intimacy of those highly child-centred institutions create very different social relationships within them. Single-sex and boarding schools, 'free' schools and those run by religious groups would all make interesting extensions to this study.

In the theorisation of sexual bullying I have dwelt heavily upon just two categories of subjectivity: sex and age. This emphasis followed the empirical findings of the data, where social differentiation seen as important by the actors in the research was based primarily upon those variables. A valuable extension of research in this area could include a greater emphasis on race and ethnicity, and on social class. A great deal of interview and observation data from this study contained detailed references to the sexual connotations of ethnic groups and their part in creating personal reputation. Much of this information was not used in the body of the study as the workplace school had very few non-white pupils with whom to develop these lines of enquiry.

The work of Troyna and Hatcher (1992) and Gillborn (1993) on children's experiences of racism in schools would provide good models for the inclusion of sexual bullying, possibly under-represented in the former's findings only because the sample was taken from primary schools. Apart from Black and Asian identities, the association of red hair with a celtic identity and thence with a devalued masculinity was strong in Blunkett Rise and presents an area of special interest for further work.

Social class was evident from the researcher's point of view in the form of a flattened economic stratum in which all but a very few of the pupils belonged, but where the internal cultural differences were profoundly significant. In these systems an extended family reputation for toughness and cohesiveness was highly important at the economic bottom end, decreasing as the better-off families enjoyed a micro-bourgeois status if one or more adults were waged or were financially successful in some illegal activity. This conceptualisation of a social-class subsystem internal to a social-class seems an interesting starting point for the further investigation of micro-social power relations both in schools and in local communities. As schools have been shown to exert an enclosing effect on their pupils, so might local working-class communities structure the social relationships of their inhabitants, albeit less constrictively and with different mechanisms and results.

Looking more deeply into the findings of this research, several areas call out for further work. These areas are subsumed by the need for a fuller account of the general disengagement of schools from their pupils' sexuality which aggravates gender conflict, and the difficulties hard-pressed staff have in managing that complex layer of working practices.

One such area of special interest is the phenomenon of 'the fall' experienced by adolescent girls. This phenomenon has been commented upon by numerous feminist researchers[6] and is manifest in a sudden drop in self-esteem and academic achievement, coinciding with the onset of eating disorders and depression.

Another process that calls for more investigation is the heterosexualisation of boys and girls through their actively produced subculture in relation to schooling systems. The effect upon adolescent attitudes of increasing availability of positive gay identities in the mass media is a seriously under-researched area, as it forms a critical nexus in the discourse of interpersonal intolerance and oppression. Indeed, the entire changing picture of gendered experience and success in UK schools calls for detailed analysis of the impact of planned interventions and unintended consequences in state education.

Theories of gender relations and sexual identity need regular feeding from research undertaken in schools themselves, but the current low esteem in which the state holds sociology of education bodes ill for new work in all the above areas. In addition, the political implications of training and resourcing greater pastoral support makes an appeal for more such research virtually hopeless, at a time when the drive in education is for quantifiable increases in academic achievement at no extra cost. Nevertheless, to make that appeal is more than a token, as certain issues occasionally seem to catch attention and result in irresistible public pressure for action; one such issue is bullying.

Much of what has previously been presented as non-sexual bullying has been demonstrated by this study to have sexualised gender conflict at its heart and systemic brutal misogyny and homophobia as its mode. It would be unfair, however, not to acknowledge the success young people have achieved in negotiating their adolescence during their time at secondary school. For most of the young people in this project, partly due to the dedicated support of parents and professionals, partly due to personal strength, this period in their lives was exciting and enjoyable despite a system that clearly needs change. It is hoped that this project will contribute to the pressure for that change which our forthcoming generations deserve.

Appendix A

Review of literature on bullying in schools

Early Scandinavian research

The phenomena that constitute the main of interest of this book can be identified as focal points for a number of different perspectives, indeed of different academic disciplines; basically they are acts of hostility between young people at school. It may sound more sensible to use the term *bullying*, but the definition of that term has always been, and remains, problematic.

For a phenomenon so widely recognised by the general public as pervasive and pernicious, bullying was surprisingly late in attracting academic attention. Only in the last three decades has the problem been the focus of serious research, and only since the late 1980s have academic studies in the English language appeared in significant number.

A great deal of the early research into bullying originated in Scandinavia, and began a tradition which has survived to the present day with the ongoing large-scale studies supervised by Professor Dan Olweus of Bergen University and the pioneering therapeutic work of Anatol Pikas. These two eminent researchers adopted a medical model of investigation, but still differed considerably regarding the definition of the behaviours they were considering. Such inconsistency was not insignificant: it had important implications for school responses to the problem of bullying as variably conceived by the experts, for example the use of individual and group psychotherapies (Pikas 1989a).

There are too many competing definitions of bullying to critique here,[1] but the problems can be illustrated by means of a few examples. The enduring definition posited by Olweus (1987), that a person is bullied when he or she is exposed, regularly and over time, to negative actions on the part of one or more persons, is so vague and catch-all it is virtually useless in assisting any understanding of the problem. Such a description could cover any situation from that of victims of passive smoking to the general public's treatment at the hands of HM government.

Subsequently, a much more verbose definition was developed by Olweus (1989), as part of his questionnaire preamble:[2]

> We say that a child or young person is being bullied, or picked on, when

another child or young person, or a group of children or young people, say nasty and unpleasant things to him or her. It is also bullying when a child or a young person is hit, kicked, threatened, locked inside a room, sent nasty notes, when no one ever talks to them and things like that. These things can happen frequently and it is difficult for the child or young person being bullied to defend himself or herself. It is also bullying when a child or young person is teased repeatedly in a nasty way. But it is not bullying when two children or young people of about the same strength have the odd fight or quarrel.

This exhausting explication has been widely used by UK researchers within adaptations of Olweus' questionnaires, but is not a suitable tool for academic or even practical discussion of bullying. It is far too long and it imposes a prefabricated definition on the respondents.

A more focused offering was made by another Scandinavian researcher: 'The long term and systematic use of violence, mental or physical, against an individual who is unable to defend himself in the actual situation' (Roland 1989: 142). In the real-life experience of the secondary school, many social scenarios occur which confound even this formulation. If one takes the example of a lone 15-year-old boy confronting a group of 11-year-old boys in a quiet school corridor and saying 'Lend me ten pence . . . each', one might well interpret the scene as one of bullying. There is an implicit menace in the request, and an improbability that it would be made to boys of his own age or in front of an adult. However, this relates only slightly if at all to Roland's definition: it is an individual approaching a group: a single event in time; random rather than systematic; it is highly contestable that the 'bully' is inflicting 'violence' either physical or mental, or that the 11-year-olds are unable to defend themselves in that situation.

Long-term practitioners have experience of thousands of scenarios that could be considered bullying but do not fit perfectly with any existing definition. My own working definition might be 'bullying is abuse of interpersonal power', but the pursuit of a gold-standard definition is, I believe, unnecessary. Now that bullying is beginning to be analysed as a series of sub-types rather than a monolithic conceit, there may be a move towards richer and more variegated treatment of the subject that draws upon disciplines outside of the psychological paradigm. In the meantime, I feel it is important to recognise the background to current mainstream theory and practice, some of the political context of which is discussed below.

The UK research imperative

In the mid- to late 1980s a number of issues concerning child welfare in British society collided to make a powerful impact at the interface of media/professional/public discourse. Public awareness had been raised with regard to new evidence of the scale of child abuse perpetrated by parents, families, professionals and strangers. Emotional, sexual, physical and satanic abusers were being exposed daily and whole social institutions (boarding schools, churches, social-services departments, clinics and police forces) were portrayed by the news media as flawed and dangerous to children (Butler Sloss 1988; King and Trowell 1993; Farmer and Owen 1995).

The contradictions and difficulties of acting positively for improvements in the quality of life for children and young people (Children Act 1989) whilst maintaining the status quo in politically sensitive areas turned campaigns against bullying in schools into a popular obsession. National consciousness was alerted to the problem of child safety in the hands of professionals, but for most adults their only experience of outside agencies handling their children was through state education. Stopping bullying in schools represented a clear-cut issue that every right-thinking person could support. It was this common-sense appeal that made this a 'safe' area for political investment, thereby creating favourable conditions for research funding into bullying in schools.

Initiatives such as Childline, Teenscape, Kidscape[3] and its anti-bullying helpline, NCH,[4] the Gulbenkian Foundation, and DfEE,[5] Scottish Office, Home Office and LEA sponsored projects (Tattum and Herbert 1993) received substantial media coverage as well as public and private money. I believe that one unintended consequence of this burst of activity was to draw away attention from the structural flaws in our society whilst chasing the new folk devils: 'the bullies'.

It seems that the pursuit of individual scapegoats in the form of school bullies was a useful (albeit temporary) diversion from many pressing but politically obnoxious tasks that would improve quality of life for children generally. Rather than tackle the economic and material deprivations, dysfunctioning family systems and culturally tolerated male violence that blight young lives, war was declared against children with a propensity to be nastier to their peers than 'normal'. This is not to dispute the need for research and action on oppressive peer behaviour in schools, but to suggest reasons for its sudden florescence at that time.

Two factors were decisive in achieving this situation. First, the funding of anti-bullying initiatives and research was influenced by public concern that in turn was fuelled by media coverage. Such coverage is most effective when it deals in stereotypes of individuals' personalities. Second, the primary extra-mural professionals dealing with pupil problems in British (and other) school systems are the educational psychologists. Their initial training and subsequent career experience promotes the investigation of the individual. It is, therefore, the work of psychologists such as Lowenstein (1978a), Arora and Thompson (1987), Besag (1989), Elliott (1992) and Sharp and Smith (1994) that form most of the work in the field of bullying in the UK. Within the psychological paradigm there are, of course, a number of themes and methods emphasised or ignored by particular researchers.

Frequency and distribution of bullying

Despite the credit for the earliest research into bullying generally being given to the Scandinavian pioneers, since the 1960s there have been a number of research projects investigating the subject of bullying in British schools, often indirectly as part of general pupil behavioural problems. Probably the earliest of these projects, and of special significance to mine, is the study into bullying levels in single- and mixed-sex secondary schools by Dale (1971).

Dale raises several points that give the impression that even by the mid-1960s there was a 'common-sense' view of several aspects of bullying that has since been empirically substantiated. This view includes:

- widespread prevalence of the problem
- a difference in type of bullying according to sex and age
- a significant variation between schools
- the effects of school ethos on levels of anti-social behaviour
- the influence of the degree of closure of the institution (for example, boarding schools versus day schools).

Dale's project was concerned with a very wide-ranging evaluation of the effects of co-education on the lives of children. The element directly related to bullying was, therefore, proportionately small, although it did draw upon a fairly large sample: about 800 student teachers who had been taught in both single- and mixed-sex secondary schools. The importance of Dale's study for mine is his data on gender relations, a dimension sorely absent from the bulk of the psychological research.

Although the report contains some references to school life, such as prefects and fagging, that seem archaic today, it is illuminating in that it reveals a great similarity to the concerns of children almost thirty years on. Some of the free responses include comments about 'boy-crazy girls', 'catty, spiteful groups', 'seniors asserting position' and so on, all of which phenomena form an important part of the ethnography in this book. As well as explicitly including girls and the relationship between them and boys at school, Dale acknowledges the sociological paradigm in the analysis of bullying – a perspective that has been largely neglected in favour of a focus on psychological characteristics of individual bullies and victims. Dale engages with the question of how behaviour and attitudes are formed by the social context as it in turn is constrained by the formal organisation of the institution.

The data provided by psychologists' quantitative research into bullying may give schools figures to test the effects of interventions, but unfortunately much of this is not helpful to parents' or teachers' wider understanding as different definitions and measurements give very different readings. For example, Lowenstein (1978b) surveyed 10,000 pupils aged 5–16 years using interviews and personality tests. The low incidence of bullying in his results, 1–5 per cent, is a partial reflection of the very strict criteria he used to define bullying. By contrast, Elliott (1992) surveyed 4,000 children and their parents over a two-year period and found that 65 per cent of the children had experienced bullying. Discrepancies such as this are common in the literature, and are usually accepted as the outcome of using different, but just as scientifically valid, criteria. Political dimensions do not feature in debates on bullying research, but Elliott's role as a long-term campaigner for children's safety and Lowenstein's more remote academic interest must be taken into account when considering the above statistical discrepancy. Elliott's agenda is served by raising public awareness of the high prevalence of bullying, whereas Lowenstein's stringent criteria are aimed at identifying extreme behaviours in a pathologising way.

The important Sheffield project involved an anonymous questionnaire-based survey of more than 6,000 pupils in all school phases in the Sheffield area (Sharp and Smith 1994). Results from that study showed that 10 per cent of pupils in secondary schools reported being bullied 'sometimes' or more frequently, but only 6 per cent reported bullying others 'sometimes' or more frequently. Boys were more likely to report as victims than girls, with the perpetrators being one or more boys. Girls were more likely to be victims of other girls or of mixed-sex groups. Girls were more likely to be victimised 'indirectly' by slanderous rumours and malicious gossip, or by social exclusion from a friendship group. Boys, generally, were remarkably over-represented in the surveys associated with the Sheffield project and all others where sex was recorded as a personal variable.

In a rare attempt to explore the role of sex in bullying, Keise researched two single-sex secondary schools focusing on racial and sexual harassment. The schools thought that: 'Whereas these may or may not have been issues for them as a whole school, bullying (seen as a form of harassment) was a common experience for all students and one with which they were immediately concerned' (Keise 1992: 5). This conception of the issues being explored here seems remarkable to me. Keise went on to consider the gender relations at work in bullying but reported little of direct relevance or interest other than:

> For some young women, seeking their feminine identity through the traditional route of boyfriends, make-up and being 'good' is simply not enough. They want these things and more besides. They seek to be equal to the male members of their families and their male friends and can match fist with fist. It would seem, moreover, in some instances that if the academic route is perceived as an impossible means of acquiring power and status then power needs to be sought by another route – and one route may be bullying.
>
> (1992: 54)

Keise's masculinisation of the phenomenon of girl-to-girl bullying is at least an effort to bring some attention to the existence of girls, but remains very isolated from the male-oriented or gender-free (gender-blind?) bullying research. There are only a few such exceptions to this tendency, including Bjorkquist et al. (1992), who have investigated manipulation as a distinctly female method of harassment, and Stein (1995), who has explored legal and educational responses to peer harassment in schools from the perspective of gendered violence.

Druet (1993) carried out a small-scale research project to investigate adolescent female bullying and sexual harassment in a girls' secondary school. Although some important details are not made clear (exactly *who* was doing the bullying in or out of school), Druet reports that confusion existed over the pupils' distinction between 'sexual harassment' and 'bullying'. This differentiation was related to the age of the girl respondents, with the older girls more likely to refer to sexualised abuse as 'sexual harassment.'

As with this study, Druet found that the most hurtful area for the girls was that of their sexual reputation. A significant finding was that, even in a female single-sex school, some girls adopted or promoted abusive masculine strategies to exert dominance over other girls. Unfortunately there are still too few works that contribute to an understanding of the complex institutional and personal dynamics in their cultural context.

Sponsorship of research into bullying

Local education authorities have a statutory duty to employ psychologists to perform certain legal functions (such as assessment and statement of special educational needs) and rarely commission research from other disciplines. Whilst there are many different theoretical perspectives to be found amongst psychologists, the administrators in LEAs tend to shape their profile by seeking value for money through measurable programmes. The culture in which the educational psychologists find themselves working with bullying leans towards a conservative quasi-medical model (Sinha 1986), with an ever-increasing requirement for 'hard facts' on which LEA officers must base their forward planning.

Both LEA psychologists and university psychology departments researching bullying have displayed a preference for large-scale questionnaire surveys to obtain 'hard data'. Statistical analysis of numerical data trends, with its proclaimed objectivity and value-freedom, keeps anonymous students under surveillance at a distance. Much of the central work done on bullying is concerned with prototypical psychological profiling, giving rise to the stereotypification of 'the bully' or 'the victim'. An image is created of the loner with poor social skills, unpopular with peers and ungratified by family relationships: finer details to be added by subsequent research. The common-sense view is then formed that if individuals do not conform to these descriptors they are unlikely to be a problem, but if they do conform they are suspects. The danger is that such an identified group of offenders or sufferers as appear in statistics can be interpreted as meaning that the other (for example) 90 per cent must be OK. It is my belief that the dominant ideology of the 90 per cent provides the climate for the existence of the 10 per cent. The key to understanding and alleviating bullying lies in the culture of the actors rather than the unrelated aberrations of a few individuals.

But such research is clearly favoured by interested purse-holders such as the government and national charities. Over the past decade quantitative research into bullying has been heavily funded by many bodies and research conclusions have been used as the basis for popular action plans at national level, for example Bullyline. Findings have been incorporated by the educational establishment into school and LEA policy, and the DfEE now uses OFSTED[6] to confirm the existence and monitor the effectiveness of schools' anti-bullying policies as part of their welfare arrangements.

There appears to me to be an affinity between the conservatism of the research into bullying (with its preoccupation with norms and standards) and its financial support. The tendency for quantitative research of this kind is to normalise one group through promotion of social conformity and marginalise another by individual deviancy: the very act of deploying means and percentiles promotes this.

In the politics of education generally, there is a concern to avoid offence to the majority by focusing on the minority. This means that teachers (generally) can be found to be at fault, whereas parents and children (generally) cannot – unless of course there can be a set of labels which appeal to the majority to describe the minority even though the two groups interpenetrate. This works best if the minority does not recognise itself by the label. In the case of research into bullying, therefore, it appears that only the most extreme cases are worthy of scrutiny. It matters not that most children actively engage in some forms of socially undesirable behaviour much of the time, but that attention is focused upon those most active within the narrow range of scientific scrutiny. The following work does not belong to the above canon: it provides a challenging range of alternative or complementary perspectives on the problem of peer group conflict which may be defined as bullying, and adds dimensions of class, race and gender.

Racism in schools

With the exception of Gillborn's (1993) work on bullying and racial violence, race and ethnicity do not feature prominently in bullying research as coherently theorised concepts. But, whilst not falling within the recognised field of bullying research, there is a body of work on racism in schools which is very pertinent to the subject.

The MacDonald Report (1989) highlighted tensions within Burnage High School, amongst others, in Manchester, in the lead-up to the fatal stabbing of an Asian youth by a white boy. The importance of the report's findings for this study lies in its recognition of a culture of unstable relationships between groups and individuals within the pupil group and the proximity of violent outburst throughout school life. The report has powerful implications for the deployment of multiculturalism in schools and communities, where official highlighting of disadvantage in one group can trigger feelings of jealousy and neglect in others. This point is an important one in the context of any school policy intended to alleviate one group's difficulty, especially when that difficulty is perceived to be directly generated by the group's relationship with another.

Mac An Ghaill (1989a) identified the differing construction of (male) racial groups by their peers at school dependent upon the institution's social/ethnic constituency. The intersection of sexual, racial and social-class identities had great bearing upon the work ethic and motivation towards academic success of groups of pupils. In this model the school can be seen as actively shaping opportunities for male pupils to develop their identities within constructions of slyness, aggressiveness, intelligence, machismo and effeminacy. Such an institutionalised construction of identity ascribed to students deeply affects their position in the hierarchy of interpersonal oppression. Mac An Ghaill's research conceptually links the abusive terms 'Paki' and 'poof' and their extension into 'Paki-bashing' and 'gay-bashing'.

Troyna and Hatcher's (1992) study into racism in primary schools develops a highly sophisticated theoretical model that offers convincing arguments for the behaviour of, and responses to, racism amongst young children. This work has enormous potential to reconceptualise bullying by:

- adopting an ethnographic approach to the problem of interpersonal hostility within a socialising institution
- recognising the difference between 'strategic' and 'non-strategic' name-calling and assaults
- acknowledging the contradictions in children's social relationships
- attributing sense of family pride and shame as motivation to the actors
- including social class as an influence on peer-culture conflict
- accepting children as active creators of racist ideology, not simply passive receivers
- cautioning against institutional interventions such as multicultural education, the effects of which can be counter-productive
- identifying the powerful influence upon children's social behaviour of the dynamic between the adult community, mass media (especially TV) and children's own lived experience with other children.

Bullying of gay and lesbian pupils

Recent work has been carried out by some psychologists investigating bullying in schools from the perspective of pupils who identify themselves or are identified by others as gay or lesbian. Often these pupils are only suspected by peers of being homosexual or bisexual, but are maltreated regardless of their actual status. Individual accounts of such persecution have been available in gay and lesbian writing for several years (Martin 1982), as well as from radical men's collectives such as Achilles Heel and associated groups (Seidler 1992).

Lately there has been increased interest within psychiatry in links between concealed or denied sexual identity and depression, self-mutilation and suicide (Silvoe et al. 1987, Rothblum 1990, Shidlo 1994). The work of Rivers (1995) is now concerned with accounts by adults of traumas suffered through homophobic sexual persecution as schoolchildren. Early reports from Rivers[7] suggest school ethos and professional competence in handling homophobic incidents are crucial to the safety not only of young gay and lesbian pupils but of all those who do not fit with the dominant conceptions of masculinity and femininity in the institution. These issues play a major part in the ethnography in this book.

Summary

Research into bullying has only a short history. The major part of the research is focused on a fairly homogeneous Scandinavian population, and this research

suffers somewhat from a lack of variety of methodologies and too narrow a definition of terms. Bullying has become recognised internationally as a problem, but
its forms are highly susceptible to cultural influence and therefore it resists simple
analysis across national boundaries.

Surveys of bullying are not always attempting to measure the same things, but
there is an increasing body of research providing comparable data. The research
and intervention programmes are carried out overwhelmingly by psychologists.
There are, however, massive differences in the philosophical approaches: from the
very humane 'no-blame approach' (Maines and Robinson 1992) to the clinical
edge of the CCM[8] (Pikas 1989a). With increased research activity in the UK a
consensus has developed amongst workers in the field that includes the following
elements:

- bullying can be either physical or psychological or both
- bullying involves a wide range of activities and intensities according to the
  circumstances
- bullying demonstrates a power imbalance between the participants
- low estimates put pupil involvement in such activity at around 10 per cent
- boys are massively over-represented in bullying activities
- girls are characterised, where they are mentioned, as more inclined to use
  emotional modes of abuse rather than physical threats or assaults.

The study of racism amongst school children has much to offer the research into
bullying, with social class, race and gender being largely overlooked by the main
body of researchers. Some current research is concerned with addressing these
omissions.

Bullying in schools has become an issue in the UK due to broadcast unease
about child protection issues. Its potential as an area of 'safe' political investment
has been exploited by state promotion, which supports inherently conservative
investigation and intervention through the psychological paradigm.

As the focus of this book is sexual bullying, the greatest omission in the research
reviewed above is the absence of girls and gender issues generally: the next section
examines the significant contribution towards an understanding of sexual bullying
made by researchers working outside the bullying research paradigm.

Review of literature on gender relations in schools

Gendered hostility in schools

The literature on gender relations amongst pupils has a very different character
from that displayed by the literature on bullying in schools. Generally it tends to
follow strongly the feminist tradition, and rejects on philosophical grounds many
aspects of the approaches to bullying discussed above.

The gender-studies methodology tends to be theory-driven into small-scale
qualitative studies. Researchers frequently work in close collaboration with their

subjects to produce detailed accounts of experiential knowledge within a democratic, empowering anti-sexist schema. The methods employed in this field are common in ethnographic work: observation, interviews and participants' diaries but, in addition, the radical character of some of the researchers encourages political consciousness-raising. Some researchers have instigated support groups and networks for their respondents following the research, thereby promoting empowerment of individuals and disadvantaged social groups.

Radical feminist work on schooling

Along with the growing research interest into bullying in schools in the 1980s, many feminists published investigations into the anti-social behaviour of boys directed at girls in schools. Sexual harassment of women in the workplace was highlighted by teachers' unions, and some action eventually took place to challenge such practices (Whitbread 1988). As part of a wider feminist interest in institutionalised sexism, the position of girls in the education system was closely scrutinised by many feminists who saw schooling as a key site for the transmission of male power: 'Patriarchy is the education paradigm' (Spender 1981: 155). Much of this writing remains fresh and vivid and shocking even after years of subsequent related research. Jones (1985) describes the male violence against women in a London comprehensive school in the early 1980s. Here she encountered pornographic graffiti, verbal sexual assault and accounts of physical molestation of girls by boys. Jones sees this set of behaviours as simply reflecting the abuse of power in society as a whole. She concludes that such male tyranny is endemic and that all boys and men benefit from it: 'As such, men/boys at school are no different from the men who buy pornography, beat women, assault their daughters (and other girls) and abuse their sisters and mothers. We, as women, cannot afford to see boys as "innocent children" or male teachers as sympathetic professionals' (Jones 1985: 33).

Mahony (another pioneering figure in this area) reviews a number of aspects of school life where male power is detrimental to the female pupils and staff: use of language; curriculum management; monopoly of space by boys and monopoly of teacher-time by boys (Mahony 1985). These practices are still neglected in the bullying literature, but two elements are particularly relevant to this book: sexual harassment and servicing.

Mahony's conception of sexual harassment includes activities such as boys acting bored when girls answer questions in class, ridicule of signs of 'cleverness' by girls and the general roughness of push and shove. Whilst these are certainly very pertinent to the general problem, the core of sexual harassment is clearly actual or threatened verbal sexual assault and unwanted sexual touching. Physical molestation is portrayed as almost pandemic, with boys grabbing breasts and buttocks, and girls continually oppressed under the appraising male gaze and commentary. The point is made that the abusive language is formed from a uniquely anti-female vocabulary: 'there are no male equivalents of "tart", "scrubber", "bitch", "cow" and "slag"' (Mahony 1985: 46). Indeed there are no precise equivalents, but there are many examples of similarly offensive epithets used exclusively against males, for example 'wanker' and 'dickhead', which appear in this study. Mahony believes, however, that boys' and girls' relationships to the language of abuse are very different: both degrade women when they use it and girls degrade themselves in a way that boys do not.

Better refined is Mahony's conception of 'servicing'. This is a feature of boy–girl relationships where girls provide materials and services that enhance the quality of life for boys in the school. Examples given by Mahony include lending pens and other stationery to boys who would otherwise be punished for not being properly equipped for school. Lending of money, cigarettes and food is also frequently observed. Mahony also offers some evidence of girls providing help with homework and classwork and settling disputes. These activities can be seen to have close links with some of the stereotypical 'mothering' duties in our society. The motivation for the girls to perform these tasks is suggested as achieving a 'good reputation' amongst the boys (Willis 1977).

Unlike the individualised psychological view of bullying, Mahony detects gendered social structures at work in schools, which impel boys' behaviour into a funnel of sexism:

> boys who do not display sufficient evidence of masculinity, or more rarely, those who actively challenge the sexist behaviour of other boys, are prime targets for a good deal of what is called in their case, bullying. Therefore, it is doubly in their interests to adopt dominant patterns of male behaviour or at least pretend to. The question here is when does the pretence become so like the real thing that it is the real thing?
>
> (Mahony 1985: 3)

No benign behaviour is attributable to schoolboys: even victims of bullying are likely to turn against girls as a selfish means of relief. The monolithic aggressiveness of masculinity is further dealt with in Mahony's later work.

Although these early contributions on interpersonal gendered hostility in schools raise awareness of some of the problems, their analysis does not fit comfortably with my observations of interplay between the genders where there appeared to be a less clear dominance of boys over girls. Mahony's unproblematic distinction between sexual harassment and bullying also seems unhelpful in the search for a better understanding of a complex of social practices that all bear upon one another within the context of the school.

Girls as deviants

Davies (1984) offers a highly nuanced exploration of the cultural interests and practices of schoolgirls, their relationships with other girls and their attitudes towards boys. She draws a picture of girls bullying one another to gain social status and openly engaging in physical violence in contest over boyfriends. Their violence is notably different from that of the boys, with the harassment and persecution involving more actors and enduring over longer periods of time than is common in disputes amongst boys.

The theme of official differentiation by sex within the school is a strong one. Davies describes the awkwardness of male staff, so confident and majestic in disciplining the boys but coming rapidly unstuck when faced with deviant femininity. Without recourse to the physical chastisement meted out so freely to the lads they found it hard to respond to the girls' misbehaviour and resorted to references to 'ladylike' norms or referred the girls to a senior female teacher.

Davies found that, in general, girls were no less resistant that boys to the school's official codes. They were just as difficult to manage in a number of key areas, but 'It is in the arena of interpersonal relationships that *some* girls can present different or greater "problems" in their heightened, longer-lasting reactions to both affront (whether from peers or teachers) and to attempted or actual disciplinary treatment from teachers' (Davies 1984: 14). This arena of girls' interpersonal relationships and their part in shaping gender conflict in school is of substantial importance for this book, but needs recasting in the light of contemporary conditions.

Language as a sexually loaded weapon

The properties and uses of language are a recurring theme throughout most of the feminist literature. Use of sexually aggressive language against schoolgirls is seen to be widespread. Walkerdine (1987) makes explicit the power that inheres in language, and Lees (1987) also considers verbal abuse to be a major weapon in the armoury of female-hating males. Lees focuses on the subjective experiences of girls at school, especially regarding their sexual reputations. She notes, as do many others (for example, Mahony and Jones), that there is an imbalance of hurt conveyed by abusive terms that favours boys: 'The language of sexual abuse, where virtually all the terms of abuse are ones which denigrate women and the only really abusive word for a man – a 'poof' – also denotes femininity, reflects the fundamental misogyny of our society' (Lees 1987: 176).

Cowie and Lees (1987) illustrate the double jeopardy facing girls in their expression of sexuality: 'Appearance is crucial: by wearing too much make-up (how do you know how much is too much): by having your skirt too slit: by not combing your hair, wearing jeans to dances or high heels to school: having your trousers too tight or tops too low . . . It is very clearly a narrow tightrope to walk to achieve sexual attractiveness without the taint of sexuality' (Cowie and Lees 1987: 109).

In her interviews with young teenage girls, Lees (1987) repeatedly found girls excusing or condoning intimate violence by boys against their girlfriends, even when they were the recipients. The girls themselves described frequent violence by girls against other girls and boys. She noted that fights between girls are usually about defending a sexual reputation more than a straight contest over a boyfriend. In one example that is uncannily echoed in this study,[9] a girl severely beats up another girl because of a suspected slander by that girl's boyfriend. After she has beaten the girl up she organises her brothers to beat the boyfriend up too.

Lees's work does, however, tend to feature boys as rather two-dimensional and also relegates the importance of school organisation raised by Mahony (1985) and Jones (1985). Wolpe (1988) also makes the criticism that Lees's analysis is neglectful of wider aspects of ideology and culture: 'While their (Mahony and Lees') interpretations are different, their conclusions converge largely because sexuality is dealt with in terms of power relations reflecting unquestioningly male domination. In this way complex relationships are reduced to a linear dimension of girls responding to boys' behaviour' (Wolpe 1988: 100).

In her more recent work Lees (1993) problematises aspects of masculinity and records some evidence that double standards are beginning to weaken, although masculinity has become entrenched and more sexist in some arenas (working-class/unemployed youth) due to changing economic factors. Others, notably Skeggs (1991), have observed a more robust challenge to sexism by young women despite recent changes in socio-economic circumstances.

Discipline and morality in schools

One of the most informative accounts of pupil gender relations in schools is the work of Wolpe (1988). In her analysis of discipline, sexuality and the school curriculum Wolpe rejects a great many of the claims that only boys sexually oppress peers at school. In her data, interpersonal abuse between genders travels both ways, and her depth analysis draws up a plethora of theories highly pertinent to this study.

Wolpe addresses the point that boys and girls develop emotionally and physically at different rates, and during their development they display different needs that have repercussions for their perceived success in the school's system: 'age related to physical maturation is an important factor' (Wolpe 1988: 248).

Concerns, interests and strategies for achieving personal goals varied greatly according to age: 11-year-olds were very different to 16-year-olds. There appeared clear evidence that boys were later developers in terms of sexual maturity than their female class-mates. Wolpe makes the case that gender identity for the girls in her study appears to become settled between the ages of 12 and 15, with some girls initially wishing to be boys, but this aspiration decaying over the period of the research. At around 13 years of age most girls were preoccupied with thoughts of older boys and how to achieve 'successful' relationships with them: 'there appears to be a lesser investment by the boys in girlfriends in early and middle adolescence than vice versa' (Wolpe 1988: 152). This romantic preoccupation distracted girls from academic work just as much as the disruptive behaviour of their male class-mates. Although Wolpe does not deal in depth with the issue of homosexuality, she does recognise its existence within the school community. She also refers to 'crushes' by boys and girls on staff, recognising too the existence of homosexual crushes (of girls on female staff), but does not develop this theme.

Two aspects of male homosexuality surface in Wolpe's study: that which is seen as deviant sexual behaviour; and 'cleverness' – the absence of overt subscription to dominant views of masculinity. The working-class/macho/thick boys are shown to operate within a gang or group ethic, but the 'elite' group of boys are shown as competitive towards each other, using cutting remarks to attack weak members of their own circle.

Wolpe's findings have a particular resonance with the substantive issues in this book. Her concern lies with the site-specificity of gender relations (the school) and the importance of cultural factors other than the universality of patriarchy. The themes of emergent sexuality within a compression chamber of conflicting adult expectations greatly encouraged the further exploration undertaken in this study.

Changing perceptions of girls and schooling

Recently, many excellent articles have appeared that develop understanding of the gendered experiences of pupils, and some of these are discussed below. The study of gender identity has opened up the alternative stereotype model generated by some of the early feminists, and the social experience of boys and girls at school is now researched from more eclectic ethnographic perspectives. Stanley (1993) reports her research in a West Midlands comprehensive school as showing that girls offer effective resistance to schooling in different forms from boys. The apparent 'withdrawnness' of several Y10 girls was investigated, with the conclusion that their quietness was a conscious strategy for achieving academically at school. These girls adopted this style to create a false impression in the eyes of the staff, whilst socially, and out of school, they considered themselves to be anything but quiet, indeed they saw themselves as rebellious.

Dubberley (1993) describes time spent in a comprehensive school in a northern coal-mining area. Much of his account concerns the back-chat given by kids to teachers and their stories of staff–pupil interactions, which are nearly all confrontational. He cites some very colourful accounts by 'the lasses' of their sexual relationships with male staff, the badinage apparently getting physical at times. Unusually in the literature, the lasses are figured as the instigators of these interactions, and, perhaps uniquely in the literature, girls are observed as sexual aggressors. The practice of 'raping' the special-needs lads is described thus: 'a number of lasses would subject an isolated lad to an investigative feeling up process' (Dubberley 1993: 91).

These actions were not, it would seem, for any sexual gratification, but a casual exercising of sexual power. The language used by pupils is described in some detail. Pupils were specific about certain words that staff used in their dictionary sense and which caused real offence to them, for example 'slut' and 'bitch', but when used by pupils amongst themselves they were meant as swear-words. In this more informal mode they were accepted as less offensive. This dual or multi-purpose meaning of language has links with Troyna and Hatcher's (1992) research into 'instrumental' and 'expressive' modes of racist verbal abuse: in other words, who says it, when and to whom is as important as what is said and how it is said.

Of special interest in this area is the work of Kehily and Nayak (1997), who explore the use of humour as a medium for verbal assault. Their schoolboy respondents use the mode of aggressive, sexualised banter to win and maintain heterosexual hierarchical status. My own observations concur with theirs, that favourite targets are the sexual reputations of the opponents' mothers.

A most illuminating account of adolescent girls' friendships is offered by Hey (1997). Against a background of schoolwork Hey draws out a detailed picture of the intensity of feelings of affiliation, alienation and rejection, generated by the girls' social practices. Hey's work is particularly interesting in terms of her data-gathering technique of analysing girls' notes. These notes represent valuable documentary evidence of what is a most elusive social practice. They constituted a feature of my own observational experience: a rich seam that I failed to mine.

Growing bodies in schools

A significant contribution to understanding gender relations in younger school children in the US has been made by Thorne (1993). Thorne studied gendered behaviour amongst elementary-school pupils in two Californian institutions, and commented on a number of features of their social organisation which are especially important.

The age-ranking of pupils, officially by the staff and formal organisation of the school, was noted to have a major effect on the children's construction of a gendered social world.

> Age is the most institutionalized principle of grouping . . . All the students in Mrs. Smith's kindergarten class were alike in being five or six years old. They differed by gender, race, ethnicity, social class, and religion, but these differences were to some degree submerged by the fact that the students were placed together because they were similar in age, confronted the same teacher, received the same work assignments, and were governed by the same rules.
>
> (Thorne 1993: 32)

Thorne does not pursue this principle of differentiation by age as a major area of investigation. It recurs, however, throughout her work as a pervasive feature of pupil life and of great significance in teacher management of difficult behaviour: naughty children are referred to as 'babies' and those who meet with approval are referred to as 'big boys and girls'.

This feature of formal organisation of gendered bodies was linked by Thorne in her presentation of schools as overwhelmingly physical sites, where young growing bodies poke, jostle, spit on and tickle each other whenever possible. The pupils in her research schools showed a preoccupation with bodies and the variations between them: size, shape, smell, colour, ability and gender were constantly being compared and commented upon by the children themselves.

Already in the elementary schools bodies are very gendered by, and within, the official schooling processes. In the lead-up to transfer to high school, by which time many girls have reached puberty, the sexualising of the body is advanced by a multitude of social practices, many of which I would call sexual bullying: bra-strap twanging, breast-grabbing and similar physical interference. Thorne describes the girls at a Halloween party as a 'sexualized troupe' playing out new social roles with newly acquired bodies, embellished by new modes of cosmetics and fashion. She notes that adolescence marks the person's moving out from parental control, and responses of parental protection and punishment can provoke greater rebellion. Paradoxically for girls, rebellion against parental control of sexuality can mean bringing that sexuality under greater oppressive control by older boys.

Hegemonic gender order

There have been several important studies on men's behaviour over the past few years, notably from Australia (among others, Walker 1988; Kenway 1995). An important reworking of feminist theory in relation to masculinity has been made by Connell (1987, 1989, 1995). Connell accepts the early feminist theorisation of patriarchy as explicatory of the social construction of gendered power, but reshapes its rejection of biological determination with a concept of body-reflexivity that admits many, but not all, possibilities of situational response. He defines gender as:

> social practice that constantly refers to bodies and what bodies do, it is not social practice reduced to the body . . . Practice that relates to (gender relations), generated as people and groups grapple with their historical situations, does not consist of isolated acts. Actions are configured in larger units, and when we speak of masculinity and femininity we are naming configuration of gender practice.
>
> (Connell 1995: 71–2)

The idea of body-reflexivity, the part that the body plays in our construction of the social world, is an important one in relation to this book's exploration of pubertal growth in adolescence. Connell also pushes the argument for multiple masculinities constructed in different social milieux at different historical periods. This supports another of his central themes: the dynamism of hegemonic masculinity.

The concept of hegemonic masculinity has been criticised by some feminist writers as bearing too heavily on masculinity and not enough on gender relations itself. I believe it is underdeveloped in several dimensions, but the concept of multiple gender identities, producible through struggle within the social practice of institutions such as schools, does assist the analysis of non-stereotypical gender relations. Although he has little to say on bullying as such, indeed he parenthesises the term,[10] Connell views the victimisation of a subdominant group entirely in terms of formation of gender identity: the construction of the superior through the positioning of the inferior.

Some of the problems with the notion of hegemonic masculinity are overcome in recent work on UK schooling by Mac An Ghaill (1994). Mac An Ghaill examines the construction of masculine identities available to boys in a West Midlands secondary school through a long-term ethnographic study which includes staff, students and parents as respondents. He posits that male hetero-sexuality is a fragile condition in the school, but endures and prevails as the dominant form by virtue of a hegemony supported by virtually all the male staff in the school irrespective of their political position *vis-à-vis* gender.

In many respects Mac An Ghaill builds upon the central themes and approaches of Wolpe, but brings into play theories of race, class and gender which were undeveloped at the time of Wolpe's project. In line with Wolpe's observa-tions of more diffuse power amongst the pupils, Mac An Ghaill's older girls show confidence in describing their superiority to their male class-mates in terms of maturity and their successful relationships with older boys. In respect of their co-education they prefer to be taught with boys as, despite their immaturity, they are 'a laugh' as well as a learning resource for information about more desirable forms of masculinity.

Unlike Wolpe, Mac An Ghaill found that sexual harassment was a source of great concern for some of the girls, but more importantly he describes the actual development of the girls' gender identity under the oppressive policing of male teachers and students. This structuring, limiting and assigning of sexual reputation forms a control on individual identity which is crucial to the manifestation of sexual bullying. Whilst not giving a great deal of time to bullying in itself, Mac An Ghaill does make an important conceptual link between bullying, sexual harass-ment, race and sexual power that goes beyond the point where most researchers on those discrete subjects stop: 'a popular discourse has been constructed that serves to depoliticize the sexual and racial violence taking place at the microcul-tural level of the playground and classroom . . . Currently the dominant official explanation of bullying excludes the dimension of power, appealing to a mixture of conventional psychology and common-sense' (Mac An Ghaill 1994: 128).

Summary

In this short review of literature there are many works that I have omitted, but the richness and diversity of approaches, perspectives and theorisations of the femi-nist-informed work on gender-hostility in schools stands in favourable contrast to the unproblematised and complacent content of most of the bullying research. In general, feminist perspectives have contributed much to a fuller understanding of the aggressive, hierarchical and competitive male ethos that prevails in many schools and other establishments. In particular, the experience of the oppressed and marginalised has a relevance to effecting a re-orientation from an officially sanctioned competitive model founded in opposition to 'otherness', towards a more inclusive, collaborative one. For victims of bullying, racism and sexual harassment, there are likely benefits to such a change in a school regime.

Compared to the extensive kudos given to the surveys on bullying, however, the gender-relations studies have received less public recognition. Any impact on official school practice has been thwarted by the diluting processes of equal oppor-tunity units with broad remits and small budgets, and institutional male resistance to the review of their power positions.

Appendix B

The Q-sort cards (see p. 162) originated as part of a set of statements drawn from brainstorm sessions at Blunkett Rise School. As an activity during a PSE session, pupils were asked to say what sorts of behaviour they disliked in the opposite sex. All the comments were noted on the whiteboard and then grouped into categories during class discussions. Some of these behaviours and practices were defined by the pupils as 'bullying', others as 'hassle' and yet others defied categorisation.

I synthesised the behaviours into forms suitable for Q-sort items to be offered to single-sex groups of different ages. The sample here was issued with the verbal prompt:

RESEARCHER: Have a look at these cards. These are all things that girls (boys) have said they don't like boys (girls) doing at school. I would like each of you to put them in order. First, put the one you think happens most often in this school at the top. Maybe you have not seen this happen, but have heard others mention it. Then put the one you think happens next often, and so on.

(When suggestions are exhausted) Now put them in the order that you think is the most serious or nasty, starting at the top for the most serious.

What do you think *(e.g.)* promiscuous means? What word would pupils actually use? *(And so on.)*

Each group had two sets of cards, one for boys' behaviour and one for girls'. Each pupil would make his/her choices whilst others made comments. Much discussion ensued about the validity of the rank orders and stimulated anecdotes and interjections. Records were made of the rank orders, which were then coded, scored and tabulated to provide some statistics for the school staff.

The Q-sort cards were most useful in generating ideas and stimulating debate, as well as obtaining data on actual frequency and perceived relative gravity of behaviours.

Q-Sort Cards: *Things boys do that girls don't like*

A) MAKING JOKES ABOUT A GIRL'S PERIODS

G) LIFTING A GIRL'S SKIRT

B) CALLING A GIRL A LESBIAN

H) A GROUP OF BOYS GRABBING A GIRL AND FEELING HER UP

C) SPREADING DIRTY RUMOURS ABOUT A GIRL

I) CALLING A GIRL PROMISCUOUS

D) TRYING TO PULL OR FLICK A GIRL'S BRA STRAPS

J) CALLING A GIRL UGLY

E) CALLING A GIRL DIRTY OR SMELLY

K) RUBBISHING A GIRL'S SEXUAL PERFORMANCE

F) CALLING A GIRL FRIGID

L) FEELING A GIRL UP WHEN SHE DOESN'T WANT IT

Things girls do that boys don't like

A) RUBBISHING A BOY'S SEXUAL PERFORMANCE

G) CALLING A BOY A WIMP

B) SAYING THAT A GIRL FINISHED WITH A BOY-FRIEND, WHEN HE FINISHED WITH HER FIRST

H) A GROUP OF GIRLS THREATENING A BOY'S GIRLFRIEND

C) MAKING FUN OF A BOY'S CLOTHES

I) A GROUP OF GIRLS DEBAGGING/KEGGING A BOY

D) THREATENING A BOY WITH THEIR HARD BOYFRIEND

J) CALLING A BOY UGLY

E) SPREADING RUMOURS THAT A BOY IS A USER

K) CALLING A BOY A VIRGIN

F) CALLING A BOY GAY

L) CALLING A BOY IMMATURE

Notes

Introduction

1 I use the term 'sexuality' to refer to a person's disposition towards any sexual matters.

2 These topics are heavily researched and numerous publications are available, perhaps due to the type of threat that boys present to teacher control. Laslett 1977, Topping 1983, Jamieson 1984 and 1988, Frude and Gault (eds) 1984 were popular texts at that time. Many more were published following the Elton Report (1989).

3 Herbert's *Talking of Silence: The Sexual Harassment of Schoolgirls* was also published that year but, although very interesting, did not deal with issues central to my concerns. A short review of literature relating to this study can be found in Appendix A.

4 By my fifth year I had worked with that year's leavers since their arrival. By my seventh year I had seen around 400 pupils right through the system, as well as working with around 1,300 for at least part of their secondary careers.

5 Gender identity here being intended to mean the subject's awareness of self as a boy or a girl within his/her immediate social context.

6 The term 'sexual bullying' is not defined here. Rather than restrict the meaning of the term to my own preconceptions (which nevertheless influence my usage of it), I have tried to allow its meaning to emerge from the data presented in the text. A discussion of the problems of definitions can be found in Appendix A and a sample list of behaviours considered to be sexual bullying in Appendix B.

7 The Q-sorts were rather like an interactive questionnaire: cut-up questions and statements that the respondents could rank, re-order, exclude, etc. See Wolf (1988) for a useful introduction to this and other Q-techniques.

8 Of the four schools that took part in this research project, the term 'host schools' refers to Baker Street, St Joseph's and Patten Avenue schools. Blunkett Rise is referred to as the 'workplace school'.

9 The terminology used for educational age groupings is as follows. Pupils transfer to secondary school at Year 7, when they are 11 years old, and leave in Year 11 when they are 16. The terms 'first years', 'second years', etc. persist with many staff, parents and even pupils. Actual ages are not obvious as pupils birthdays can fall anywhere in the academic year. The term 'lower school' refers to Key Stage 3, i.e. years 7, 8 and 9. 'Upper school' refers to Key Stage 4, or years 10 and 11.

10 There are variations in the title of this subject depending on school and local education authority (LEA), but the lessons deal with issues as diverse as citizenship, bullying, consumer rights and bereavement. Sex education is usually part of the PSE syllabus for at least some of the year groups, but it is also covered formally in science.

11 I was extremely fortunate to have the support of a female collaborator, Rhiannon, who had worked as equal opportunities advisory teacher to a LEA and was active in a variety of anti-sexist, anti-racist spheres. Her practical help in conducting the interviews

was outmatched by her sage advice on a number of sensitive matters which otherwise would have eluded me.

12 Conditions of anonymity and confidentiality were discussed and it was stressed that, although the ultimate aim of research like this was to improve the quality of life for those attending school, there should be no expectation that complaints would be taken up on their behalf. The only exception to this would be the disclosure of matters requiring us by law (Children Act 1989) to inform the school's statutory 'named person' to whom all matters of child protection must be referred.

13 These items were behaviours that had been generated during the pilot sessions. The pupils were asked 'What do boys/girls do that girls/boys don't like?' The brainstormed responses were then categorised and synthesised into batteries of Q-sort cards.

1 Boy troubles

1 Sharp and Smith 1994, and Wolverhampton Borough Council's Safer Cities project.

2 Remafedi et al. (1993) found that boys at 12 years of age were three times more likely to state uncertainty of sexual orientation than young men of 18.

3 One report calculates the ratio of time spent by 4-year-old boys playing with either sex as 3:1 in favour of other males. By age six and a half, the preference had increased to 11:1. Maccoby and Jacklin (1987).

4 I found the task of relaying the shifting meaning of this term a real problem. Wherever possible, I have used speech marks to specify the use of the word in the pupils' sense of an unpopular or weak boy. Otherwise I have used it to mean homosexual.

5 Grassing: originally telling tales, but now simply complaining to authority.

6 Case studies on two such young people feature in later chapters.

7 'Cool' meaning attractive, casual and in control.

8 'Wedging' was another, similar form of assault, but considered more playful. This practice entailed reaching beneath the waistband of skirt or trousers and pulling the victim's underwear sharply up between their buttocks. Not only was this embarrassing and sometimes painful, but, if successful, necessitated a hobbling trip to the toilet for the victim to rearrange their underclothes.

9 The term 'hard' girl or boy described reputation and attitude rather than physical strength.

10 Although the etymology here appears to be gypsy, the pupils in some of the schools were clear that this was not what they meant – they meant a very poor or scruffy person. They also tied this to notions of rejection of their fashion system, evidenced by references to some pupils who spent money on alternative styles, whether 'scruffy' or not.

11 Gilbert and Taylor (1992) discuss the prominence of girls as 'helpers' in popular teen fiction. Leading characters are frequently engaged in such exploits as going out with a boy to facilitate a relationship for another couple or to reveal the bad character of a friend's suitor.

12 The pupils themselves referred to a bewildering and shifting system of categorising themselves and others according to religion, country or continent of parental origin, colour and youth subculture. The strength of this identification was attested to by the fact that many to whom I refer as African-Caribbean called themselves Jamaican, though even their parents had never been to Jamaica.

13 'Neither does the process of symbolically elevating and/or emulating young Black men give them a more privileged place on the hierarchy of pupil identities' (Wright et al. 1998).

14 'far from being mindless entertainment, music is a key site in everyday life where males and females reflect on their gendered and sexual identities and make adjustments to the images they have of themselves' (Mercer and Julien 1995: 192).

15 'Computer geeks' and 'anoraks' also fell into this category. These were solitary boys, or

small cliques, who showed great, but introjected, interest in and knowledge of these activities and who created their own cultural space within them. Such knowledge and interest was evident amongst the more dominant boys, but in a more socialised mode, such as playing electronic games in amusement arcades.

16 Neither boys nor girls showed much erotic interest in pornography, but prized it for its educative and carnival qualities: 'look at him', 'imagine wearing that to school', etc.

17 Cf. Section headed 'School-gate gallants' in Chapter 4.

2 Girl troubles

1 Stella was a girl of Asian origin; the boy's ethnicity was not recorded. Khanum (1995) provides an interesting account of ethnicity, gender, sex and religion in a British school.

2 Mussen et al. (1990) found that girls who matured earlier than their cohort were often the subjects of much sexual attention from their peers: prurient attempts at intimacy from the boys and jealousy from the girls.

3 See Simmons et al. 1979; Petersen 1988; Conger 1991, and Thorne 1993.

4 The phenomenon of red-headed boys' victimisation was especially strong at Blunkett Rise, close to the Welsh border. Many of the boys made a connection between Celtic ethnicity and red hair, and associated certain unmasculine traits – inability to take a joke, spitefulness, etc. – with that ethnic identity. The abusive comment 'he's a right Ginge' was levelled at boys who did not have red hair but were somehow associated with those disapproved traits.

5 This word has a number of meanings, very different to one another. Hey (1997: 66) notes its definition by her girl respondents as a noun, 'a girl who is unreliable, who makes arrangements and then breaks them'.

6 See Courtman (1994) for a discussion of resistance to PSE.

7 'Raping' was one behaviour named during brainstorms by younger pupils in the pilot interviews. Their understanding was of (usually a mob of) either sex grabbing an individual of the opposite sex and rummaging about in their underclothes. Many pupils remembered this as an activity more common in primary school. The item's inclusion was very helpful in stimulating discussion of what actually constituted rape, sexual assault, etc.

3 Age differences in adolescent relationships

1 See, e.g., the journals of the National Association of Pastoral Care in Education.

2 Girls, on average, undergo their pubertal growth spurt at age 11, whilst boys generally undergo theirs around age 13. The cultural effects of this phenomenon are made more difficult to cope with due to the 'secular trend', each generation being physically bigger and maturing earlier than the last (Coleman and Hendry 1990). This trend can cause confusion to parental expectations.

3 Another indicator of social behaviour that shows strong maturational differences by gender is criminal offending. Girls' offending behaviour peaks at age 14/15, but males' at age 20 years – with a rate four times greater than the girls' (Home Office 1995).

4 See Wolpe (1988), Mac An Ghaill (1994) and especially Wellings et al. (1994). In a sample of 789 females who reported having sexual intercourse between the ages of 13 and 15, 75 per cent said their partners were older than themselves, the mean difference being two years. These differentials remained throughout the rest of the 8,000+ sample irrespective of age at first intercourse. The sexually active under-16s were asked to name the main factor in the sexual relationship; amongst the variety of responses 39 per cent of girls said it was because they were in love, compared to only 6.2 per cent of boys (Wellings et al. 1994: 68–72).

5 Homosexual relationships were not apparent and were not acknowledged by any of the interviewees.

6   See, for example, Gilbert and Taylor 1992 and Martin 1996.
7   Add to this list forearms, cuffs, desk lids, computer screensavers, corridor walls and steamed windows, and one might get the impression that the advertising industry is not nearly as creative as it reckons.
8   For readers frustrated in understanding these messages: Julie loves Barky, and Karen and Kippa will be together for ever because their love is strong.

4 The ideology of age seniority

1   See later section on 'school-gate gallants'. Pinxi had transferred from another secondary school in Y8 as part of a witness-protection scheme following the stabbing of one pupil by another.
2   The number of pupils that a school can officially have on roll. 'Difficult pupils' always find their way into undersubscribed schools, altering the balance of their original intake and, it is claimed, reducing the school's popularity even further.
3   The last official school day for leavers is usually just before their exam study leave, about seven or eight weeks before the end of the school year for everyone else.
4   This practice was in operation when Cheeva was insulted by her male class-mate by the suggestion that her boyfriend had 'come' over her arm (Chapter 2).
5   See Gaddis and Brooks-Gunn 1985; Coleman and Hendry 1990; Mac An Ghaill 1994.
6   It is important to note that, at that time, school security was given a very low priority. Considering the large numbers of potentially vulnerable young people on school sites and their accessibility to visiting strangers, schools have always had less money spent on protection than, say, shops or offices. It took the combination of rocketing insurance premiums against arson, and the tragedies at Dunblane Primary and St Luke's Infants', Wolverhampton in 1996 to release funds for security fencing and video surveillance for schools across the country.
7   See Askew and Ross (1988), especially ch. 4 on the experience of women teachers.

5 The culture of feminine violence

1   Nilan's (1989) superb analysis of Australian girls' hierarchies is highly recommended on this topic.
2   Pinxi had brought this matter up during an earlier interview, then repeated it almost verbatim in this meeting.
3   Roza's mother and older sisters housed a succession of male partners. The local community included a number of such homes, where a matriarch presided over her children, extended younger family and transient adult males.
4   Cf. Chapter 8.
5   'What girlfighters fight for, and those who fear girls fall back on, is dyadic intimacy: the one boy or man on whom they lay all their chips of life. In the empathy of first love, they get this from the boys they will fight to keep for ever. This is their great hope – the achievement that will make up for everything else: for being raised to serve men, for being their mothers' daughters' (Thompson 1995, quoted in Martin 1996).

6 Homophobias: intra-gender policing

1   Having written this, I later read the headline 'Pervert label puts men off teaching' in the *Times Education Supplement* (28 August 1998).
2   Corporal punishment was still prevalent in schools until the mid-1980s.
3   See Willis 1977; Woods 1975 and 1990, and Corrigan 1979, amongst others, for classic accounts of boys' strategies. Hargreaves 1975, Saunders 1979, Kyriacou 1989 and others have produced textbooks on this subject. Practical manuals on controlling

disruptive teaching groups have also been prolific, and are often published by LEA advisory teams.

4 Lees (1993) was surprised to find so many girls troubled by thoughts of being seduced by lesbians. Although the girls in this study were not generally disposed to violence towards lesbians, they were suspicious and afraid of their influence unless they were already friends.

5 See Mac An Ghaill 1994: 166.

6 Research into the families of boys permanently excluded from school has shown that those from single-parent families are twice as likely to have behaviour problems than those from families where there are both biological parents. But children with one biological parent and a step-parent are ten times more likely to have behavioural difficulties at school (Ashford 1994). Adult males attempting to exercise authority over adolescent boys have serious conflictual potential.

7 Mac An Ghaill (1994) and Mills (1996) both give examples of the disruption created in schools when there is an easing of the 'normal' homophobic relationships between males.

7 Summary of findings: the importance of being gendered

1 During the period of this research I was aware of several cases of rape and of serious sexual assault against pupils on roll at one or other of the participating schools. These crimes were all committed outside school hours and off the premises but had welfare implications for the schools none the less. I was impressed by the schools' sensitive handling of their role. Given the high level of confidentiality, there may have been many other incidents of which I was not aware.

2 For example, Jenny Eclair, Jo Brand and Jeremy Hardy.

3 You don't notice how many people have red Volkswagen Beetles until you buy one yourself.

4 Official regulations did exist (until recent deregulation) for the allocation of space per pupil in schools. The current DfEE recommendations are very complicated, but, seemingly, the general teaching space for groups of up to thirty secondary-age children is reckoned to be a minimum of 45 square metres, or 1.5 square metres per person.

8 Analysis, discussion and wild speculation

1 For example, eating disorders such as *anorexia nervosa* and *bulimia* (Millstein and Litt 1993).

2 See Martin's (1996) ethnography for a discussion of how adolescent girls' failure to achieve weight loss can slide from body-hate into self-hate.

3 See Younger and Warrington (1996) for an introduction to a number of related issues.

4 The 15–24-year-old male group was stable from 1971 until 1992, since when it has risen from 6 to 15 per 100,000 (Home Office 1995).

5 At a Baker Street School staff meeting, the head asked, 'How can we raise our A to C exam grades by that vital 12 per cent?' The male deputy for upper school answered, 'Get rid of all the boys'.

6 See Thorne 1993.

Appendix A

1 See Duncan 1991. The debate on definitions continues both in the UK and elsewhere: Terry (1998) raises a number of the prevailing difficulties.

2 See Ahmad, Whitney and Smith (1991).

3 Kidscape's original *raison d'être* was promoting child safety on a general level but it quickly became primarily associated with bullying as media interest in that area grew.

4 National Children's Homes, a Methodist charity lately running down the residential aspect of its operations in favour of community projects.

5 Department for Education and Employment. This department evolved from the old Department of Education and Science.

6 OFSTED (the Office for Standards in Education) replaced Her Majesty's Inspectors of Schools in 1993.

7 Personal communication.

8 CCM: Common Concern Method. Pikas's embracing of the medical model is apparent in the title of his article: 'A pure concept of mobbing gives the best results in treatment'.

9 See the section headed 'The school disco: breaking tradition'.

10 In his recounting of the persecution of 'Cyrils' (weak academic boys) by 'Bloods' (tough sporting boys) at a private school in Australia (Connell 1987).

References and bibliography

Ahmad, Y., Whitney, I. and Smith, P. (1991) 'A survey service for schools on bully/victim problems', in P. Smith and D. Thompson *Practical Approaches to Bullying*, London: Fulton.

Arnot, M. and Weiner, G. (1987) *Gender and the politics of schooling*. London: Hutchinson.

Arora, C.M.J. and Thompson, D.A. (1987) 'Defining bullying for a secondary school', *Education and Child Psychology*, 4: 110–20.

Ashford, P. (1994) 'Who is excluded from school? Does family status have an influence?' *Journal of the Association for Pastoral Care in Education*, 12 (4): 10–12.

Askew, S. and Ross, C. (1988) *Boys Don't Cry: Boys and Sexism in Education*, Milton Keynes: Open University Press.

Ball, S. (1981) *Beachside Comprehensive: A Case Study of Secondary Schooling*, Cambridge: Cambridge University Press.

Besag, V. (1989) *Bullies and Victims in Schools*, Milton Keynes: Open University Press.

Beynon, J. (1989) 'A school for men: an ethnographic case study of routine violence in schooling', in S. Walker and L. Barton (eds) *Politics and Processes of Schooling*, Milton Keynes: Open University Press.

Bjorkquist, K., Lagerspertz, K.M.J., Berto, M. and King, E. (1982) 'Group aggression among schoolchildren in three schools', *Scandinavian Journal of Psychology*, 23 (1): 45–52.

Bjorkquist, K., Lagerspertz, K.M.J. and Kaukainen, A. (1992) 'Do girls manipulate and boys fight? Developmental trends in regard to direct and indirect aggression', *Aggressive Behaviour*, 18: 117–27.

Brooks-Gunn, J. and Ruble, D.N. (1983) 'The experience of menarche from a developmental perspective' in J. Brooks-Gunn and A.C. Petersen (eds) *Girls at Puberty: Biological, Psychological and Social Perspectives*, New York: Plenum.

Brooks-Gunn, J. and Warren, M.P. (1985) 'Effects of delayed menarche in different contexts: dance and non-dance students', *Journal of Youth and Adolescence*, 14: 285–300.

Brown, L.M. and Gilligan, C. (1992) *Meeting at the Crossroads: Women's Psychology and Girls' Development*, Cambridge, Mass.: Harvard University Press.

Butler-Sloss, E. (1988) *Report of the Inquiry into Child Abuse in Cleveland, 1987*, London: HMSO.

Cahill, S. (1982) 'Becoming boys and girls', PhD diss., UCLA, cited in B. Thorne (1993) *Gender Play*, Milton Keynes: Open University Press.

Cherry, T. (1984) 'Bradford', in Y. Roberts, *Man Enough*, London: Chatto.

Coleman, J.C. and Hendry, L. (1990) *The Nature of Adolescence*, London: Routledge.

Conger, J.J. (1991) *Adolescence and Youth: Psychological Development in a Changing World*, New York: Harper Collins.

Connell, R.W. (1987) *Gender and Power*, Cambridge: Polity Press.

Connell, R.W. (1989) 'Cool guys, swots and wimps: the interplay of masculinity and education', *Oxford Review of Education*, 15 (3): 291–303.

Connell, R.W. (1995) *Masculinities*, Cambridge: Polity Press.

Corrigan, P. (1979) *Schooling the Smash Street Kids*, London: Macmillan.

Courtman, D. (1994) 'Understanding resistance to PSE', *Careers Education and Guidance*, 8 (2): 15–16.

Cowie, C. and Lees, S. (1987) 'Slags or drags', in Feminist Review (ed.) *Sexuality: A Reader*, London: Virago Press.

Dale, R.R. (1971) *Mixed or Single Sex School? Vol. II: Some Social Aspects*, London: Routledge and Kegan Paul.

Davies, L. (1984) *Pupil Power: Deviance and Gender in School*, London: Falmer.

de Kruif, N. (1989) 'Bullying in the Dutch school system', in E. Roland and E. Munthe (eds) *Bullying: An International Perspective*, London: David Fulton.

DES (1987) *Sex Education at School*, London: HMSO.

Druet, D. (1993) 'Adolescent female bullying and sexual harassment', in D. Tattum (ed.) *Understanding and Managing Bullying*, London: Heinemann.

Dubberley, W.S. (1993) 'Humour as resistance', in P. Woods and M. Hammersley (eds) *Gender and Ethnicity in Schools: Ethnographic Accounts*, London: Routledge.

Duncan, N.S. (1991) 'Bullying in Schools', unpub. MEd. diss., Manchester University.

Eichler, I. (1991) *Nonsexist Research Methods: A Practical Guide*, London: Allen and Unwin.

Elliot, M. (1992) *Bullying: A Practical Guide to Coping for Schools*, Harlow: Longman.

Elton (Chair) Report (1989) *Discipline in Schools*, London: HMSO.

Farmer, E. and Owen, M. (1995) *Child Protection Practice: Private Risks, Public Remedies*, London: HMSO.

Foucault, M. (1990) *The History of Sexuality, Vol. 1*, London: Penguin.

Frude, N. and Gault, H. (eds) (1984) *Disruptive Behaviour in Schools*, Chichester: John Wiley.

Gaddis, A. and Brooks-Gunn, J. (1985) 'The male experience of pubertal change', *Journal of Youth and Adolescence*, 14 (1): 61–9.

Garner, P. (1994) 'Exclusions from school: towards a new agenda', *Journal of the Association for Pastoral Care in Education*, 12 (4): 3–9.

Gilbert, P. and Taylor, S. (1992) *Fashioning the Feminine: Girls, Popular Culture and Schooling*, Sydney: Allen and Unwin.

Gillborn, D. (1993) 'Racial violence and bullying', in D. Tattum (ed.) *Understanding and Managing Bullying*, London: Heinemann.

Gilroy, P. (1987) *There Ain't No Black in the Union Jack*, London: Hutchinson.

Hargreaves, D.H. (1975) *Interpersonal Relations and Education*, London: Routledge and Kegan Paul.

Harris, S. (1990) *Lesbian and Gay Issues in the English Classroom*, Milton Keynes: Open University Press.

Herbert, C.M.H. (1989) *Talking of Silence: The Sexual Harassment of Schoolgirls*, London: Falmer.

Hey, V. (1997) *The Company She Keeps: An Ethnography of Girls' Friendships*, Buckingham: Open University Press.

Holland, J. (1993) *Sexuality and Ethnicity: Variations in Young Women's Sexual Knowledge and Practice*, London: Tufnell Press.

Holland, J., Ramazanoglu, C., Sharpe, S. and Thomson, R. (1994) *Pressured Pleasure: Young Women and the Negotiation of Sexual Boundaries*, London: Tufnell Press.

Home Office (1995) *Social Trends*, London: HMSO.

Humphries, M. (1992) 'Live dangerously: homophobia and gay power', in V.J. Seidler (ed.) *Men, Sex and Relationships*, London: (Achilles Heel) Routledge.

Jamieson, J.H. (1984) 'Coping with physical violence', *Maladjustment and Therapeutic Education*, 2 (2): 39–45.

Jamieson, J.H. (1988) 'Violence at home: life outside residential care', *Maladjustment and Therapeutic Education*, 6 (1): 3–13.

Jones, C. (1985) 'Sexual tyranny in mixed-sex schools', in G. Weiner (ed.) *Just a Bunch of Girls*, Milton Keynes: Open University Press.

Jones, C. and Mahony, P. (1989) *Learning Our Lines: Sexuality and Social Control*, London: The Women's Press.

Jones, M.C. and Bayley, N. (1950) 'Physical maturing amongst boys as related to behaviour', *Journal of Educational Psychology*, 41: 129–48.

Kehily, M.J. and Nayak, A. (1997) '"Lads and laughter": Humour and the production of heterosexual hierarchies', *Gender and Education*, 9 (1): 69–87.

Keise, C. (1992) *Sugar and Spice? Bullying in Single-Sex Schools*, London: Trentham.

Kelly, L., Burton, S. and Regan, L. (1994) 'Researching women's lives or studying women's oppression', in M. Maynard and J. Purvis (eds) *Researching Women's Lives from a Feminist Perspective*, London: Taylor and Francis.

Kenway, J. (1995) 'Masculinities in schools: under siege, on the defensive and under reconstruction?' *Discourse: Studies in the Cultural Politics of Education*, 16 (1): 59–79.

Khanum, S. (1995) 'Education and the Muslim girl', in M. Blair, J. Holland and S. Sheldon (eds) *Identity and Diversity: Gender and the Experience of Education*, Milton Keynes: Open University Press.

King, M. and Trowell, J. (1993) *Children's Welfare and the Law*, London: Sage.

Kyriacou, C. (1989) *Effective Teaching in Schools*, Oxford: Basil Blackwell.

Laing, A.F. and Chazan, M. (1986) 'The management of aggressive behaviour in young children', in D.P. Tatum (ed.) *Management of Disruptive Pupil Behaviour in Schools*, London: John Wiley.

Laslett, R. (1977) *Educating Maladjusted Children*, London: Crosby, Lockwood Staples.

Lees, S. (1987) 'The structure of sexual relations in school', in M. Arnot and G. Weiner (eds) *Gender and the politics of schooling*, London: Hutchinson.

Lees, S. (1993) *Sugar and Spice: Sexuality and Adolescence*, London: Penguin.

Lowenstein, L.F. (1978a) 'Who is the bully?', *Bulletin of the B.P.S.*, 31.

Lowenstein, L.F. (1978b) 'The bullied and non-bullied child', *Bulletin of the B.P.S.*, 3: 316–18.

Lukes, J.R. (1986) 'Finance and policy-making in special education', in W. Swann (ed.) *The Practice of Special Education*, Oxford: Basil Blackwell.

Mac An Ghaill, M. (1989a) 'Coming of age in 1980s England: reconceptualizing black students' schooling experiences', *British Journal of Sociology of Education*, 10 (3): 273–86.

Mac An Ghaill, M. (1989b) 'Beyond the white norm: the use of qualitative research in the study of black youths' schooling in England', *Qualitative Studies in Education*, 2 (3): 75–189.

Mac An Ghaill, M. (1994) *The Making of Men: Masculinities, Sexualities and Schooling*, Milton Keynes: Open University Press.

Mac An Ghaill, M. (1995) '(In)visibility: "race", sexuality and masculinity in the school context', in M. Blair, J. Holland and S. Sheldon (eds) *Identity and Diversity: Gender and the Experience of Education*, Milton Keynes: Open University Press.

Maccoby, E.E. and Jacklin, C.N. (1987) 'Gender segregation in childhood', in H.W. Reese (ed.) *Advances in Child Development and Behaviour*, 20, New York: Academic Press.

MacDonald, I., Bhavnani, R., Khan, L. and John, G. (1989) *Murder in the Playground: Report of the Inquiry into Racism and Violence in Manchester Schools*, London: Longsight.

Mahony, P. (1985) *Schools for the Boys? Co-education Reassessed*, London: Hutchinson.

Maines, B. and Robinson, G. (1992) *Michael's Story: The No Blame Approach*, Bristol: Lame Duck Publishing.

Martin, A.D. (1982) 'Learning to hide: the socialization of the gay adolescent', in J. Feinstein, A. Looney, T. Schwartzberg and A. Sorosky (eds) *Adolescent Psychiatry*, Chicago: University of Chicago Press.

Martin, K. (1996) *Puberty, Sexuality and the Self: Girls and Boys at Adolescence*, London: Routledge.

McRobbie, A. and Nava, M. (eds) *Gender and Generation*, London: Macmillan.

Mercer, K. and Julien, I. (1995) 'True confessions: a discourse on images of Black male sexuality', in M. Blair, J. Holland and S. Sheldon (eds) *Identity and Diversity: Gender and the Experience of Education*, Milton Keynes: Open University Press.

Mills, M. (1996) 'Homophobia kills: a disruptive moment in the educational politics of legitimisation', *British Journal of Sociology of Education*, 17 (3): 315–26.

Millstein, S.G. and Litt, I.F. (1993) 'Adolescent health', in S. Feldman and G. Elliott, *At the Threshold: The Developing Adolescent*, Cambridge, Mass.: Harvard University Press.

Mussen, P.H., Conger, J.J., Kagan, J. and Huston, A.C. (1990) *Child Development and Personality*, New York: Harper and Row.

Neubauer, P.B. (ed.) (1976) *The Process of Child Development*, New York: Meridian.

Newson, J. and Newson, E. (1978) *Seven-Year-Olds in the Home Environment*, London: Penguin.

Nilan, P. (1989) 'Kazzies, DBTs and tryhards: categorisations of style in adolescent girls' sex talk', *British Journal of Sociology of Education*, 15 (2): 201–13.

Okley, J. (1978) 'Privileged, schooled and finished: boarding education for girls', in S. Ardener, *Defining Females*, London: Croom Helm.

Olweus, D. (1978) *Aggression in Schools: Bullies and Whipping Boys*, Washington DC: Hemisphere Press.

Olweus, D. (1987) 'Bully/victim problems among school-children in Scandinavia', in J.P. Myklebust and R. Ommundsen (eds) *Psykologprofesjonen mot ar 2000*, Oslo: Universitetsforlaget. Quoted in V. Besag (1989) *Bullies and Victims in Schools*, Milton Keynes: Open University Press.

Olweus, D. (1989) 'Bully/victim problems amongst schoolchildren', in K. Reuben and D. Pepler (eds) *The Development and Treatment of Childhood Aggression*, New Jersey: Erlbaum.

Pagelow, M.D. (1981) *Woman Battering: Victims and their Experiences*, London: Sage.

Patterson, G.R. and Stouthamer-Loeber, M. (1984) 'The correlation of family management practices and delinquency', *Child Development*, 55 (4): 1299–1307.

Petersen, A.C. (1988) 'Adolescent development', *Annual Review of Psychology*, 39: 583–608, cited in J.J. Conger (1991) *Adolescence and Youth: Psychological Development in a Changing World*, New York: Harper Collins.

Piaget, J. (1972) *Psychology and Epistemology*, Harmondsworth: Penguin.

Pikas, A. (1989a) 'The common concern method for the treatment of mobbing', in E. Roland and E. Munthe (eds) *Bullying: An International Perspective*, London: David Fulton.

Pikas, A. (1989b) 'A pure concept of mobbing gives the best results in treatment', *School Psychology International*, 10 (2): 95–104.

Power, S., Whitty, G., Edwards, T. and Whigfall, V. (1998) 'Schoolboys and schoolwork:

gender identification and academic achievement', *International Journal of Inclusive Education* 2(2).

Prendergast, S. (1992) *This is the Time to Grow Up: Girls' Experiences of Menstruation in School*, Cambridge: Health Promotion Research Trust.

Remafedi, G., Resnick, M., Blum, R. and Harris, L. (1993) *Death by Denial: Preventing Suicide in Gay and Lesbian Teenagers*, Los Angeles: Alyson Publications, quoted by R.C. Savin-Williams and R.C. Rodriguez in T. Gullotta, G. Adams and R. Montemayor (eds) *Adolescent Sexuality*, London: Sage.

Rivers, I. (1995) 'Protecting the gay adolescent at school', paper presented at *Second International Congress on Adolescentology*, Milan.

Roland, E. (1989) 'Bullying: the Scandinavian research tradition', in D. Tattum and D.A. Lane (eds) *Bullying in Schools*, Stoke on Trent: Trentham Books.

Rothblum, E.D. (1990) 'Depression amongst lesbians: an unresearched phenomenon', *Journal of Lesbian and Gay Psychotherapy*, 1 (1): 66–87.

Salisbury, J. and Jackson, D. (1996) *Challenging Macho Values: Practical Ways of Working with Adolescent Boys*, London: Falmer.

Saunders, M. (1979) *Class Control and Behaviour Problems*, Maidenhead: McGraw-Hill.

Savin-Williams, R.C. and Rodriguez, R.C. (1993) 'A developmental, clinical perspective on lesbian, gay male and bisexual youths', in T. Gullotta, G. Adams and R. Montemayor (eds) *Adolescent Sexuality*, London: Sage.

Seidler, V. J. (1992) *Men, Sex and Relationships*, London: (Achilles Heel) Routledge.

Seltzer, V.C. (1982) *Adolescent Social Development: Dynamic Functional Interaction*, Lexington, Mass.: Lexington Books.

Sharp, S. and Smith, P.K. (1994) *Bullying in U.K. Schools: The DES Sheffield Bullying Project*, Dept. of Psychology, University of Sheffield.

Shidlo, A. (1994) 'Internalized homophobia', in B. Greene and G. M. Herek (eds) *Lesbian and Gay Psychology: Theory, Research and Clinical Applications*, London: Sage.

Shilling, C. (1993) *The Body and Social Theory*, London: Sage.

Silove, D., George, G. and Bhavani-Sankaram, V. (1987) 'Parasuicide: interaction between inadequate parenting and recent interpersonal stress', *Australian and New Zealand Journal of Psychiatry*, 21: 221–8.

Simmons, R.G., Blyth, D.A., Van Cleeve, E.F. and Bush, D.M. (1979) 'Entry into early adolescence: the impact of school structure, puberty, and early dating on self-esteem', *American Sociological Review*, 44: 948–67.

Singer, M. (1992) 'Sex and male sexuality', in V.J. Seidler (ed.) *Men, Sex and Relationships*, London: (Achilles Heel) Routledge.

Sinha, C. (1986) 'The role of psychological research in special education', in W. Swann (ed.) *The Practice of Special Education*, Oxford: Basil Blackwell.

Skeggs, B. (1991) 'Challenging masculinity and using sexuality', *British Journal of Sociology of Education*, 12 (2): 127–39.

Skeggs, B. (1993) 'The cultural production of "learning to labour"', in M. Barker and A. Breezer (eds) *Readings in Culture*, London: Routledge.

Skinner, A. (1992) *Bullying: An Annotated Bibliography of Literature and Resources*, Leicester: Youthwork Press.

Smith, G.T. (1991) Bullying in schools survey, Wolverhampton Borough Council Safer Schools Project, Unpub.

Smith, G.T. (1993) personal communication.

Smith, P.K. and Sharp, S. (eds) (1994) *School Bullying: Insights and Perspectives*, London: Routledge.

Spender, D. (1981) *Men's Studies Modified*, Oxford: Pergamon Press.

Stanley, J. (1993) 'Sex and the quiet schoolgirl', in P. Woods and M. Hammersley (eds) *Gender and Ethnicity in Schools: Ethnographic Accounts*, London: Routledge.

Stein, N. (1995) 'Sexual harassment in school: the public performance of gendered violence', *Harvard Review of Education*, 65 (2): 145–62.

Strauss, S. (1988) 'Sexual harassment in the school: legal implications for the principals', *NASSP Bulletin*, March.

Tattum, D. and Herbert, G. (1993) *Countering Bullying: Initiatives by Schools and Local Authorities*, Stoke on Trent: Trentham Books.

Terry, A.A. (1998) 'Teachers as targets of bullying by their pupils: a study to investigate incidence', *British Journal of Educational Psychology*, 68: 225–68.

Thorne, B. (1993) *Gender Play*, Milton Keynes: Open University Press.

Topping, K. (1983) *Education Systems for Disruptive Adolescents*, London: Croom Helm.

Troyna, B. and Hatcher, R. (1992) *Racism in Children's Lives: A Study of Mainly-White Primary Schools*, London: Routledge.

Walker, J.C. (1988) 'The way men act: dominant and subordinate male cultures in an inner-city school', *British Journal of Sociology of Education*, 9 (1): 3–18.

Walkerdine, V. (1987) 'Sex power and pedagogy', in M. Arnot and G.Weiner (eds) *Gender and the politics of Schooling*, London: Hutchinson.

Walsh, J. 'Back to school: the best days of your life, the worst of mine', *Independent*, 4 Sept. 1998.

Weiner, G. (1994) *Feminisms in Education: An Introduction*, Buckingham: Open University Press.

Weiner, G. (ed.) (1985) *Just a Bunch of Girls*, Milton Keynes: Open University Press.

Welford, H. 'Dirt, distress and danger . . . I think I'll take the car', *Independent*, 4 Sept. 1998.

Wellings, K., Field, J., Johnson, A. and Wadsworth, J. (1994) *Sexual Behaviour in Britain: The National Survey of Sexual Attitudes and Lifestyles*, London: Penguin.

Wetherell, M. and Griffin, C. (1992) 'Feminist psychology and the study of men and masculinity: assumptions and perspectives', *Feminism and Psychology*, 2 (2): 361–91.

Whitbread, A. (1988) 'Female teachers are women first: sexual harassment at work', in D. Spender and E. Sarah (eds) *Learning to Lose: Sexism and Education*, London: The Women's Press.

Wild, J.V. and Taylor, J.M. (1994) 'Sexuality education for immigrant and minority students: developing a culturally appropriate curriculum', in J. Irvine (ed.) *Sexual Culture and the Construction of Adolescent Identities*, Philadelphia: Temple University Press.

Willis, P. (1977) *Learning to Labour: How Working Class Kids Get Working Class Jobs*, Aldershot: Saxon House.

Willis, P. (1980) 'Notes on method', in S. Hall, D. Hobson, A. Lowe and P. Willis (eds) *Culture, Media, Language*, (CCCS) London: Hutchinson.

Wolf, R.M. (1988) 'Q-methodology', in J. Keeves (ed.) *Educational Research Methodology and Measurement: An International Handbook*, London: Pergamon.

Wolpe, A.M. (1988) *Within School Walls: The Role of Discipline, Sexuality and the Curriculum*, London: Routledge.

Wood, J. (1984) 'Groping towards sexism: boys' sex talk', in A. McRobbie and M. Nava (eds) *Gender and Education*, London: Macmillan.

Woods, P. (1975) '"Showing them up" in secondary school', in S. Delamont (ed.) *Frontiers of Classroom Research*, London: NFER.

Woods, P. (1979) *The Divided School*, London: Routledge and Kegan Paul.

Woods, P. (1990) *The Happiest Days: How Pupils Cope with Schools*, London: Falmer Press.

Wright, C., Weekes, D., McGlaughlin, A. and Webb, D. (1998) 'Masculinised discourses within education and the construction of Black male identities amongst African Caribbean youth', *British Journal of Sociology of Education*, 19 (1): 75–87.

Younger, M. and Warrington, M. (1996) 'Differential achievement of girls and boys at GCSE: some observations from the perspective of one school', *British Journal of Sociology of Education*, 17 (3): 299–313.

Index